Th tion
tion

The New Information Literacy Instruction

Best Practices

Edited by Patrick Ragains
M. Sandra Wood

ROWMAN & LITTLEFIELD
Lanham • Boulder • New York • London

Published by Rowman & Littlefield
A wholly owned subsidiary of The Rowman & Littlefield Publishing Group, Inc.
4501 Forbes Boulevard, Suite 200, Lanham, Maryland 20706
www.rowman.com

Unit A, Whitacre Mews, 26-34 Stannary Street, London SE11 4AB

British Library Cataloguing in Publication Information Available

Library of Congress Cataloging-in-Publication Data

Names: Ragains, Patrick, editor. | Wood, M. Sandra, editor.
Title: The new information literacy instruction : best practices / edited by Patrick Ragains and M. Sandra Wood.
Description: Lanham : Rowman & Littlefield, [2016] | Series: Best practices in library services | Includes bibliographical references and index.
Identifiers: LCCN 2015025833| ISBN 9781442257924 (cloth : alk. paper) | ISBN 9781442257931 (pbk. : alk. paper) | ISBN 9781442257948 (ebook)
Subjects: LCSH: Information literacy—Study and teaching (Higher)—United States. | Research—Methodology—Study and teaching (Higher)—United States. | Academic libraries—Relations with faculty and curriculum—United States.
Classification: LCC ZA3075 .N493 2016 | DDC 028.7071/173—dc23 LC record available at http://lccn.loc.gov/2015025833

∞™ The paper used in this publication meets the minimum requirements of American National Standard for Information Sciences—Permanence of Paper for Printed Library Materials, ANSI/NISO Z39.48-1992.

Printed in the United States of America

Contents

Part II: Innovative Models for Information Literacy Instruction

Part III: Branching Out: Teaching Special Literacies

Figures and Tables

FIGURES

TABLES

Preface

Dynamic, service-oriented librarians constantly look for ideas to improve and promote their services. This is certainly true of instructional librarians, who study pedagogy, and share and absorb both time-tested and new practices via conference presentations and published literature. *The New Information Literacy Instruction: Best Practices* presents best practices in information literacy instruction (ILI) in higher education, divided into three parts, each representing a broad theme:

Part I: Supporting Specific Academic Programs
Part II: Innovative Models for Information Literacy Instruction
Part III: Branching Out: Teaching Special Literacies

Each chapter describes instructional practice in the context of professionally accepted frames or standards, which will aid librarians in creating lessons and programs of their own, focused on selected themes. The *Framework for Information Literacy for Higher Education* (2015) and "Characteristics of Programs of Information Literacy That Illustrate Best Practices" (2012), both from the Association of College & Research Libraries (ACRL), are prominent among these frames. These two recent ACRL documents, together with other familiar benchmarks, such as Bruce's seven faces of information literacy (Bruce, 1997) and ACRL's "Information Literacy Competency Standards for Higher Education" (2000), will help readers generalize the experiences recorded herein.

This book was developed for the following professionals:

- **Instructional librarians** at the college and university levels, who will find many examples to use or modify for their own lessons, programs, and assessments

- **Library administrators** in higher education—deans and directors will find much to consider for instructional programs
- **Middle and high school librarians**, who can adapt many lessons and assessments for their students and settings
- **Public librarians**, who will find examples pertinent to supporting student research; programming ideas for science, geographic, media, and visual literacy; and more

The five chapters in part I emphasize ILI delivered to students in particular courses and programs. In chapter 1, Susan Mikkelsen and Elizabeth McMunn-Tetangco discuss their collaboration with the University of California (UC) Merced Merritt Writing Program to teach students in introductory composition courses to "think like a researcher." This effort was part of ACRL's "Assessment in Action" program, which seeks to develop and disseminate best practices in information literacy instruction. Heidi Slater, Michelle Rachal, and Patrick Ragains summarize a rigorous programmatic assessment in chapter 2, "Pairing Course Assessment with Library Instruction Assessment of Freshman Composition: A Collaborative Project." Information literacy instruction in health science education is the focus of chapter 3, wherein Suzanne Shurtz and Laura Ferguson articulate strong connections between information literacy competencies and the concepts underlying evidence-based medicine. In chapter 4, Patrick Ragains describes developing, teaching, and revising a credit-bearing information literacy course in an undergraduate Honors curriculum over several years. Cindy A. Gruwell's "Building Bridges for Student Success," chapter 5, summarizes the evolution of ILI for the nursing curriculum at St. Cloud State University in Minnesota, emphasizing connections between evidence-based nursing practice and information literacy.

Part II covers two models for information literacy instruction. In chapter 6, Heidi Buchanan and Beth McDonough describe how one-shot instruction can be an effective and flexible programmatic basis for ILI while being amenable to innovation. Sara Arnold-Garza discusses "flipped" instruction in chapter 7, whereby students complete background assignments out of class and engage in more productive, higher-level work when the librarian meets with them.

Part III concludes the book, with six chapters on teaching special literacies. For decades, librarians have curated and provided access to archives, manuscripts, maps, images, and other nontextual forms of information. Likewise, librarians with substantial subject knowledge are teaching students how to find, select, and use information in disciplines like science and history. These chapters will widen librarians' horizons and, in turn, those of students and faculty whom they serve. In chapter 8, Benjamin R. Harris presents several sample lessons that vividly illustrate how to teach elements of visual literacy.

Chapter 9, by Michele R. Tennant, Mary E. Edwards, Hannah F. Norton, and Sara Russell Gonzalez, describes both course- and program-level support for scientific literacy. In chapter 10, Scott Martin and Jo Angela Oehrli summarize a library-wide professional development program at the University of Michigan to share and build librarians' data-related skills. In chapter 11, Eva Dodsworth and Larry Laliberté discuss librarians' roles in teaching spatial literacy, which is the use of maps and visualizations to interpret location, distance, direction, relationships, movement, and change through space (Sinton, 2011). Ellen D. Swain, in chapter 12, presents compelling examples of archivists' teaching roles, introducing students to rich troves of primary sources, which they are challenged to interpret. Finally, chapter 13, by Patrick Ragains, describes how a team of history faculty, librarians, and instructional design and media development professionals created, taught, assessed, and revised a new course teaching digital media production skills in the context of researching and presenting historical topics.

Best practices in information literacy instruction continue to evolve. The vignettes in *The New Information Literacy Instruction: Best Practices* are mileposts, but, more importantly, they are guides to planning and delivering ILI in a future where students, teachers, workers, and citizens need the cognitive and technical skills to learn, produce, and participate in an evolving, information-rich society.

REFERENCES

ACRL (Association of College & Research Libraries). 2000. "Information Literacy Competency Standards for Higher Education." American Library Association. Association of College & Research Libraries. http://www.ala.org/acrl/standards/informationliteracycompetency.

———. 2012. "Characteristics of Programs of Information Literacy That Illustrate Best Practices: A Guideline." American Library Association. Association of College & Research Libraries. http://www.ala.org/acrl/standards/characteristics.

———. 2015. *Framework for Information Literacy for Higher Education*. American Library Association. Association of College & Research Libraries. http://acrl.ala.org/ilstandards/wp-content/uploads/2015/01/Framework-MW15-Board-Docs.pdf.

Bruce, Christine S. 1997. *The Seven Faces of Information Literacy*. Adelaide: Auslib Press.

Sinton, D. S. 2011. "Spatial Thinking." In *21st Century Geography: A Reference Handbook*, edited by J. Stoltman, 733–44. Thousand Oaks, CA: Sage.

Acknowledgments

The editors gratefully acknowledge the contributions of all of the chapter authors, all experienced instructors, who provided their best work for this book.

I

SUPPORTING SPECIFIC ACADEMIC PROGRAMS

1

Think Like a Researcher

Integrating the Research Process into the Introductory Composition Curriculum

Susan Mikkelsen and Elizabeth McMunn-Tetangco,
University of California, Merced, Library

Academic librarians strive to help students develop good research and critical thinking skills but are often hindered by short instruction sessions and limited face-to-face time with the students who need help most. Busy academic calendars frequently mean that time for library instruction is carved out of scheduled class time, forcing faculty to give up precious instruction minutes. The typical one-shot instruction session severely restricts what librarians are able to teach, often forcing us to spend valuable time demonstrating database searches and teaching the mechanics of citing sources. Furthermore, one-shot library instruction may give students the mistaken impression that research is an event rather than a process. And once the library session is over, librarians rarely have the opportunity to observe whether students continue to use the skills they have been taught.

Recognizing the limitations of the one-shot library instruction model, librarians and lecturers from the UC Merced Merritt Writing Program joined forces to integrate teaching the research process within the curriculum of an introductory writing composition course. During a pilot program called Teaching Research and Information Literacy (TRAIL), conducted in the spring and fall semesters of 2014, faculty and librarians collaborated to develop lessons and activities that emphasized the need for students to "think like a researcher." This mantra, repeated often throughout the semester, helped provide context for students—mostly first-years—who came to the writing classes with varying degrees of research preparation from high school and community college.

THE ONE-SHOT LIBRARY SESSION

Challenges of One-Shot Library Instruction

The literature suggests that though common in academic libraries, the one-shot library session is considered less effective than a longer, credit-based class (Mery, Newby, and Peng, 2012). One-shot sessions make it difficult to emphasize that research is an iterative process, likely giving students the false impression that finding information for their research assignments is like a shopping trip to the grocery store. Additionally, because these sessions can end up as data dumps, with librarians trying valiantly—possibly desperately—to impart everything students will need to know in an hour or two, students may end up buried in an avalanche of new information, leaving them confused, overwhelmed, and more stressed than when they first arrived in the library for instruction. Indeed, a study carried out by University of Alabama Libraries assistant professors Kevin W. Walker and Michael Pearce suggests that one-shot sessions are too short to make appreciable differences in information literacy acquisition at all (Walker and Pearce, 2014).

Alternatives to the One-Shot Library Session

Looking for alternatives to the one-shot instruction session, academic librarians at many institutions have initiated collaborations with faculty to make library instruction time more authentic and valuable. A 2011 study revealed that faculty have a high degree of interest in improving students' information literacy skills and agree that collaborating with librarians is important (Bury, 2011). Librarian/faculty collaboration can take many forms, including multiple in-person library sessions or scaffolded instruction sessions, preinstruction tutorials, train-the-trainer sessions, and curriculum redesign.

Information literacy librarian Heidi L. M. Jacobs and associate professor Dale Jacobs, both at the University of Windsor, describe a collaboration between a librarian and a composition and rhetoric professor in "Transforming the One-Shot Library Session into Pedagogical Collaboration: Information Literacy and the English Composition Class." Their collaboration centered on the idea that "research is as much a process as writing" (Jacobs and Jacobs, 2009: 72). By working together across departments, they were able not only to open a more nuanced conversation about research and writing, but also to work to develop an assignment that more closely engaged students with these two connected processes (Jacobs and Jacobs, 2009). Similarly, a study at Western Carolina University underscored the increased effectiveness of information literacy instruction when it results from a targeted collaboration between faculty and librarians, concluding that "effective inclusion of information literacy requires buy-in from the faculty and students; therefore a solid and collaborative relationship between faculty, students, and liaison are essential for success" (Zanin-Yost, 2012: 455).

At Gettysburg College, reference and instruction librarian Meggan D. Smith and assistant professor Amy B. Dailey describe a collaboration between librarians and faculty that allowed them to incorporate three information literacy sessions for a class over the course of a semester. Adding three scheduled library sessions focused on in-class information literacy in addition to students getting help from librarians during regularly scheduled office hours allowed them to see improvement in student research and attainment of information literacy skills (Smith and Dailey, 2013).

Outside of collaborations that focus on curriculum, librarians and faculty have also partnered to work together in various ways to increase their knowledge of information literacy. At CSU (California State University) San Marcos, for instance, librarians developed a several-days-long workshop for new faculty in order to communicate how best to incorporate librarians and information literacy into course instruction (Meulemans and Carr, 2013). Discussions between faculty and librarians at other campuses have also proved fruitful. In an exploration carried out at York University in Canada, researchers found that faculty beliefs and teaching practices do not always necessarily match (Bury, 2011). At Westminster College, academic librarians Dianne VanderPol and Emily A. B. Swanson describe the development of a faculty/staff learning community designed to increase communication between groups. They conclude by noting, "It is unreasonable to think that one librarian can teach every outcome in the ACRL standards. A reasonable goal, and one that librarians should strive for, is to work with faculty members to assure that these outcomes are being taught effectively throughout a student's career" (VanderPol and Swanson, 2013: 146).

INTRODUCTORY COMPOSITION AT THE UNIVERSITY OF CALIFORNIA, MERCED

UC Merced, the newest of the University of California campuses, opened in 2005. Situated in California's Central Valley, UC Merced enrolled 6,195 students in fall 2013. An overwhelming majority of students hail from California, and student average age is twenty, with only 3 percent of undergraduates over the age of twenty-five; 90 percent of students receive some form of financial aid (UC Merced Institutional Research and Decision Support, 2013). In fall of 2014, 68.2 percent of new freshmen were first-generation college students (UC Merced Institutional Research and Decision Support, 2015).

Writing 10, the semester-long introductory writing composition course at UC Merced, is required for most students, making it an ideal place to embed information literacy in the curriculum. Writing 10 is centered on reading and composition (Merritt Writing Program, 2014) with most sections completing a research paper as the culminating project for the semester. The vast majority of students enrolled in Writing 10 are freshmen, and they come to UC Merced with varying degrees of library proficiency. While some students are fairly adept at writing and also at using library resources, many others have never written a research paper. Prior to the TRAIL project, the typical one-shot session for Writing 10 focused on helping students manage topics, evaluate source credibility, determine keywords, and develop search strategies to navigate UC Merced's over 580 databases and other holdings.

Because Writing 10 is a foundational course attended by large numbers of students each semester, instructors are encouraged to follow a common syllabus. They do, however, retain a degree of autonomy in developing assignments and in choosing themes for their class sections. There is no common textbook; instead, individual professors often select books and readings focused on particular themes. Though faculty do have latitude in selecting the overall theme, all sections of Writing 10 are expected to assign an argument paper as the culminating project for the course.

CURRICULUM REDESIGN FOR WRITING 10

The TRAIL program began at UC Merced in the summer of 2013 when Matt Moberly, a Merritt Writing Program instructor who had previously participated in a similar project at New Mexico State University (NMSU), approached librarians about redesigning the Writing 10 curriculum to reflect an emphasis on research. The groundwork laid by Moberly and NMSU librarians during this original collaboration was pivotal to the success of TRAIL at UC Merced. Based on his previous experience with curriculum redesign, Moberly was able to help us outline the goals of the project and obtain a modest grant from the UC Merced Center for Research and Teaching Excellence to pay five Merritt Writing Program faculty a small stipend to work in cooperation with one of our librarians on the curriculum redesign.

The primary goals of the curriculum redesign were to

- better integrate information literacy skills in Writing 10
- teach research as a process rather than an event
- improve the effectiveness and quality of one-shot library instruction sessions

- improve the quality of student research papers
- prepare students for research beyond Writing 10

The first step in redesigning the composition curriculum was to standardize the writing assignments used by TRAIL faculty. After much negotiation, the faculty agreed that the formal writing assignments for the course would be a rhetorical analysis; a research topic proposal; an annotated bibliography; and the culminating assignment, an argument essay structured as a problem/solution paper. Students also wrote regularly in reflective journals; however, these were low-stakes assignments graded on a credit/no credit basis.

Once the faculty reached consensus on the writing assignments, librarians stepped in to build information literacy lessons, activities, and tutorials. Using a flipped classroom approach and a train-the-trainer model, UCM librarians developed curricular interventions that would help writing faculty prepare students from the beginning of the semester for a more meaningful in-person session in the library. Along with lessons, tutorials, and assignments, we identified information literacy–related articles from the academic literature to use as course readings during the semester (see appendix A).

The redesigned curriculum was piloted in six sections of Writing 10 in spring 2014. At the same time, the lead librarian for the TRAIL project embedded herself in one of the pilot sections, attending nearly every class for the entire semester. This allowed the librarian to see how students responded to assignments, readings, and discussions, and proved to be invaluable to the success of the project. Among the most interesting observations, the lead librarian saw firsthand that:

- Students struggle to read the academic texts they are being asked to use for their own research assignments.
- Students struggle to distinguish between opinion and fact (evidence).
- Students struggle to identify the problem that underlies their research topic or question.
- Students struggle to recognize their own research bias.

Based on these observations, several additional lessons and assignments were developed and the curriculum underwent a second revision during the summer of 2014 before it was used again in fall 2014. All interventions were assigned to students or taught in class by TRAIL faculty throughout the semester. During the second phase of the pilot, the lead librarian met biweekly with TRAIL faculty to review the previous two weeks' research-focused activities and assignments and to address issues or concerns that may have arisen. These meetings also gave the librarian the opportunity to preview

TRAIL INFORMATION LITERACY LESSONS AND ASSIGNMENTS

The full text of assignments is available at http://libguides.ucmerced.edu/think_like_a_researcher.

- **Think Like a Researcher!**—a lesson designed to help students understand the difference between opinion and fact, and to develop critical thinking skills related to research and information
- **How to Read a Scholarly Article**—an in-class activity designed to help minimize students' discomfort with scholarly articles by giving them strategies to use when reading academic texts
- **What Kind of Information Do I Need? Understanding the Knowledge/Information Cycle**—a tutorial designed to help students understand various information formats, the timeline for information development, and how to determine what formats are best for different information needs
- **Using Google for Academic Research**—a series of short tutorials designed to help students use Google more effectively for academic research
- **Avoiding Researcher Bias**—an activity developed to help students understand research bias and begin to develop an awareness of how to avoid bias in their own research
- **Discovering Key Words in Credo Reference**—an online tutorial and assignment designed to teach students how to glean keywords from reference articles to use when searching for scholarly information in library databases
- **What Makes a Good Research Topic?**—an in-class activity developed to help students (1) turn a broad topic into a narrowed research question; (2) identify the underlying social problem associated with their research question; and (3) determine whether their chosen topic/question is actually researchable
- **Database Tutorials: Academic Search Complete and Opposing Viewpoints in Context**—interactive tutorials developed using Guide on the Side software, designed to help students learn the mechanics of database searching prior to in-person library instruction. Tutorials were completed during class or assigned as homework.
- **Chat with a Librarian on 24/7 Chat Reference**—a class demonstration/activity wherein one student asked a research question using a chat reference service as a way to introduce this service to students

upcoming assignments and activities, provide pedagogical strategies, and lend other types of support as needed.

INFORMATION LITERACY THRESHOLD CONCEPTS

Embedding information literacy training directly into the course curriculum gave the UC Merced librarians the opportunity to address many of the core ideas, or threshold concepts, associated with information literacy that would otherwise be neglected in a one-shot session. Threshold concepts are the foundational paradigms in any discipline that must be understood in order to fully master the subject. According to Meyer and Land, threshold concepts are (1) transformative—they change our perspective; (2) integrative—they help us unify separate concepts; (3) irreversible—they cannot be "ungrasped"; (4) bounded—they are often unique to a discipline; and (5) troublesome—they are often difficult to understand and can be roadblocks to learning. For example, in the area of information literacy, intellectual property might be considered a threshold concept because when understood, it gives perspective and meaning to the purpose of copyright law, avoiding plagiarism, and citing sources (Meyer, Land, and ETL Project, 2003).

Based on their shared experience and a survey conducted in 2010, academic librarians Lori Townsend, Korey Brunetti, and Amy R. Hofer (2011) proposed seven information literacy threshold concepts that are closely aligned with the recently approved ACRL *Framework for Information Literacy in Higher Education* (2015). The UC Merced librarians considered both of these documents during the TRAIL curriculum redesign, introducing several threshold concepts through lessons and activities taught during writing class time and others during the in-person instruction sessions taught by the lead librarian.

INFORMATION LITERACY THRESHOLD CONCEPTS

- Metadata = findability
- Good searches use database structure
- Format is process
- Authority is constructed and contextual
- "Primary source" is an exact and conditional category
- Information as a commodity
- Research solves problems

(Townsend, Brunetti, and Hofer, 2011)

In-Person Library Instruction Sessions

The faculty from all nine Writing 10 sections piloting the new curriculum brought their students to the library for in-person instruction about halfway through the semester. All of these two-hour instruction sessions were taught by the lead TRAIL librarian. Because of the extensive preparation students received prior to coming to the library, in-person instruction sessions were completely restructured. Rather than spending the bulk of the session demonstrating database searches, discussing the difference between popular and scholarly articles, and explaining Boolean logic, the librarian focused on higher-ordered skills relating to information literacy threshold concepts and frames, knowledge practices, and dispositions from the new ACRL *Framework for Information Literacy*.

One activity from the in-person library instruction sessions successfully introduced the threshold concepts of "Metadata = findability" and "Good searches use database structure." Metadata is defined as "information about information"; metadata attached to any object makes it findable online. During previous one-shot instruction sessions, librarians often focused on teaching students about keyword searches, subject headings, and controlled vocabulary in order to help them understand metadata and how it is used to find relevant information. Unfortunately, our experience showed that these high-level discussions often left many students confused because they lacked the background knowledge to make sense of these concepts. To give students a better understanding of metadata as an overarching threshold concept, the TRAIL librarian took a different approach when she met with students face-to-face. Since students had already completed multiple tutorials on how to conduct database searches, the focus of in-person instruction was to teach a general understanding of databases and metadata. The librarian began the discussion by identifying databases that students are very familiar with, like Amazon.com. By demonstrating a search in Amazon for a laptop (something that many students have actually done), the librarian was able to point out how this **database** uses **fields** that are specific to the product to describe the particular item they are trying to find. Using the limiters provided by Amazon, it was easy to identify fields for laptops such as Laptop Display Size, Hard Disk Size, Graphics Processor, RAM Capacity, and so forth. The specific information added to each of these fields is the **metadata**; for example, Ram Capacity metadata included 12GB & Up, 8GB, 6GB, and so forth. Students could easily grasp these concepts when they were described using a search tool they were already familiar with.

To further develop their understanding of metadata, students were then asked to generate metadata about themselves. Asked to imagine that they were going to enroll in an online dating service like Match.com, students were instructed to write down five pieces of metadata they would use to describe themselves that would make them findable to a potential partner. As students volunteered to share their metadata, themes quickly emerged in their responses: age, ethnicity, college major, hobbies, and gender were common personal descriptors. Students quickly grasped that these themes or descriptor categories would actually be the fields used in an online dating service to help a searcher find the type of person the searcher was looking for. It was easy for them to understand that the more specifics included in a search, the better the results would match exactly the type of person a searcher would be looking for. Generating metadata about themselves also gave them a deeper understanding of how information is tagged or described for discovery.

Building on these two activities, the TRAIL librarian easily transitioned into a general discussion/demonstration of how to construct good searches in library databases. Search fields such as Keyword, Title, Subject, and Document Type now made more sense. A quick mention of Boolean logic was all that was needed to help them understand how to narrow or broaden a search. Students easily applied strategies they had learned for searching in Amazon to searching in library databases like Academic Search Complete. Based on feedback from writing faculty and students, the shift away from teaching the mechanics of database searching to focusing on these high-level threshold concepts during library instruction sessions was very well received.

INTEGRATION OF ACRL *FRAMEWORK FOR INFORMATION LITERACY*

Along with the threshold concepts identified by Townsend, Brunetti, and Hofer, the new ACRL *Framework for Information Literacy* standards were consulted during the redesign of the TRAIL curriculum. As mentioned previously, there is close alignment between these two sets of standards, but the ACRL frames Authority Is Constructed and Contextual, Research as Inquiry, and Searching Is Strategic were especially useful to our process and were ultimately emphasized in the new curriculum. The specific knowledge practices (learner behaviors that demonstrate understanding of information literacy concepts) and dispositions (which describe the affective, attitudinal, or valuing dimension of learning) were directly tied to the assignments and activities used in TRAIL. Most of these learning experiences were introduced in the writing classroom, leaving time for the librarian to review, reinforce, and extend the concepts when students came to the library for a one-shot session (see tables 1.1, 1.2, and 1.3).

ASSESSING THE TRAIL CURRICULUM

The TRAIL project was selected to be part of the second cohort of "Assessment in Action," an ACRL-sponsored program aimed at supporting the assessment of teaching and learning in academic libraries (ACRL, 2015). Multiple assessments of the curriculum were conducted for Assessment in Action, including a qualitative analysis of students' final reflection responses and final argument papers. In addition, TRAIL instructors completed a post-semester survey that provided insights into the faculty perspective on the effectiveness of the new curriculum.

Final Reflection Evaluation

At the end of the semester, 157 TRAIL students responded in writing to six questions/prompts that assessed their perceived learning about the research process over the course of the semester. These final reflections were scored by librarians using a four-point-scale rubric (1 = Marginal, 2 = Emerging, 3 = Developing, 4 = Advanced) (see appendix B).

Rubric scores showed that the vast majority of students responded positively to the TRAIL curriculum. Scores generally clustered in a normal distribution, with the majority of students scoring in the middle of the scale. Based on the reflection comments and resulting scores, it is evident that most students felt they had experienced growth in their ability to do academic research as a result of participating in TRAIL (see table 1.4).

Final Paper Evaluation

A random sample of forty final papers from TRAIL sections will be evaluated by Merritt Writing Program faculty in spring 2015. Papers will be scored using a four-point-scale rubric designed to measure four criteria related to information literacy: source suitability, argument and evidence, citation style, and source integration (see appendix C). As a basis for comparison, forty randomly selected papers from Writing 10 sections that came to the library for traditional one-shot library sessions and forty more papers from Writing 10 sections that received no library instruction will also be scored using the same rubric. Results of this assessment measure are forthcoming.

Table 1.1. Authority Is Constructed and Contextual

Frame: Authority Is Constructed and Contextual

"Authority Is Constructed and Contextual refers to the recognition that information resources are drawn from their creator's expertise and credibility based on the information need and the context in which the information will be used. Experts view authority with an attitude of informed skepticism and an openness to new perspectives, additional voices, and changes in schools of thought."

Experts understand the need to determine the validity of the information created by different authorities and to acknowledge biases that privilege some sources of authority over others, especially in terms of others' worldview, gender, sexual orientation, and cultural orientations. ("Threshold Concepts and Information Literacy," 2015)

Classroom Instruction	*Library Instruction*	*Knowledge Practices*	*Dispositions*
Think Like a Researcher!		acknowledge that they themselves are developing their own authoritative voices in a particular area and recognize the responsibilities this entails, including seeking accuracy and honesty, respecting intellectual property, and participating in communities of practice	
Avoiding Researcher Bias			develop awareness of the importance of assessing content with a skeptical stance and with a self-awareness of their own biases and worldview develop and maintain an open mind when encountering varied and sometimes conflicting perspectives
What Kind of Information Do I Need? Understanding the Knowledge/Information Cycle		recognize that authoritative content may be packaged formally or informally and may include audio, visual, and other nonprint sources	
	Evaluating Sources		motivate themselves to find authoritative sources, recognizing that authority may be conferred or manifested in unexpected ways

Table 1.2. Research as Inquiry

Frame: Research as Inquiry

"Research as Inquiry refers to an understanding that research is iterative and depends upon asking increasingly complex or new questions whose answers develop additional questions or lines of inquiry in any field."

Experts see inquiry as a process that focuses on problems or questions in a discipline or between disciplines that are open or unresolved. ("Threshold Concepts and Information Literacy," 2015)

Classroom Instruction	*Library Instruction*	*Knowledge Practices*	*Dispositions*
How to Read a Scholarly Article		employ critical skills to evaluate information	
Developing Successful Research Topics/ Questions/ Proposals	Discussion: What does it mean to "Think Like a Researcher"? Discussion: Manage Your Topic Video: Picking Your Topic IS Research	formulate questions for research based on information gaps or reexamination of existing, possibly conflicting, information	appreciate that a question may be more complex than it initially appears value intellectual curiosity in developing questions and learning new investigative methods value persistence, adaptability, and flexibility and recognize that ambiguity can be beneficial
Opposing Viewpoints Tutorial Avoiding Researcher Bias			seek divergent perspectives during information gathering and assessment are willing to refine or change the direction, method, or scope of research based on new insights maintain both an open mind and a critical stance
Reflection Journal Prompts			practice self-reflection and metacognition
Student Conferences with Writing Instructors		monitor gathered information and assess for gaps or weaknesses	
Chat with a Librarian Classroom Demonstration			seek appropriate help when needed

Table 1.3. Searching Is Strategic

Frame: Searching Is Strategic

"Searching Is Strategic refers to the understanding that information searching is often nonlinear and iterative, requiring the evaluation of a broad range of information sources and the mental flexibility to pursue alternate avenues as new understanding is developed."

The act of searching begins with a question and directs the act of finding needed information. Encompassing inquiry, discovery, and serendipity, searching identifies both possible relevant sources as well as the means to access those sources. ("Threshold Concepts and Information Literacy," 2015)

Classroom Instruction	*Library Instruction*	*Knowledge Practices*	*Dispositions*
	What Is a Database?	understand how information systems (i.e., collections of recorded information) are organized in order to access relevant information	
Discovering Key Words in Credo Reference	Key Words & Search Terms	use different types of searching language (e.g., controlled vocabulary, keywords, natural language) appropriately	
Credo Reference Tutorial Academic Search Complete Tutorial	Search Tips	design searches strategically, considering and selecting a system to search and reviewing search results recognize that some tools may be searched using both basic and advanced strategies and understand the potential of each type of strategy evaluate and make connections between different sources and ideas	exhibit mental flexibility and creativity understand that first attempts at searching do not always produce adequate results persist in the face of search challenges and know when to stop searching
	Citing Sources		respect intellectual property by consistently attributing the published and unpublished words, ideas, and products of other creators

Table 1.4. Final Reflection Rubric Scores

	Final Reflection Rubric Scores				
	4=Advanced	*3=Developing*	*2=Emerging*	*1=Marginal*	*No Score*
Changes in Research Process	20%	31%	34%	13%	2%
Evaluating and Selecting Sources	23%	32%	33%	11%	1%
Overcoming Research Challenges	4%	11%	66%	15%	4%
Changes in Attitude and Confidence Level	17%	29%	33%	17%	4%
Transferability of Research Skills	17%	43%	26%	11%	3%
Understanding of "Think Like a Researcher"	23%	30%	33%	9%	5%

TRAIL FINAL REFLECTION PROMPTS

- How has your process for doing academic research changed since the beginning of the semester?
- Describe your process for evaluating and selecting sources for your research assignments in Writing 10. How did you decide which sources to use and which not to use? Did you add or change sources for your final assignment after turning in your annotated bibliography?
- What challenges did you encounter when doing research for your assignments in this class? What strategies did you use to overcome them?
- Have your attitudes and perceptions (confidence level) about doing research changed over the course of the semester?
- Did learning more about the research process in this class help you in other classes this semester? Do you think it will help you in future classes?
- Think about the research you've done this semester, and describe what you think it means to "think like a researcher."

Postsemester Faculty Questionnaire

All five TRAIL faculty participants completed a short Qualtrics survey to assess their impressions of the effectiveness of the new curriculum (see appendix D). Based on responses to one question on the survey, four out of five TRAIL instructors indicated that students in TRAIL sections thought and wrote more like emerging researchers than students they had previously taught in Writing 10 sections at UC Merced that did not follow the TRAIL curriculum. In addition, faculty responses were overwhelmingly positive when asked whether TRAIL students performed better at multiple information literacy tasks than non-TRAIL students in Writing 10 classes in previous semesters (see table 1.5).

THE FUTURE OF WRITING COMPOSITION AND TRAIL: WHERE DO WE GO FROM HERE?

Based on student reflections and faculty surveys, UC Merced librarians are confident that the TRAIL curriculum has achieved four of the five initial goals of the project, that is, to better integrate information literacy skills in Writing 10, to teach research as a process, to improve the quality of one-shot

Table 1.5. TRAIL Faculty Questionnaire Responses

	TRAIL Faculty Questionnaire Responses		
Based on your previous experience did your students	*Yes, more so than previous students*	*No, less so than previous students*	*Unsure, no discernable differences*
. . . view research as an ongoing process?	5	0	0
. . . select suitable resources for their assignments?	4	0	1
. . . write strong research questions?	4	0	1
. . . incorporate evidence from multiple viewpoints?	3	0	2
. . . demonstrate persistence in information finding?	4	0	1

sessions, and to prepare students for research beyond Writing 10. We will know if the curriculum impacted the quality of student research papers in the coming months when TRAIL papers are evaluated and compared with papers from non-TRAIL Writing 10 sections. Whatever the outcome of this final assessment measure, the question now is, where do we go from here? Although we have had outstanding support from the Merritt Writing Program for the TRAIL program, changing the Writing 10 curriculum at the institutional level will likely be challenging. The success of this program will be determined largely by the commitment of the writing faculty who, if they adopt this model, will be responsible for teaching the bulk of the information literacy lessons during their class time. It will be up to librarians to provide assessment data showing that the benefit to students is sufficient to warrant adoption of the new curriculum.

APPENDIX A: INFORMATION LITERACY–FOCUSED TRAIL COURSE READINGS

Carr, Nicholas. 2008. "Is Google Making Us Stupid?" *Yearbook of the National Society for the Study of Education* 107, no. 2: 89–94.

Head, Alison J. 2012. "Learning Curve: How College Graduates Solve Information Problems Once They Join the Workplace." *Available at SSRN 2165031.*

———. 2013. "Learning the Ropes: How Freshmen Conduct Course Research Once They Enter College." *Available at SSRN 2364080.*

Howard, Rebecca Moore, Tricia Serviss, and Tanya K. Rodrigue. 2010. "Writing from Sources, Writing from Sentences." *Writing & Pedagogy* 2, no. 2: 177–92.

Stedman, Kyle D. 2011. "Annoying Ways People Use Sources." *Writing Spaces: Readings on Writing*, 242–46.

APPENDIX B

Student Reflection Rubric: Writing 10 TRAIL Sections. *If students do not meet the marginal level, please score as 0.

Student ID: Evaluator Initials:

Concept	*Guiding Question*	*4=Advanced*	*3=Developing*	*2=Emerging*	*1=Marginal*	*Score*
Academic Research Changes	To what extent has a student incorporated new practices into the academic research process?	Clearly exhibits a **minimum of two** new or increasingly sophisticated research practices. Demonstrates **maturity** in the research process.	Clearly exhibits a **minimum of two** new or increasingly sophisticated research practices. Demonstrates **strong progress** in the research process.	Exhibits a **minimum of one** new or increasingly sophisticated research practice. Demonstrates **some progress** in the research process.	**May or may not outline a minimum** of one new or increasingly sophisticated research practice. Demonstrates **minimal progress** in the research process.	
Source Selection	Is the student using good judgment to select appropriate sources?	Provides a thoughtful rationale for determining the selection of sources. Refers to a **minimum of three** appropriate criteria in source selection considerations.w	Provides a thoughtful rationale for determining the selection of sources. Refers to a **minimum of two** appropriate criteria in source selection considerations.	Provides an adequate rationale for determining the selection of sources. Refers to a **minimum of one** appropriate criterion in source selection considerations.	Provides a limited, incomplete, or superficial rationale for determining the selection of sources. May or may not refer to using appropriate criteria in source selection considerations.	

(continued)

Concept	*Guiding Question*	*4=Advanced*	*3=Developing*	*2=Emerging*	*1=Marginal*	*Score*
Challenges	Is the student overcoming research challenges with useful strategies?	Clearly identifies a **minimum of two** research challenges and provides **highly useful** strategies for overcoming them.	Clearly identifies a **minimum of two** research challenges and provides some useful strategies for overcoming them.	Identifies a **minimum of one** research challenge and provides at **least one** useful strategy for overcoming it.	Identifies **one or more** challenges but lacks useful strategies for overcoming challenges.	
Attitude	Does the student convey the attitudes required of a researcher?	Tone and text **clearly convey a** positive attitude about the research process. Changes in research practices clearly indicate growth.	Tone and text **usually convey** a positive attitude about the research process. Changes in research practices clearly indicate growth.	Tone and text convey, at minimum, **some** positive attitudes about the research process. Changes in research practices indicate **some** growth.	Tone and text convey **some or limited** positive attitudes about the research process. Changes in research practices indicate **limited** growth.	
Transferability	Is the student applying research to other academic research needs?	Demonstrates **a strong understanding** of the applicability of the research process to other academic needs. Clearly identifies and illustrates with a **minimum of two** specific examples.	Demonstrates a **solid understanding** of the applicability of the research process to other academic needs. Clearly identifies and illustrates with a **minimum of one** specific example.	Demonstrates **some understanding** of the applicability of the research process to other academic needs. **May or may not illustrate** with one or more examples.	Makes a **limited connection** between the applicability of the research process to meeting other academic needs. **May or may not illustrate** with one or more relevant examples.	

Concept	*Guiding Question*	*4=Advanced*	*3=Developing*	*2=Emerging*	*1=Marginal*	*Score*
Think Like a Researcher	Does the student understand the thinking required of a researcher?	Illustrates a **strong understanding** of the researcher mind-set. Refers to a **minimum of three** higher-level thinking characteristics required of researchers.	Illustrates a **solid understanding** of the researcher mind-set. Refers to a **minimum of two** higher-level thinking characteristics required of researchers.	Illustrates **some understanding** of the researcher mind-set. Refers to a **minimum of one** higher-level thinking characteristic required of researchers.	Illustrates a **limited understanding** of the researcher mind-set. May tangentially refer to higher-level thinking characteristics required of researchers.	
Comments/ Observations/ Student Quotes:					Total:	

APPENDIX C

Final Paper Evaluation Rubric: Writing 10

Rubric—Evaluating Final WRI 10 Student Papers

Student ID: Evaluator Initials:

If students do not meet the marginal level, please score as 0.
Highlighted rows are of greatest interest for the Assessment in Action project

Concept	*Guiding Question*	*4=Advanced*	*3=Developing*	*2=Emerging*	*1=Marginal*
Source Suitability	To what extent have students used suitable sources (credible, relevant) in their papers for evidence?	**All** sources are relevant and credible.	**Most** sources are relevant and credible.	**Some** sources are credible and relevant.	**Few sources** are credible or relevant.
Argument & Evidence	Are students presenting arguments and counterarguments supported with evidence?	Multiple viewpoints are presented with **strong evidence** provided for each/all side(s).	Multiple viewpoints are presented with **supporting evidence** provided for each/all side(s).	Multiple viewpoints are presented, but **evidence is weak or lacking** for one (or both) sides.	A **single viewpoint** is presented with **some or limited evidence.**
Citation Style	Do students cite source sources accurately?	**All** in-text citations and bibliography references are consistently formatted in a standard citation style with **minor or no errors.** Citations include information	In-text citations and bibliography references are consistently formatted in a standard	In-text citations and bibliography references are formatted in a standard citation style with **some errors**. Citations may be **missing** information needed for	In-text citations and bibliography references are **often inconsistently formatted,** incomplete, and/or missing. Citations

		needed for readers to locate the resources.	citation style with **few errors**. Citations include **most, if not all**, information needed for readers to locate the resources.	readers to locate the resources.	are **missing some** information needed for readers to locate the resources.
Source Integration	Do students successfully incorporate sources in their papers?	Sources receive attribution. **Content is highly appropriate and expertly incorporated** into the text.	Sources receive attribution. **Most content is appropriate and satisfactorily incorporated** into the text.	Sources receive attribution. **Some or all content is appropriate but may not be smoothly integrated** into the text.	Sources **may not always receive attribution**. Source integration is **attempted** but is often unsuccessful due to poor content choice and/or poor mechanics.
					Total:

Comments/Observations:

Student Quotes:

Source Selection Observation: (not formally part of the rubric)	**All or most** sources are selected from library collections or databases rather than the free web.	**Many** sources are selected from library collections or databases rather than the free web.	**Few** sources are selected from library collections or databases rather than the free web.

APPENDIX D: TRAIL FACULTY QUESTIONNAIRE—FALL 2014

Instructions:
Please complete the following questions. You will be asked to (a) share your observations of student practices and (b) reflect on the collaborative endeavor of integrating the research process with the writing process in selected Writing 10 sections (TRAIL).

1. Based on your own observations, did students in your TRAIL section(s) think and write like emerging researchers more so than your students in previous classes (particularly WRI 10 students at UC Merced)?

   Yes / No / Unsure

2. Specifically did your students . . .
   - view research as an ongoing process?
   - select suitable resources for their assignments?
   - write strong research questions?
   - incorporate evidence from multiple viewpoints?
   - demonstrate persistence in information finding?

   Yes, more so than previous students / No, less so than previous students / Unsure, no discernable differences

3. Were there any particular activities, readings, or approaches from the TRAIL resources that seemed particularly effective in helping students learn? If so, please highlight one or two of these.

4. Based on your experience, would you promote this model of integrating research and writing skills to other writing faculty? Why or why not?

5. Feel free to mention any other observations, challenges, or successes as a result of this collaboration and teaching experience.

REFERENCES

ACRL (Association of College & Research Libraries). 2015. "Assessment in Action: Academic Libraries and Student Success." American Library Association. Association of College & Research Libraries. http://www.ala.org/acrl/AiA.

Bury, Sophie. 2011. "Faculty Attitudes, Perceptions and Experiences of Information Literacy: A Study across Multiple Disciplines at York University, Canada." *Journal of Information Literacy* 5, no. 1 (June): 45–64.

Jacobs, Heidi L. M., and Dale Jacobs. 2009. "Transforming the One-Shot Library Session into Pedagogical Collaboration: Information Literacy and the English Composition Class." *Reference & User Services Quarterly* 49, no. 1 (Fall): 72–82.

Merritt Writing Program. 2014. UC Merced. http://writingprogram.ucmerced.edu/.

Mery, Yvonne, Jill Newby, and Ke Peng. 2012. "Why One-Shot Information Literacy Sessions Are Not the Future of Instruction: A Case for Online Credit Courses." *College & Research Libraries* 73, no. 4 (July): 366–77.

Meulemans, Yvonne Nalani, and Allison Carr. 2013. "Not at Your Service: Building Genuine Faculty-Librarian Partnerships." *Reference Services Review* 41, no. 1: 80–90.

Meyer, Jan, Ray Land, and ETL Project. 2003. *Threshold Concepts and Troublesome Knowledge: Linkages to Ways of Thinking and Practising within the Disciplines*. Edinburgh: University of Edinburgh.

Smith, Meggan D., and Amy B. Dailey. 2013. "Improving and Assessing Information Literacy Skills through Faculty-Librarian Collaboration." *College & Undergraduate Libraries* 20, no. 3–4 (September): 314–26.

"Threshold Concepts and Information Literacy." 2015. *Threshold Concepts and Information Literacy*. http://www.ilthresholdconcepts.com/.

Townsend, Lori, Korey Brunetti, and Amy R Hofer. 2011. "Threshold Concepts and Information Literacy." *portal: Libraries and the Academy* 11, no. 3 (July): 853–69.

UC Merced Institutional Research and Decision Support. 2013. "UC Merced Profile." http://ipa.ucmerced.edu/docs/facts/UC%20Merced%20Profile.pdf.

———. 2015. "Undergraduate Enrollment by First Generation Status." http://ipa.ucmerced.edu/docs/Undergraduates/undergrad%20enrollment%20first%20gen%20status.pdf.

VanderPol, Dianne, and Emily A. B. Swanson. 2013. "Rethinking Roles: Librarians and Faculty Collaborate to Develop Students' Information Literacy." *Journal of Library Innovation* 4, no. 2 (July): 134–48.

Walker, Kevin W., and Michael Pearce. 2014. "Student Engagement in One-Shot Library Instruction." *Journal of Academic Librarianship* 40, no. 3–4 (May): 281–90.

Zanin-Yost, Alessia. 2012. "Designing Information Literacy: Teaching, Collaborating and Growing." *New Library World* 113, no. 9–10: 448–61.

2

Pairing Course Assessment with Library Instruction Assessment of Freshman Composition

A Collaborative Project

Heidi Slater, Michelle Rachal, and Patrick Ragains,
University of Nevada, Reno

In the summer of 2013, the Core Writing (CW) program at the University of Nevada, Reno, situated in the English Department, began preparation for a programmatic assessment of its Composition II course (English 102). Since students in this course need to gather authoritative sources in order to write a research-based persuasive paper, the assessment provided the perfect opportunity to collaborate with the library. Three librarians, comprising the Core Writing Library Group, joined in a yearlong process to plan and implement the project. This effort provided the library with (1) a means to assess students' research skills, confidence, and attitudes on a larger scale and over a longer time frame than ever before; (2) a chance to learn more about the Core Writing curriculum and its desired student learning outcomes; (3) a setting to build on established relationships and form new ones with instructors; and (4) an opportunity to teach mutually identified information literacy concepts such as Scholarship Is a Conversation in partnership with Core Writing instructors (ACRL, 2015). The assessment also supported the library program's strategic outcome that "all first year students will learn how to access core library resources and research assistance both onsite and online" (UNR, Libraries and Teaching & Learning Technologies, 2015: 1). Although this project stands apart from the library's regular evaluation process, its results inform all aspects of the freshman library instruction curriculum, policies, and practice.

PLANNING AND IMPLEMENTATION

The most recent assessment of English 102 (2005–2006) had identified three relatively weak writing areas among students: (1) documentation skills,

(2) use and acknowledgment of alternative perspectives, and (3) students' acknowledgment of their own biases and assumptions (UNR, Core Writing Program, 2006: 15). To address these weaknesses, the CW directors proposed a project in which library research and the writing process would be systematically integrated and contextualized around rhetorician Kenneth Burke's parlor metaphor:

> Imagine that you enter a parlor. You come late. When you arrive, others have long preceded you, and they are engaged in a heated discussion, a discussion too heated for them to pause and tell you exactly what it is about. In fact, the discussion had already begun long before any of them got there, so that no one present is qualified to retrace for you all the steps that had gone before. You listen for a while, until you decide that you have caught the tenor of the argument; then you put in your oar. Someone answers; you answer him; another comes to your defense; another aligns himself against you, to either the embarrassment or gratification of your opponent, depending upon the quality of your ally's assistance. However, the discussion is interminable. The hour grows late, you must depart. And you do depart, with the discussion still vigorously in progress. (Burke, 1974: 110–11)

The Core Writing directors hypothesized that "if students understand that documentation, use of others' ideas, and awareness of their own assumptions were all connected—and were all crucial to the purpose of persuading readers—we would see improvement in the weak areas" (Walsh et al., 2014: 2). Specifically, students were expected to demonstrate the following outcomes: (1) find sufficient, authoritative, and relevant sources; (2) articulate an original rhetorical purpose that acknowledges and extends previous work on their topic; (3) use correct documentation and format; and (4) evaluate others' perspectives (Walsh et al., 2014: 4).

To test the hypothesis, half of the ENG 102 instructors (the Burkean Parlor group) would (1) introduce the parlor metaphor of scholarship as a conversation; (2) implement four curriculum modules that required information literacy instruction (ILI), both in class and via a LibGuide populated with links to vetted databases and locally created instructional documents and videos; and (3) require each student to create a concept map of the academic conversation on their chosen topic. The other half of the sections (the control group) would be taught as usual, most often with ILI, but with no exposure to the Burkean Parlor metaphor or the related curriculum.

In addition to supporting the English Department's assessment goals, the librarians sought a deeper understanding of the expectations of the English 102 program related to students' writing and selection of information sources. For instance, how do Core Writing instructors define both scholarly and authoritative sources? Do these definitions match those of the librarians? Do the instructors themselves agree on what constitutes scholarly and authoritative sources? Insight into questions like these could inform the librarians' own curriculum and teaching practice.

Librarians and English faculty at Oregon State University had conducted a similar study that introduced the Burkean Parlor metaphor to freshman composition classes, although they noted anecdotal reports of success (McMillen and Hill, 2004) rather than a "systematic qualitative analysis of the impact of the metaphor" (Walsh et al., 2014: 3). UNR's assessment study extends this research to include empirical analyses of students' final papers and their responses to a pre- and postsurvey of information literacy skills and attitudes.

After several months of planning, the Core Writing faculty designed the assessment study and received institutional review board (IRB) approval; two librarians also received IRB certification in order to collect and analyze the data from pre- and post-library instruction surveys. The CW directors, taking the librarians' suggestions, (1) outlined the curriculum modules; (2) developed supplemental teaching materials; (3) wrote the script for a video illustrating how to map a scholarly conversation; and (4) drafted the rubric that would be used to score a sample of the final papers. The librarians (1) created instructional videos and handouts for the modules, including a video explaining how to create a concept map of a scholarly conversation; (2) created a LibGuide for instructors to access the resources (http://guides.library.unr.edu/burkeanparlor); (3) developed the library instruction curriculum, which included a standardized lesson, a multiple-choice skills assessment (see the appendix), and time for individual work and assistance; (4) selected Bubbl.us to use as a concept mapping tool; and (5) created, administered, and tabulated the pre- and postinstruction surveys. Although the surveys for the Burkean and control groups were almost identical, the librarians created two separate surveys in order to segregate the anonymous responses from the two groups.

Prior to the start of the spring 2014 semester, the Core Writing director divided ENG 102 instructors in half by their last names; those in the first half of the alphabet would be in the Burkean Parlor group and those in the second half would be in the control group. Instructors selected for the study could opt out if they wished, but those remaining attended a meeting with the Core Writing director and with the Core Writing Library Group (CWLG) to discuss the requirements of the study and the curriculum. Twenty-one instructors participated in the Burkean Parlor group and eighteen remained in the control group. Roughly 900 students were included in the Burkean Parlor group with an almost equal number in the control group. Because of the need to restrict the online curriculum access to the Burkean course sections, the CWLG set the Burkean Parlor LibGuide to private and provided the link only to the Burkean Parlor instructors. However, the librarians did encourage the control group to watch the introductory library videos. Also, many of the supplemental materials on the Burkean Parlor LibGuide were available on the general Core Writing LibGuide.

The four curriculum modules corresponded with the parlor metaphor: Module One: "Listening"; Module Two: "Catching the Tenor"; Module Three: "Mapping the Parlor/Putting In Your Oar"; and Module Four: "Framing Sources." Module One occurred as students developed their topics. Most course instructors assigned students to watch two library videos, the first introducing the Mathewson-IGT Knowledge Center and its services, and the second showing how to begin searching and gathering sources using the library website. Instructors encouraged students to use the web and resources like *Wikipedia* to gain background knowledge and locate several preliminary sources. In Module Two, the students watched videos on evaluating sources and then came to the Knowledge Center for an instruction session. Concurring with Davidson and Crateau that "students have difficulty determining source credibility and rhetorical positioning without assistance" (Davidson and Crateau, 1998: 251), librarians framed their teaching around the Burkean Parlor metaphor, emphasizing that library catalogs, search engines, and databases are tools to enable students to discover, evaluate, and select sources necessary to understand their conversations and produce an annotated bibliography of authoritative sources.

In Module Three ("Mapping the Parlor/Putting In Your Oar"), after students finished their annotated bibliographies, they created concept maps of their chosen "conversations." The concept mapping assignment was intended to help students see how their argument fit within a larger scholarly conversation. Students mapped their sources along one of several argument lines that were introduced by the instructors. These lines included (1) compare/contrast; (2) cause/effect; (3) historical development; (4) division of a topic into subtopics; and (5) unification of multiple perspectives. In the last module, "Framing Sources," students watched a video identifying plagiarism and providing guidance on avoiding it, after which instructors taught their students how to properly integrate and cite sources.

Course instructors distributed the pre-library instruction surveys either electronically or in print, during class, prior to a library instruction session. Printed copies of the completed surveys were accepted because most classes do not meet in a computer lab and not all students have a device of their own that provides web access. Although the preinstruction surveys were optional, librarians and instructors encouraged students in both the Burkean and control groups to complete them.

As mentioned above, library instruction sessions were delivered to the Burkean classes after Module One ("Listening"). There was no preferred point in the semester for a librarian to meet with classes in the control group. Some of the control group and Burkean Parlor sections were fifty minutes long, while others were seventy-five minutes. This meant that the library instruction lesson had to fit within a fifty-minute class period. Librarians gave students in the seventy-five-minute sessions more time both for individual work and group discussion of questions or problems encountered. During sessions with the Burkean classes, the librarians often had to spend unplanned time at the beginning introducing the Knowledge Center and library website after discovering that students had not viewed the introductory library videos. In either case, once these preliminaries were covered, the librarians taught a standardized lesson that included instruction on evaluating resources and introductions to key search interfaces and databases. Using the parlor metaphor, they discussed the function of the library as an organized set of tools to tap into a conversation, the librarian's role as "wingman" in the parlor, generation of keywords, and execution of search queries using the library's different search interfaces. The session also included three in-class multiple-choice questions to check for understanding (see the appendix). Library instruction sessions were not required and not necessarily standardized for classes in the control group, but instruction delivered to both groups included discussions of students' information needs, an introduction of the library's home page, prominent discovery interfaces (Summon, the library catalog, and selected databases), and the Core Writing LibGuide.

After an initial library session, Burkean instructors had the opportunity to request another class meeting for the librarian to help students create their concept maps on Bubbl.us. However, due to Bubbl's simplicity, most did not ask for help. These instructors continued to implement Modules Three and Four until the end of the semester, when papers were collected and post-instruction surveys distributed.

ASSESSMENTS

Following are summaries of the rubric-based assessment of students' final research papers and results of the library instruction surveys. Scoring a sample of student essays yielded important information about their performance, while the surveys revealed attitudes toward research and using the library system.

Final Research Papers

English 102 instructors were asked to provide anonymous copies of final research papers for a random sample of five to seven students, stratified by gender, from each of their class sections. This produced a sample of 252 papers (13 percent of the 1,896 students enrolled in English 102 classes for spring 2014). This was calculated as a reliable sample size for the population given a 95 percent confidence level, a 5 percent margin of error, and the assumption that the mean would skew high from the norm at about 75 percent. Not all students turned in work, so the final sample available for rating was 232 papers or 12 percent of the total population. Student papers were assigned numbers, recorded as belonging to Burkean Parlor or control sections, then uploaded to a restricted SharePoint site available to faculty who would rate the papers (Walsh et al., 2014).

The Core Writing director recruited a group of six raters. Five were English 102 instructors and the sixth was one of the participating librarians. Before the group's first meeting, three sample papers (student work from previous semesters) were distributed by e-mail as examples of high, mid, and low levels of student writing. A six-point scale was used, with a score of one as the lowest, and a score of four considered proficient. The first iteration of the norming rubric included the following eight categories:

1. Relevant Sources
2. Sufficient Sources
3. Reliable Sources
4. Purpose: students provide an original rhetorical purpose that acknowledges and extends previous work on their topic.
5. Documentation: accurate attribution; citations follow assigned style.
6. Framing: students will introduce and explain paraphrases and quotations from source material to demonstrate the credibility of the sources and how they relate to the students' research argument.
7. Own: evaluation of own perspectives and assumptions. Students understand and acknowledge their own beliefs and biases without relying exclusively on the views of others.
8. Other: students recognize, respect, and analyze differing perspectives and question the authority of others' assumptions. (UNR, Core Writing Program, [2013])

During these preliminary sessions, the raters agreed to score student papers using the eight categories. Discussions prompted extensive revision of the rubric to facilitate agreement among the raters and to clarify Core Writing standards. Much attention was centered on defining the scope of "authoritative sources" when applied to the materials students cited. The group agreed on the following definition:

> Authoritative sources are written by people or groups who are qualified to build knowledge on—or understanding of—a subject. The most common authoritative sources include peer-reviewed scholarly articles, high-quality investigative journalism (for developing events), and governmental or inter-governmental agency reports. However, if students are engaging in analysis or philosophical argument, they may cite cultural authorities such as philosophers, literary critics, or social activists. (Walsh et al., 2014: 6)

The next step in the process was for the raters to individually assess the same subset of five student papers and submit the scores to the director for evaluation of inter-rater reliability. After all scores were submitted, the director wrote in an e-mail message to the raters that "in all but three criteria . . . inter-rater reliability was in the 'excellent' range . . . there were problems in the first three source criteria (poor or fair inter-rater reliability)." Based on previous discussions in the norming meetings, the group agreed to collapse the three source categories into one category: "Sources: students will assemble sufficient credible and relevant sources to ground their research argument." The new rubric was given to the raters who then rated a second subset of five papers. The director noted in another e-mail that the raters scored in the "high excellent range for inter-rater reliability."

With the norming successfully concluded, the team was now ready to begin rating student papers. Each paper would be read by two raters and the scores for that paper averaged. Each rater was randomly assigned seventy-five papers. The estimated time to rate was twenty minutes per paper for a total of twenty-five hours. Scoring took the librarian closer to thirty hours, because she had less prior experience grading student compositions than did the other raters. Table 2.1 below shows the mean score and t-test results of this assessment.

Table 2.1. Rating of Student Papers

	Control Mean Score	*Standard Deviation*	*BP Mean Score*	*Standard Deviation*	*T-test Probability*
Sources	3.50	1.09	3.68	1.10	0.11
Purpose	3.97	0.76	4.17	0.92	0.04
Documentation	3.32	1.21	3.25	1.20	0.32
Framing	3.37	1.07	3.50	1.09	0.18
OWN	3.39	1.01	3.47	1.01	0.28
OTH	3.08	1.09	3.09	1.15	0.48

Papers written by students in the Burkean Parlor course sections showed significantly better expression of rhetorical purpose—that is, joining a scholarly conversation by acknowledging and extending previous research in a field. These papers also had higher average scores on source use and framing of sources, although not sufficiently higher to be statistically significant. A proficient score of four was achieved only in one area (rhetorical purpose) and by only the Burkean Parlor group. This suggests the need for improved instruction in all other areas. Although the Burkean Parlor paper results were not significantly different from those of the control group, the final report strongly encourages instructors to

> make full use of MIKC [i.e., UNR Libraries] research support and to utilize an explicit curriculum such as the Burkean Parlor Modules to teach research, documentation, framing, and qualification skills in context—as a set of moves required to successfully "put an oar in" to an ongoing scholarly conversation on a subject of interest. (Walsh et al., 2014: 1)

Pre- and Post-Library Instruction Surveys

As discussed above, the surveys were designed to assess students' confidence conducting library research, their likelihood of using library resources, and their receptiveness to a variety of library tools such as Summon (which the library brands as OneSearch). There were also three skills-related questions: evaluation of a sample source, identifying an effective search query, and a question requiring distinctions between Summon, the library catalog, and databases as preferred sources for particular types of information. The post-instruction survey included an added question, which asked students to rate the importance of specific local resources and services, including the library videos, the library instruction session, the Core Writing LibGuide, opportunities to get help from a librarian (chat, e-mail, in person, or telephone), and the Knowledge Center website. The librarians received 883 preinstruction survey responses and 257 responses to the postinstruction survey.

The Core Writing director drew the following conclusions from the survey responses and the sample of papers rated:

> Both Burkean Parlor and Control groups reported sizeable gains in confidence in using search engines, finding sources, and judging quality of resources. There were few differences between Burkean Parlor and Control sections overall, but BP participants did show better ability to use search logic and to judge the quality of Internet sources [nonlicensed sources] than did Control participants. They also reported increased willingness to use the library to find quality sources and reported themselves more likely to think about the quality of source material

> and to mine quality sources in-hand for additional material [tracking citations] than did Control participants. Although we don't know yet if these differences were statistically significant, they do speak to the spirit of the BP Intervention, which was to contextualize library research as a rhetorical conversation among scholars. (Walsh et al., 2014: 7)

Three more concerns surfaced. First, only about half of the students in both groups felt confident or highly confident they could locate a book on the library shelves. Since these were second-semester freshmen, this was not a surprise to find in responses to the preinstruction survey. However, there was little change by the end of the semester. Although the Knowledge Center has many access points for help, including an online guide that explains how to read a call number, many first-year students still are not confident they can find a book on the shelf. Should they be, or, is the skill of locating a book in print becoming obsolete? What does this say about students' actual use of print books? Were they using online instead of available print sources? Did this bias influence the quality and variety of sources they used? This trend in students' responses caused the librarians to wonder if they should address this in Core Writing instruction or wait until later in their undergraduate careers, when more sources would be required for research papers.

Second, in the pre-library instruction survey, about 60 percent of the students said they were likely or very likely to ask a librarian for research help, but by the end of the semester that number decreased by as much as 15 percent. Although the number of post-library instruction survey responses was much smaller than those received earlier in the semester, the decrease seemed significant. One librarian remarked, "Great. They hated us." Further, if at least half say they are likely to ask for help, why do we see a very small percentage of freshmen at the reference desk, chatting online, or requesting individual consultations? Upon reflection, the librarians realized that many students may feel they know it "all," or at least enough, that they don't need to ask for help any longer. Our service ethic and accumulated experience lead us to keep encouraging them to seek help, because freshmen often "don't know what they don't know." This was evidenced by the inconsistency between low-scoring student papers and the high levels of confidence revealed in the surveys.

Finally, there was a significant difference between the Burkean Parlor and control groups in the search interfaces or databases they considered the easiest to use and provided the best results. Students in both groups chose Summon as their favored tool (Burkean Parlor: 64 percent; control: 57 percent). Students in the Burkean classes chose specialized databases second (15 percent) and then a tie for third between the library catalog (8 percent) and Google Scholar (8 percent). These results also support the higher scores for rhetorical purpose among the Burkean Parlor students. Perhaps this speaks to the combined success of the parlor metaphor, the concept mapping assignment, and the library instruction session in strengthening a culture of scholarship in which library tools play a significant and necessary role. The control group chose Internet search engines second (16 percent) and Google Scholar third (14 percent); preference for the library catalog and databases lagged far behind.

Quantitative Indicators

Because the assessment required half of the ENG 102 spring semester 2014 instructors to include a face-to-face library instruction session and to incorporate a selection of the library's resources in their curriculum, usage of related online resources increased significantly from the previous spring semester. In addition, the Core Writing/library collaboration caused the highest percentage ever of ENG 102 sections to request an instruction session: 91 percent of all ENG 102 sections received at least one library session (up from 59 percent the previous spring).

CHANGES PLANNED AND IMPLEMENTED

Working as a coordinated team to plan and implement the assessment led the Core Writing librarians to examine all aspects of their instruction and recommend changes to instructors or, when possible, to implement changes on their own. One modification concerned the best time in the semester to meet with an ENG 102 class. Visiting classes around the fifth through seventh weeks in the semester, the librarians discovered that most students had not previously gathered enough background information to "catch the tenor" of conversation on their prospective topics. In light of this, librarians now encourage instructors to schedule an instruction session at the beginning of the research process and another one as the students move further along and have had more time to modify their early perspectives on their topics. Doing so can help students make the best start possible by building their background knowledge with appropriate sources and learning that different sources provide different kinds of information, which are useful at different times in the research process.

The survey results suggest several other directions for freshman instruction. First, librarians should continue to teach and promote Summon as the primary discovery tool used by first-year students. Summon was a relatively new service at the time of the assessment, and this feedback was an important indicator of its acceptance. The librarians also wish to explore why very small numbers of freshmen seek research assistance, when half say they are likely or very likely to ask a librarian for help. Furthermore, there is a need to promote reference management systems and teach more students how to use them, since neither the Burkean nor the control group achieved a proficient mean score for documentation of sources. Perhaps teaching students to use fairly simple reference management systems, such as EasyBib or ProQuest Flow, can improve students' documentation skills and ultimately help them distinguish their own arguments from those of others.

Based on the positive results of the surveys and instructors' predominant expectations of how library research skills are delivered, the librarians believe the one-shot session has value. Although undergraduate enrollment is rising dramatically, staffing and computer lab classroom availability currently allows the library to provide one or two sessions to all English 102 classes. Within this structure, librarians can introduce students to a wide range of vetted sources and teach basic processes for conducting effective literature reviews, doing so within an accepted rhetorical context. Although freshmen are not writing as proficiently as desired, both the Core Writing program and the library system now have evidence that students value library resources and the librarians' teaching role. The Core Writing director expressed confidence that the librarians had consistently helped students locate more authoritative sources, which had helped students frame stronger arguments. As long as the Core Writing program teaches the parlor metaphor, librarians will coach students to identify authoritative sources (instead of just "scholarly" sources) and present lessons within the context of a conversation. This may help freshmen transition from merely reporting on sources they find to entering a scholarly conversation using their own voices. Looking forward, the university's planned implementation of a "Writing in the Disciplines" program holds promise for providing students with more guided practice and opportunities to improve their composition skills throughout their undergraduate careers.

LESSONS LEARNED FOR PROGRAM-LEVEL INFORMATION LITERACY COLLABORATIONS

The collaboration described here provided opportunities to plan, teach, and assess a curriculum, including planning and delivering revised information literacy lessons. A number of general points can be drawn from this experience:

- A close collaboration between an academic program and instruction librarians can greatly strengthen relationships between the participants, thereby increasing students' exposure to information literacy concepts and practices.

- Participating in an instructional assessment allows librarians to develop a greater understanding of the curriculum and faculty's expectations for student performance.
- Librarians need not be deeply integrated in order to have a positive effect on student learning.
- Collaboration is often time intensive. Strive to make good use of your time and be sensitive to the opportunity costs for everyone who participates.
- It is important to be alert to collateral information, such as students' lack of confidence finding books, or the disparity between freshmen's stated willingness to approach reference services for help and their actual use of available services. This sort of information is valuable and can lead to improvements in user services and library instruction.
- Lower-level university students appear to have higher opinions of their ability to evaluate, integrate, and cite sources than their actual ability to do so. This affirms the importance of introducing information literacy concepts and skills to freshmen and guiding them as they practice.
- When collecting data, it is important to select and use survey and analysis software that will meet your needs. In our case, Google Forms was adequate for collecting and analyzing the student survey responses. However, it is not without drawbacks, since it is ultimately unsecure, its interface changes without notice, reports are difficult to format for printing and presentation, and its analysis capabilities are relatively limited. On the positive side, it is easy to export a Google Form to Excel.
- Review your assessment data periodically, to see it with fresh eyes. Implications may not become clear for months or even longer.

CONCLUSION

After the sampled student essays were scored and results analyzed, the Core Writing director concluded that "collaborative assessment of ENG 102 produced better integration between Core Writing and MIKC [library] curriculum and demonstrated that the BP [Burkean Parlor] Intervention significantly increased student ability to articulate a rhetorical purpose that fits in with and extends previous research in the field." She urged "ENG 102 instructors to make full use of MIKC research support and to utilize an explicit curriculum such as the Burkean Parlor Modules to teach research, documentation, framing, and qualification skills in context" (Walsh et al., 2014: 9). Challenges remain, since improvements are desired in students' documentation, their framing of sources, evaluating their own assumptions, and their ability to address differing perspectives. Further, the incumbent Core Writing director rotated out of that position at the end of the assessment. Historically, Core Writing has had new leadership every one to three years, which requires librarians to build new relationships, promote their instructional program, and renegotiate the content of Core Writing library instruction with each new director. Moving forward, Core Writing faculty and librarians alike are aided by the results of the program assessment described above.

APPENDIX

In-class Multiple Choice Skills Assessment

1. Scenario:
   You are researching the implications of testing cosmetics on animals and you find a recent article by Joe Wolfpack from People for the Ethical Treatment of Animals. **Which of the following statements is true?** Think particularly about Authority, Accuracy, and Purpose in this scenario and how it relates to the objectivity, the neutrality, of the information that will be provided by the article.
   a. The source is likely NOT objective because it is an article
   b. This source is likely objective because the author's name is included
   c. This source is likely NOT objective because the sponsor of the article is a group that advocates for animal rights
   d. This source is likely objective because People for the Ethical Treatment of Animals is a non-profit organization
2. Scenario:
   Which search query will provide the best results in ***Academic Search Premier*** for this question: Should concealed weapons be allowed on college campuses?
   a. [The exact words] Should concealed weapons be allowed on college campuses
   b. "concealed weapon" AND (universit* OR "college campus")
   c. concealed weapon AND (university OR college campus)
   d. guns and (higher education OR universities)
3. What will you do? Use a library tool to locate expert information in scholarly or trade publications.
   a. Circle what you will be looking for: Books Articles
   b. Circle which tool you will use: OneSearch Catalog Research Database
   c. Write an effective search query for your research question or thesis statement below:
   d. Now search

REFERENCES

ACRL (Association of College & Research Libraries). 2015. *Framework for Information Literacy for Higher Education*. American Library Association. Association of College & Research Libraries. http://acrl.ala.org/ilstandards/wp-content/uploads/2015/01/Framework-MW15-Board-Docs.pdf.

Burke, Kenneth. 1974. *The Philosophy of Literary Form*. Berkeley: University of California Press.

Davidson, Jeanne R., and Carole Ann Crateau. 1998. "Intersections: Teaching Research through a Rhetorical Lens." *Research Strategies* 16, no. 4: 245–57.

McMillen, Paula S., and Eric Hill. 2004. "Why Teach Research as a Conversation in Freshman Composition Courses? A Metaphor to Help Librarians and Composition Instructors Develop a Shared Model." *Research Strategies* 20, no. 1–2: 3–22.

UNR (University of Nevada, Reno), Core Writing Program. 2006. *Core Writing Program Assessment Report: 2006*. Reno, NV: The University.

———. [2013]. *ENG 102 Assessment Project 2013–2014: Information for Participating Instructors*. Reno, NV: The University.

UNR (University of Nevada, Reno), Libraries and Teaching & Learning Technologies. 2015. *Strategic Priorities, 2009–2015*. Reno, NV: The University.

Walsh, Lynda, Matt Zytkoskee, Michelle Rachal, et al. 2014. *ENG 102 Assessment 2013–2014*. Reno, NV: The University.

3

Best Practices in Information Literacy Instruction in Health Science Education

Case Study of Developing an Information Literacy Program in a College of Medicine

Suzanne Shurtz,
Texas A&M University Medical Sciences Library
Laura Ferguson,
Texas A&M Health Science Center College of Medicine

Developing an information literacy program in a health science professional program requires an understanding of the nature of health information and of the information needs of health professionals. Librarians can use the Association of College & Research Libraries best practices for information literacy programs as a framework to tie outcomes to the institution's mission and student competencies, while collaborating with faculty. This chapter will provide a case study of developing an information literacy program in a college of medicine while applying best practices of the information literacy standards. Some issues related to locating, choosing, and applying health information are unique from utilizing information in other fields. Prior to considering best practices of teaching information literacy skills in health science education, it is helpful to have an understanding of the definition of health information literacy and of the general goals of information literacy skills for health professional students.

What is information literacy? "Information literacy is the ability to find, evaluate, and use information efficiently, effectively, and ethically to answer an information need" (Lanning, 2012: 2). The American Library Association (ALA) and its associated organization, Association of College & Research Libraries (ACRL), have standards for information literacy, which include being able to describe an information need, to identify and locate information sources to answer that need, to search information resources, to assess the information found, and to ethically apply the information (ACRL, 2000; ACRL, 2012; ACRL, 2015). Key drivers for renewed interest in information literacy instruction in health science education have been efforts at enhancing patient safety and advancing the other tenets of health care quality improvement with the landmark publications *To Err Is Human: Building a Safer*

Healthcare System (Kohn, Corrigan, and Donaldson, 2000) and *Crossing the Quality Chasm* (Institute of Medicine and Committee on Quality of Health Care in America, 2001). Physicians and other health care professionals are encouraged to use research evidence to make clinical decisions and to assist patients and families in understanding their choices in care with respect to diagnostic and therapeutic interventions via the process of shared decision making.

With the abundance of health information available and with the potential that the information will be utilized to help make decisions for patient care and population health, it is imperative that health professionals gain information literacy skills. Many health professional education programs include information literacy competencies. There are parallels between these competencies and the information literacy ACRL standards. However, rather than referring to "information literacy," most health professional programs call these skills "evidence-based practice" or the application of evidence/research to patient care. Medicine was the first health field to coin the term *evidence-based medicine*, explaining that this process is "the conscientious, explicitly, and judicious use of current best evidence in making decisions about the care of individual patients" (Sackett et al., 1996: 71). Other health professional fields followed medicine's lead of considering research studies when making decisions regarding patient/population health. Evidence-based practice is a process that can be summarized in the following steps: (1) Ask a searchable clinical question; (2) Acquire the best evidence; (3) Appraise the evidence found; (4) Apply the evidence to the patient; and (5) Assess the impact (Straus et al., 2004). Once the impact of applied evidence is assessed, a new question may be asked and the cycle begun again. Health professionals must be taught this process and the skills inherent with each step. Following are the steps of evidence-based practice and how they parallel with the ACRL "Information Literacy Competency Standards for Higher Education" (2000).

The first ACRL literacy competency standard is: "The information literate student determines the nature and extent of the information needed" (2000). Health professional students are often taught to ask "the answerable question," or one in which the information need is clearly articulated (Onady and Raslich, 2003: 265). To do this, students must distinguish between whether the need is for background information, such as what are the known pathological or physiological contributions of a particular complaint or disease; or, whether the question is a foreground or patient-specific one, such as what is the most effective treatment for a particular population or is there new information about risk factors or causal associations for a particular concern (Onady and Raslich, 2003). A standard format by which health professional students learn to articulate an information need for patient care is to formulate a question using the PICO format. This acronym stands for patient/problem (P), intervention (I), comparison of intervention (C), and outcome (O) (Straus et al., 2004). A clinical question describes the patient and problem, what potential intervention may be considered to diagnose or treat or prognosticate the problem, whether there is a comparative intervention, and what measurable outcome would be used to determine if the intervention was effective. Developing a PICO question also aligns with the ACRL threshold concept Research as Inquiry (2015).

The second ACRL literacy competency standard is: "The information literate student accesses needed information effectively and efficiently" (2000). Health professional students must learn how to be strategic in searching for information, and how to select the most appropriate search tools based on the type of information sought. If the question is a patient-centered question, using the PICO "format provides an efficient framework for searching electronic databases, one designed to retrieve those articles most relevant to the clinical question" (Melnyk et al., 2010: 52). The PICO terms, in effect, become the brainstormed search terms. The evidence-based practice step of searching to find the best evidence also parallels the ACRL concept Searching Is Strategic (2015).

The information literate student, according to the ACRL's literacy competency standard three, "evaluates information and its sources critically and incorporates selected information into his or her knowledge base and value system" (2000). "A lack of information literacy skills means that users can become quickly overwhelmed by nonspecific, irrelevant or unreliable information" (Kelham, 2014: 235). Such is the case with the abundance of health information. Students should be taught to critically appraise information they find. Some general principles that may be taught to health professional students when looking at health information can be summarized in four Rs: recent, reliable, relevant, and readable.

The next step of evidence-based practice parallels the fourth literacy competency standard, "The information literate student, individually or as a member of a group, uses information effectively to accomplish a specific purpose" (ACRL, 2000). Once information is located and evaluated, health professional students must learn how to apply it to patients or populations. The concept of "decision analysis" takes into account the evidence-based literature outcomes, the values of patients and their families, and the value and cost of diagnostic and therapeutic interventions (Hunink et al., 2014).

"The information literate student understands many of the economic, legal, and social issues surrounding the use of information and accesses and uses information ethically and legally" according to literacy competency standard five (ACRL, 2000). The final step in the evidence-based process is to assess how well the application of evidence worked and to consider if additional information is needed. In addition to considerations about individual patients, families, and communities, the impact of application of evidence to health care decision making must include the economic impact. Newer concepts of economic analyses are important and are better summarized as "value" (Porter, 2010; Hunink et al., 2014). Value takes into account outcomes as well as costs (such things as survival, quality of life, etc.)

Accreditation standards for many health science professional programs specify requirements of information resources and services, necessitating a library to support the program (LCME, 2014). Librarians are often involved in teaching information literacy competencies within the curricula. Dorsch and Perry found that "librarians are actively engaged in curriculum development, deployment, and assessment" including instructing how to articulate a clinical question in a PICO format (patient/problem, intervention, comparison, outcome), teaching how and where to search effectively, and educating how to appraise evidence found (2012: 255). Cooper and Crum mention that librarians teach not only how to effectively search for information, often in for-credit classes, but also "how to use new technology to access information" (2013: 274).

CASE STUDY OF AN INFORMATION LITERACY PROGRAM AT A COLLEGE OF MEDICINE

Background

The Texas A&M University's Medical Sciences Library serves the Texas A&M Health Science Center's (TAMHSC) Colleges of Medicine, Nursing, and Pharmacy, as well as the university's Colleges of Veterinary Medicine and Biomedical Sciences, Agriculture and Life Sciences, and Department of Health and Kinesiology. The TAMHSC's College of Medicine has included information literacy and evidence-based medicine (EBM) instruction in its curriculum for many years with support from the Medical Sciences Library, but with no systematic plan and few opportunities for assessment or evaluation. Librarians have regularly been invited during student orientation to share basic information literacy skills, such as navigating to and using the library's website and electronic resources. A librarian taught how to search PubMed for a research project in a second-year course. Third-year students rotating through their internal medicine clerkship for several years met in small groups with a librarian to cover basics of EBM. Other clerkships incorporated EBM assignments, although not consistently across clerkships or campuses. A fourth-year informatics elective, also offered by a librarian, was entitled "Computers in Medicine," about using computer resources effectively. Because the opportunities for teaching within the curriculum were limited, librarians also offered informal, nonmandatory instructional sessions to show how to use specific library resources more in depth (Shurtz, 2009).

In addition to this instruction from librarians, students had four hours of review/lecture covering the basics of epidemiology and biostatistics to help them evaluate evidence and to prepare them for related questions on Step I of their United States Medical Licensing Examination (USMLE, 2015). Because EBM curriculum was delivered in a piecemeal fashion, with much of the content delivered in lecture format rather than in self-directed or active learning activities, students struggled to retain the content. Students in the college historically scored at or below national averages in the USMLE section on epidemiology and biostatistics. Also, the curriculum did not provide consistent research opportunities for all students, a disadvantage for students when applying for a shrinking number of residencies, as scholarly activities set students apart to be more competitive with "matching" to residency programs.

In 2011, College of Medicine leadership, looking to prepare for accreditation visits from the Liaison Committee on Medical Education, assessed the curriculum. Among other curriculum reform initiatives, the leadership created an Evidence-based Medicine (EBM)/Scholarship and Research Curriculum Taskforce. Participants on the task force acknowledged weaknesses in the current curriculum and decided on targeted improvements, including better integration of evidence-based medicine content, improved teaching of epidemiology and biostatistics to improve scores on the USMLE, and increased research opportunities to develop "clinician scientists" (TAMHSC College of Medicine, 2014). Because of their previous involvement with teaching, librarians were invited to participate in the redesign of EBM/Scholarship and Research curriculum. Since 2011, the EBM/Scholarship & Research curriculum components have undergone continual revisions to improve student learning and retention. While the curricular development is ongoing, lessons learned from the process may be instructive for other health science programs and librarians supporting similar programs. Following is an outline of the development of the College of Medicine's information literacy program, using the framework of ACRL's Best Practices Initiative (2012).

Mission, Goals, and Objectives

ACRL best practices explain that the mission, goals, and objectives of an effective information literacy program should correspond with that of the institution and the library (2012). The TAMHSC College of Medicine developed a strategic plan in 2014 with increased focus on self-directed and lifelong learning, and with curricular competencies including evidence-based methods to solve clinical problems and utilization of information technology in providing medical care. Articulated in the College of Medicine's strategic plan is a goal to "improve the integration of research and scholarly activity into the curriculum with intentional design and resource support" (TAMHSC College of Medicine, 2014: 16). The Texas A&M Medical Sciences Library's strategic plan follows a similar vein to those of the College of Medicine, with goals such as expanding and enhancing evidence-based activities and critical thinking through its instructional efforts.

In May 2014, the Association of American Medical Colleges (AAMC) produced a report entitled "Core Entrustable Professional Activities for Entering Residency." Some of the core activities that AAMC has identified as being essential for medical students entering residencies is the ability to "identify strengths, deficiencies, and limits in one's knowledge and expertise"; to "form clinical questions and retrieve evidence to advance patient care"; to "apply principles of epidemiological sciences to the identification of health problems"; and to "make informed decisions about diagnostic and therapeutic interventions based on patient information and preferences, up-to-date scientific evidence, and clinical judgment" (AAMC, 2014: 22, 21, 44, 26). These principles of lifelong learning also tie into the College of Medicine's and Medical Sciences Library's goals, as well as the ACRL Characteristics of Programs of Information Literacy that Illustrate Best Practices (ACRL, 2012).

The focus of information literacy for the program described in this case study has been on critical thinking and evidence-based medicine skills to support institutional competencies and goals. To achieve this, the overarching goals for the College of Medicine EBM/Scholarship & Research program have included ensuring students can do the following:

1. Define and illustrate the basic concepts and tools of epidemiology
2. Define and illustrate the basic concepts and tools of biostatistics
3. Understand research study design
4. Apply epidemiologic and biostatistical principles in critical evaluation of the medical literature to determine its validity and reliability
5. Incorporate the principles and skills of evidence-based medicine into practice
6. Demonstrate lifelong learning skills, including keeping up with current research, and recognizing and addressing personal knowledge gaps

Planning

When planning an information literacy curriculum, ACRL best practices include defining opportunities and challenges, tying planning to an institution and library's strategic plan, using information from environmental scans, and planning for regular assessment (2012). In addition, best practices in the planning process include defining available resources facilitating teamwork between librarians, faculty, and administrators, and leveraging librarians as leaders in the information literacy program. During the development of the EBM/Scholarship and Research Curriculum, there has been much discussion about opportunities and challenges to achieve the program's goals. To assist with planning curriculum, librarians on the EBM/Scholarship and Research Curriculum redesign task force conducted a literature review and compiled best practices in teaching evidence-based medicine and biostatistics. Using this information and the outline of biostatistics concepts covered on the USMLE, the task force developed learning objectives, as well as the lectures, assignments, and activities to teach the objectives. One of the greatest challenges to the planning process has been finding a "home" for the EBM/scholarship curriculum, or time within the curriculum, while trying to determine whether it would be best as a stand-alone course or embedded in other courses, or a combination of these options. Other obstacles to curriculum planning have included how to deliver content across distributed campuses; how to engage faculty, especially clinicians competent in EBM concepts and biostatistics; and how to create EBM/Scholarship and Research opportunities within clinical years across locations.

From academic year 2012–2013, the "medical humanities" (nonscience content) were offered as separate courses with a course on professionalism, another on patient communication, another on EBM, and so forth. The EBM course was taught in both the first- and second-year curriculum by faculty including epidemiologists, biostatisticians, and librarians. A librarian was asked to serve as a co-course director and has continued in the role during curriculum reform planning. Because students struggled to keep up with the model of several small courses, it was proposed that nonbasic science content be rolled into a single course, leading to the creation of the "Becoming a Physician" (BAP) course. For academic years 2013–2014 and 2014–2015, EBM was embedded within the BAP course, which also included topics such as palliative care, ethics, patient communication, professionalism, health literacy, and history of medicine. A new clinical faculty member trained in evidence-based medicine served as a codirector for the EBM curriculum, and a biostatistician was also added to the team. Being embedded within the BAP course, however, did not allow for coverage of all EBM/scholarship learning objectives or for robust assessment of knowledge. Ideally, the content would have both the time appropriate to content delivery as well as opportunities to be integrated into appropriate courses.

An opportunity for the EBM/Scholarship and Research leadership was a redesign of the entire medical curriculum beginning fall 2015, allocating four hours a month throughout the first year and a half for the EBM/scholarship curriculum. In preparation for this redesign, the College of Medicine's Office of Medical Education collected all course learning objectives to create a curriculum map. This was beneficial, and the reform planning process has required an even more granular understanding of when basic science faculty introduces research and clinical literature to allow concomitant teaching of content and EBM methods. Gradually, faculty have been able to add information about their curricular use of reading material from the body of research literature (as opposed to textbooks and other information) to enable the process. Faculty development in techniques to choose appropriate articles for teaching basic science and clinical content, as well as assessment of faculty competency in teaching EBM methodology, will be new program goals.

During the transition to this new curriculum, EBM leaders have coordinated with basic science and clinical faculty to include EBM concepts in their courses, as well as in the Clinical Synthesis Integrated Exercises (CSIEs), which are case-based, facilitator-guided, small-group sessions piloted in 2014 to integrate basic science, clinical information, critical thinking, and decision-making skills. Simultaneously, continued efforts to provide curriculum for humanism in medical education have led to an initiative for trainees to learn to reappreciate literature, ethics, patient experience, and provider viewpoints in intellectual, moral, and philosophical grounds shaped by culture, religion, and experience such that reading books, articles, and qualitative research from the social sciences is also being taught. Several strategies have been used to enhance faculty comfort with content, including developing facilitator guides for small-group sessions, holding online meetings (due to distributed campuses) to answer questions and prepare faculty for teaching, and making instructional resources (modules, student study guides, textbooks) available to the faculty for their own review.

Administrative and Institutional Support and Collaboration

When developing an information literacy program, additional considerations should be made to administrative and institutional support and collaboration (ACRL, 2012). The EBM/Scholarship and Research curriculum task force described here has been fortunate to have backing from the College of Medicine's administration, curriculum committee, and other curriculum reform subcommittees and task forces. While EBM content has been housed in the BAP course, EBM instructors have received support from those course faculty and coordinators. At times, there have been difficulties enlisting facilitators and establishing clear communication channels between EBM leaders and course faculty, but perseverance in attendance at course and curriculum meetings and continued communication with program leaders has resulted in enhanced understanding of the importance of attention to this portion of the curriculum. New faculty have begun to assist in module/content creation and small-group session facilitation. Within clinical settings, EBM leadership has learned of evidence-based assignments ongoing in some clerkship sites of which they were previously unaware. Clinical faculty at sites without such activities are considering the resources required for implementation of EBM in their locations.

Articulation and Pedagogy

Another essential element of planning an information literacy program is determining the breadth of the learning objectives and the order in which they should be taught (ACRL, 2012). The sequence of content for this case study was identified early on in the planning process, focusing on the order of the steps of evidence-based practice (ask, acquire, appraise, apply, and assess) (Melnyk et al., 2010). Discerning the scope of content for the teaching of evidence-based medicine has been more problematic, as there has been no precedent for a comprehensive EBM/Scholarship and Research curriculum in the college, and there have been significant time restrictions on dedicated EBM content delivery. Strides have been made to address the lack of time in the curriculum through delivery of some content via self-directed learning activities. The College of Medicine's strategic plan recognized the need to advance the constructs of adult learning theory particularly as it relates to "self-paced learning" and "flipped classroom" methodology (TAMHSC College of Medicine, 2014: 32). The reformed EBM curriculum will incorporate a variety of learning modalities, including development of online modules, readings (both articles and the required textbook, *Jekel's Epidemiology, Biostatistics, Preventive Medicine, and Public Health*, 4th edition), assignments/exercises, team-based learning sessions in "flipped" format, interactive lectures, journal clubs, and small-group discussions. Content is sequential, building upon previous concepts and tying to clinical experiences via a case-based focus, demanding critical thinking, and developing skills for lifelong learning.

Assessment/Evaluation

Inclusion of various types of student assessment in measuring educational outcomes of an information literacy curriculum is ideal. Additionally, principles of program evaluation must include curriculum goals, delivery, and learners' "process and product" (ACRL, 2015). The EBM concepts are often introduced via an online module, reinforced and practiced in guided sessions, and then performed independently in assignments. The online modules, embedded within the College of Medicine's Blackboard Learning System, include quizzes that provide options to generate reports analyzing quiz questions and students' responses. Instructors identify those questions most frequently missed and determine if there is a need to revise the question or to refine instruction. Team-based learning sessions begin with a quiz to provide for student self-assessment. Interactive lectures include using online polling software to engage students and conduct informal assessments of students' understanding of concepts in "real time." Students are asked to apply EBM concepts to complete assignments, such as writing a clinical question in PICO format, searching for an answer using authoritative library resources including point-of-care tools, and then critically appraising the information found using critical appraisal worksheets. Grading rubrics for these assignments allow for standardization of scores and feedback among multiple graders. In small-group discussions, students complete self-assessment grading rubrics about their participation, and group facilitators also assess student engagement. The Office of Medical Education conducts course assessments after each completed course, providing feedback used to make course improvements. Anecdotal student comments and faculty feedback have contributed to modify the EBM/Scholarship and Research curriculum content and delivery. USMLE Step I student epidemiology and biostatistics scores are also tracked over time, with the goal of raising scores to at or above the national average over a period of five years.

LESSONS LEARNED

When implementing an information literacy program in health science curricula, librarians should consider how to do the following:

- Leverage the related accreditation and professionalism competencies to show the value of information literacy skills
- Tie in "valued-added" skills that support institutional goals, such as improving students' standardized exam performance and increasing opportunities for scholarly activity to improve competitiveness for post-graduation opportunities
- Work to develop collaborations and embed content into the curriculum with or without a stand-alone course
- Establish regular lines of communication with administration and curriculum leaders

- Begin by teaching critical thinking skills, such as utilizing the 4 Rs (relevant, recent, reliable, readable) when evaluating health information
- Focus on the steps of evidence-based practice (ask, acquire, appraise, apply, assess)
- Consider how to present the information in a real-world context and connection (using cases and specific examples)
- Deliver materials using multiple modalities (online modules, readings, group work, interactive lectures, "flipped" instruction, assignments, and projects)
- Plan for optimal student assessment and program evaluation

CONCLUSION

Finding time in an already full health science curriculum to explicitly and systematically teach appropriate use of information resources may be a challenge and may require flexibility, creativity, and collaboration between librarians and other faculty. However, health science education is recognizing that skill development is more important than content memorization when medical science knowledge continues to exponentially increase, especially with regard to highly specialized constructs such as genetics/epigenetics, molecular biology, and technological advancements. Information management and information literacy skills are being recognized as crucial to the success of health care professionals. An information literacy program within a health science curriculum can be developed to incorporate ACRL best practices, while teaching evidence-based practice and other skill sets supporting school/college strategic plans, program accreditation, and core competencies to empower health science students to efficiently and effectively locate, appraise, and apply relevant and reliable evidence for patient care and population health.

REFERENCES

AAMC (Association of American Medical Colleges). 2014. "Core Entrustable Professional Activities for Entering Residency: Curriculum Developers' Guide." https://members.aamc.org/eweb/upload/Core%20EPA%20Curriculum%20Dev%20Guide.pdf.

ACRL (Association of College & Research Libraries). 2000. "Information Literacy Competency Standards for Higher Education." American Library Association. Association of College & Research Libraries. http://www.ala.org/acrl/standards/informationliteracycompetency.

———. 2012. "Characteristics of Programs of Information Literacy That Illustrate Best Practices: A Guideline." American Library Association. Association of College & Research Libraries. http://www.ala.org/acrl/standards/characteristics.

———. 2015. *Framework for Information Literacy for Higher Education*. American Library Association. Association of College & Research Libraries. http://acrl.ala.org/ilstandards/wp-content/uploads/2015/01/Framework-MW15-Board-Docs.pdf.

Cooper, I. Diane, and Janet A. Crum. 2013. "New Activities and Changing Roles of Health Sciences Librarians: A Systematic Review, 1990–2012." *Journal of the Medical Library Association* 101, no. 4 (October): 268–77.

Dorsch, Josephine L., and Gerald Perry. 2012. "Evidence-Based Medicine at the Intersection of Research Interests between Academic Health Sciences Librarians and Medical Educators: A Review of the Literature." *Journal of the Medical Library Association* 100, no. 4 (October): 251–57.

Hunink, M. G. Myriam, Milton C. Weinstein, Eve Wittenberg, Michael F. Drummond, Joseph S. Pliskin, John B. Wong, and Paul P. Glasziou. 2014. *Decision Making in Health and Medicine: Integrating Evidence and Values*. Cambridge: Cambridge University Press.

Institute of Medicine (U.S.) and Committee on Quality of Health Care in America. 2001. *Crossing the Quality Chasm: A New Health System for the 21st Century*. Washington, DC: National Academies Press.

Kelham, Charlotte. 2014. "Health Care Librarians and Information Literacy: An Investigation." *Health Information & Libraries Journal* 31, no. 3 (September): 235–38.

Kohn, Linda T., Janet M. Corrigan, and Molla S. Donaldson, eds. 2000. *To Err Is Human: Building a Safer Health System*. Washington, DC: National Academies Press.

Lanning, Scott. 2012. *Concise Guide to Information Literacy*. Santa Barbara, CA: ABC-CLIO. ProQuest ebrary.

LCME (Liaison Committee on Medical Education). 2014. "Functions and Structure of a Medical School: Standards for Accreditation of Medical Education Programs Leading to the M.D. Degree." http://www.lcme.org/publications.htm.

Melnyk, Bernadette M., Ellen Fineout-Overholt, Susan B. Stillwell, and Kathleen M. Williamson. 2010. "The Seven Steps of Evidence-Based Practice." *American Journal of Nursing* 110, no. 1 (January): 51–53.

Onady, Gary M., and Marc A. Raslich. 2003. "Evidence-Based Medicine: Asking the Answerable Question (Question Templates as Tools)." *Pediatrics in Review* 24, no. 8 (August): 265–68.

Porter, Michael E. 2010. "What Is Value in Health Care?" *New England Journal of Medicine* 363, no. 26 (December): 2477–81.

Sackett, David L., William M. C. Rosenburg, J. A. Muir Gray, and W. Scott Richardson. 1996. "Evidence Based Medicine: What It Is and What It Isn't." *BMJ* 312, no.7023 (January): 71–72.

Shurtz, Suzanne. 2009. "Thinking Outside the Classroom: Providing Student-Centered Informatics Instruction to First- and Second-Year Medical Students." *Medical Reference Services Quarterly* 28, no. 3 (July–September): 275–81.

Straus, Sharon E., Michael L. Green, Douglas S. Bell, Robert Badgett, Dave Davis, Martha Gerrity, Eduardo Ortiz, Terrence M. Shaneyfelt, Chad Whelan, and Rajesh Mangrulkar. 2004. "Evaluating the Teaching of Evidence Based Medicine: Conceptual Framework." *BMJ* 329, no. 7473 (October): 1029–32.

TAMHSC College of Medicine (Texas A&M Health Science Center College of Medicine). 2014. "Transforming Medicine: A Strategic Plan for the Texas A&M Health Science Center College of Medicine." http://medicine.tamhsc.edu/strategic-plan/docs/strategic-plan.pdf.

USMLE (United States Medical Licensing Examination). 2015. "USMLE Content Outline." http://www.usmle.org/pdfs/usmlecontentoutline.pdf.

4

Developing, Teaching, and Revising a Credit-Bearing Information Literacy Course

Research in the Information Age

Patrick Ragains,
University of Nevada, Reno

This chapter describes the development and delivery of Research in the Information Age (Honors 235), a one-credit sophomore-level course at the University of Nevada, Reno (UNR), designed to prepare Honors students to conduct a literature review for a required senior thesis. Related goals include learning to formulate good research questions; effectively searching library catalogs, licensed databases, and other interfaces; understanding how to analyze scholarly literature; and practicing scholarly integrity (including citation practice, quoting, paraphrasing, avoiding plagiarism, and understanding the purpose and scope of institutional review board approval of research). Librarians created the course and have taught it since its inception in 2010. Although a number of the Association of College & Research Libraries' "Characteristics of Programs of Information Literacy That Illustrate Best Practices" (ACRL, 2012) are applicable to this course, articulation and pedagogy will be highlighted, to describe its place in the Honors curriculum and the teaching methods employed, which include online learning modules, active learning, and group discussion. Librarians who teach Honors 235 have recently modified the course to increase its relevance to science majors in the Honors Program, primarily students in biology, engineering, and nursing. The chapter concludes with recommendations for librarians planning to teach credit-bearing courses in Honors or similar programs.

DEVELOPING THE COURSE

The idea of offering a new course to help Honors students learn how to conduct a scholarly literature review emerged in 2008, after librarians taught a series of course-related workshops for seniors in the program, and soon after the opening of UNR's new library, the Mathewson-IGT Knowledge Center. The new building provided a promotional "big bang" for library instructional services, study and computer lab space, and digital media production, generating interest across the university community. The Honors director wanted students in the program to use the new facility to their best advantage. In the workshops, students were exposed to the library catalog, scholarly resources (subject-specific databases, Web of Science and ProQuest Dissertations & Theses Global), basic and advanced search techniques, techniques of properly quoting and paraphrasing, and citation principles and styles. The Honors director saw the sessions as beneficial but wanted students to develop these skills before their senior year. A credit-bearing course could include assignments in each of these areas and thereby give students guided practice in discovering and entering scholarly conversations. This interest also reflected the Honors director's general desire for students to learn practices that could better prepare them for graduate and professional programs. Research and instruction librarians saw this interest as a dual opportunity to teach information competencies at students' common point of need while also covering advanced topics that would serve students well in the future.

Taking the Honors director's goals for the new course as a starting point, librarians developed learning objectives. Below is the latest iteration of student learning objectives for Honors 235:

> Students will prepare for the research involved in writing an Honors senior thesis by learning the following:
>
> 1. How to develop preliminary research questions
> 2. How to explore topics and develop problem statements/research questions
> 3. How to find a wide range of information sources, including: scholarly, popular, and government-produced sources
> 4. How to evaluate sources of information
> 5. How to conduct advanced searches for information in a variety of research databases
> 6. How to keep track of information sources through a citation manager
> 7. How to cite sources in accordance with scholarly standards
> 8. How to use information and creative works in accordance with copyright and other pertinent intellectual property laws
> 9. Principles of scholarly integrity, including institutional review and avoiding plagiarism
> 10. Sources for research guidance and assistance, including finding a thesis advisor and getting help from librarians

Scheduling factors influenced the course design to a degree. Honors students are typically quite busy, since each student has a content major (sometimes a double major), takes Honors classes, participates in required campus events, and performs service learning activities. With these commitments in mind, the Honors director and librarians decided to conduct the course mostly online, using the university's licensed Blackboard learning management system. Weekly, students would complete an assignment, such as drafting preliminary research questions, examining licensed databases and websites linked from the lessons, and other activities within the course's online framework. By about the sixth week of the course, students would attend a workshop on the EndNote online reference management tool and create an account in the system. Also, starting in the course's fifth semester, several readings were assigned and a midsemester in-person class session was added to discuss a reading. Thus, three in-person meetings are required, but students receive and submit all other course work online. Students can achieve the stated learning outcomes of the course within this structure, but without the burden of another weekly classroom session.

Librarians in the Knowledge Center's Research Services department divided responsibility for developing fourteen weekly lessons. Individual librarians created videos introducing their lesson's concepts and developed an assignment requiring students to apply ideas covered in the lesson (such as drafting research questions or considering one's research plan in light of the institutional review board overview) or use a licensed online resource. The course was initially offered on a pass/fail basis, with the stipulation that each assignment must be completed in order to pass.

For the first three semesters of the course, the dean of libraries was the instructor of record. One Research Services librarian coordinated the course, communicating with students and grading their assignments. This model worked, since the coordinating librarian maintained good schedules for reminding students about due dates for the assignments, each of which she graded within two days of its deadline, and maintained contact with the contributing librarians to let them know how students performed on their lessons and requested any changes to lessons for the following semester. Near the end of the third semester (spring 2011), the librarian announced she was leaving the university to work abroad.

The coordinating librarian's departure created a gap to be filled by another librarian and, once someone had assumed that responsibility, an opportunity to revise the course. Two Research Services librarians, each with prior experience and strong interests in teaching, volunteered to take over the course. Over the summer they revised the syllabus, created new online lessons, and prepared to teach the course in the upcoming academic year. This new phase of development improved the course in a number of ways. First, the two librarians created new lessons on formulating research questions, using images, and examining authorial misrepresentation in the context of academic integrity. Also, the dean of libraries, whose involvement was limited to addressing the class at its first meeting, stepped aside as the instructor of record about this time, thereby giving the newly involved librarians more control and creating a more typical teaching environment.

In keeping with the early history of the course, the two librarians decided, in their first year of involvement, to offer one section per semester. They would alternate as instructors each semester; that is, one would teach the course in the fall and the other in the spring. However, due to student demand, two sections per semester were offered beginning in the fall of 2012, establishing a practice that has since continued. Also at this time, the instructor-librarians requested to convert the course from a pass/fail option to letter grading (i.e., traditional A–F grades), in order to incentivize students and better differentiate their performance. The Honors director and University Courses and Curriculum Committee approved this request, and letter grading took effect in the fall 2012 semester.

TEACHING

The following textbox shows the author's typical sequence of lessons over the course of a semester. The course begins with an overview of concepts to be covered and an introduction to the university library website. In the weeks immediately following, students draft research questions, identify keywords and primary sources, and evaluate a website. In the next four weeks, students focus closely on licensed online databases and attend a workshop on EndNote online, in which they set up an EndNote account. Another resource-related assignment introduces government information sources, and the remaining lessons require students to analyze a social science article, discuss information ethics and scholarly integrity, learn more about citing sources, make contacts with faculty and librarians related to their planned senior thesis, consider whether their topic may require institutional review, and write a statement describing how they plan to use what they have learned in the course. The other instructor-librarian who taught the course through 2013 reordered some of the lessons in weeks nine through eleven and replaced the lesson shown in the sidebar for week nine with another on using and interpreting images.

RESEARCH IN THE INFORMATION AGE: COURSE CALENDAR AND TOPICS

Week	*Topic*	*Assignment*
1	Introduction to the Course IN PERSON: Getting Started with Research	In-class discussion: 1. Research and the role of the literature review 2. Introduction to the library website Topic and background sources
2	The Research Question	Research question and keywords
3	Information Sources	Identifying primary sources in your discipline
4	Evaluating Sources	Website evaluation
5	The Purpose and Function of Scholarly Journals	Web of Science search
6	Using EndNote Web IN-PERSON workshop	(Times/locations listed) Sign in at the workshop
7	Disciplinary Paradigms: Sciences, Social Sciences, Humanities	Choose a database from the library website and search it
8	The Role of Dissertations in Your Literature Review	ProQuest Dissertations & Theses Global search exercise
	MIDSEMESTER BREAK	No discussion posting
9	IN PERSON: 1. Review of Database Searching 2. Discuss Article: The association between cyber victimization and subsequent cyber aggression: The moderating effect of peer rejection. Journal of Youth and Adolescence 42(5): 662–74.	Identify the author's argument. Are his conclusions warranted? Why or why not?
10	Information Ethics and Scholarly Integrity	Consequences of misrepresentation
11	Government Information	Government website evaluation
12	Citing Sources	Note taking and source citation
13	Next Steps in Preparing for Your Thesis: 1. Finding a thesis advisor 2. Getting help from a Subject librarian 3. Research proposals and institutional review	Meeting with a librarian in preparation for final synthesis Discussion postings: meeting with librarian; your research and institutional review.
14	Final Synthesis	Discussion posting

RESEARCH IN THE INFORMATION AGE: COURSE CALENDAR AND TOPICS

The lessons covering information discovery were relatively easy to develop. Experienced instructional librarians are quite used to teaching students to use available resources like the local library catalog and licensed databases. For this part of the course, the librarian-instructors simply needed to craft and deliver resource overviews that would provide students with a good foundation to use in the context of junior- and senior-level courses, including their thesis research. It was more challenging to develop lessons representing other parts of the research process. Summaries of several such lessons follow.

What Is Research?

An early lesson in the course defines research. As articulated, this is congruent with the information literacy threshold concept that "scholarship is a conversation" (ACRL, 2015). The lesson presented the concept as follows:

> Research is the systematic investigation into and study of phenomena, materials, and sources in order to establish facts and reach new conclusions. Students sometimes think their research projects should involve gathering lots of information, reading and synthesizing, and then restating it. A project of this kind is not original research, although it may provide you with useful background and a good starting point for original research. Below are some other characteristics of good and bad research. Keep these in mind when you are thinking about your own project and reading other people's research.
>
> **Good research:**
> - Identifies a problem or justifies a scope of inquiry and states its limitations;
> - Reviews pertinent literature and other communication, placing the present study in context;
> - Uses sound methods of investigation, which are explained to the reader;
> - Discusses and interprets results of the investigation;
> - Presents well-supported conclusions and offers implications for future research and practice.
>
> **Bad research may:**
> - Fail to define a clear scope of inquiry;
> - Ignore existing knowledge pertinent to the present study;
> - Use flawed or biased methods or methods that are not disclosed to the reader;
> - Misinterpret the results of the investigation;
> - Make unwarranted conclusions, perhaps departing from the original scope of inquiry.

To guide students in drafting preliminary research questions, the instructors further advised students that "research uses pertinent data and information to answer a question or solve a problem. Therefore, a good research question is a clear, focused question that you will attempt to answer." For guidance on types of questions to avoid, they adapted Badke's framework for "bad" research questions (Badke, 2014):

1. The fuzzy question. The question isn't well defined, such as "Why are people so paranoid these days?" This question could be improved with more specificity and focus. Here's a possible revision: "If crime rates are going down, why do so many people believe that there is more crime in their neighborhoods than before?"
2. The multipart question. It's best to limit your question to one issue only; otherwise, your purpose may be unclear. Here's an example: "What are we doing about the use of illegal guns and how can we prevent so many young people from dying in our cities?" A possible revision of this multipart question would be: "What is the best way to decrease the number of shooting deaths among urban youths?"
3. The question that will not fly. You may start out with an interesting and inventive question and then discover that it is unanswerable with available data. For example, "What is the effect of the Internet on the prevalence of schizophrenia in the American population?" This might be an interesting question, but how would you go about gathering the data to answer it? Are there already research studies or data that support a causal link between the Internet and schizophrenia? Can you design and carry out a research study to investigate this question?
4. The question that isn't there. If you simply compile and summarize others' research, then you've conducted a literature review, but you haven't done original research. Review and analyze literature related to your question and methods; then try to determine what questions remain unanswered.

To conclude this lesson, the librarians emphasized two points: that faculty in one's discipline and librarians can help students review existing literature, and that faculty can also help them formulate good research questions and avoid starting investigations that "won't fly."

Identifying Primary Sources

In the third week, students viewed a video defining primary and secondary sources and showing examples of both in different disciplines, including an advertisement for a runaway slave and a research article published in a psychology journal—both primary sources. A patent describing an invention is identified as a primary source, while a manual describing how to use the invention is secondary. The video lesson emphasized that a "primary source is the one that has the closest relationship in both time and space to the subject you are studying" (Wagstaff and Gant, 2015). Sample searches for primary sources in the local library catalog and WorldCat followed. The lesson went on to define secondary sources and stressed the importance of this type of information in allowing researchers to contextualize their arguments properly. Students were assigned to list at least two primary sources in their subject areas (examples could be datasets, literary works, paintings, or observational data). The instructor told students they could consult with an instructor or librarian in their field for guidance.

This assignment has given students more difficulty than most others in the course. Many science majors could correctly identify an empirical research article as a primary source, although an engineering student interested in drones and the laws governing them initially was unable to identify related primary sources (the instructor suggested patents and court decisions as possible sources). Students often cited editorials, popular magazine articles, and websites. After reading such an assignment submission, the instructors would reply to the student, explain why one or more of the sources did not qualify as "primary," and provide guidelines for selecting other sources and resubmitting the assignment. Most students who failed at first eventually succeeded in locating some primary sources. As such, the assignment itself was not a failure, but the course instructors have flagged it for examination and possible revision before the next fall term. It could be that varying definitions of primary sources in different disciplines confounds students, yet it is important for them to grasp these concepts in order to better understand authority, perspective, and other conventions in their field of study.

Analyzing a Research Article

About midsemester, students in the course were assigned to read a social science article, which would be discussed in an in-person class meeting. This assignment was added in the course's fifth semester in order to expose students to an empirical research article and teach techniques for reading one, as opposed to reading articles in the popular press. Students in the fall 2012 course read a 2012 article by sociologist Gordon Gauchat, titled "Politicization of Science in the Public Sphere: A Study of Public Trust in the United States, 1974 to 2010." Gauchat examined responses collected over time to a question in the General Social Survey (GSS) about the respondents' level of trust in certain societal institutions, "scientific institutions" among them (although the GSS did not define "scientific institutions," which, Gauchat recognized, could easily result in differing interpretations influencing respondents' answers). In class, students identified the author's main arguments, discussed whether they were warranted, and suggested sources to check for other viewpoints related to public trust in science.

Most students could identify the author's key argument—that conservatives experienced the greatest decline of confidence in science from 1974 until 2010. Also, most believed the author's arguments were warranted. However, in both semesters this article was used, a small but significant number of students said in class or wrote in their online submissions that Gauchat's perceived bias against conservatives influenced his conclusions, rendering them unreliable. This level of response from a portion of the class led the instructor to select a different empirical article for subsequent semesters ("The Association between Cyber Victimization and Subsequent Cyber Aggression," listed in the sidebar on page 59), hoping to reduce emotional responses and possible perceptions that students with conservative political beliefs were being treated dismissively.

Finally, the instructor asked students where they might look for other viewpoints on the issue discussed in the article. Several suggested political websites or news sources; although this lesson followed their introduction to citation tracking in Web of Science and Google Scholar, none suggested checking those sources. This provided a good opportunity to review techniques for finding citing literature. It also reflects the threshold concept that "searching is strategic" (ACRL, 2015).

ASSESSING AND REVISING THE COURSE

UNR solicits student evaluations for every course section, and these provide much of the basis for formative assessment. Students were asked to evaluate the instructor's teaching behavior and the course, such as the following:

- The requirements of this course were clear.
- The amount of work required for this course was appropriate.
- The instructor presented the material in an effective manner.
- Classroom discussion encouraged diverse opinions, insights, and perspectives.

Based on responses gathered over four semesters for course sections taught by one librarian, on a scale of one to four, where a score of three indicates agreement with the question asked, students' overall evaluation of teaching was 3.19 and their evaluation of the course was 3.09. Students' narrative comments indicated mixed satisfaction with lessons and assignments related to resource instruction. Some wrote that they learned much that was valuable, while others saw those components either as too simple for their academic level or not pertinent to their discipline. More than one student commented that the course should better address the research needs of science and engineering students, who perform more laboratory- or field-related work than do social science and humanities majors. Past and prospective instructors discussed this last point and revised some assignments for the 2014/2015 academic year to relate literature reviews more closely to the work of science and engineering majors. Four liaison librarians serving those disciplines taught sections of Honors 235 that year and plan to discuss their experience with the larger cohort of librarians who will teach it in the future. Thus, a feedback loop exists within this group of librarian-instructors, all of whom want to improve the course.

Articulation, or the position of "Research in the Information Age" as a sophomore course in the Honors curriculum seems appropriate, although it is early for some students who may be two or more semesters away from choosing a thesis topic, joining a lab, and starting their research. This need not be a problem, since students in the course are required to identify at least one potential thesis advisor and meet their designated liaison librarian, thereby gaining knowledge of networking and establishing connections that will aid their future thesis work. At the request of the Honors director, an instructor-librarian taught a refresher for students in a senior-level class, concentrating on students retrieving sources for their literature reviews, focusing on tracking citations and searching dissertations. This seems appropriate, as it is responsive to students' immediate needs and recognizes the need for some review and repeated practice. The librarian-instructors envision this pattern will continue; that is, the course will continue at the sophomore level and will be followed, later in the Honors curriculum, by in-class instruction as needed for reinforcement of the concepts taught.

LESSONS LEARNED

In addition to the previous discussion on assessment and revising this particular course, here are some general points to consider as takeaways:

1. When developing a course, work with faculty and others to write clear, relevant, and realistic student learning objectives. Describe how students will demonstrate the knowledge and skills you intend to teach.
2. Include timely topics in your lessons, and present them in ways that promote analytical thinking and discussion.

3. Vary the activities in your lessons. For instance, if you have three or four lessons focused on search and retrieval, devise different tasks for students to complete.
4. Include collaborative learning experiences, especially those that require students to discuss important concepts. Provide class time or online forums for summing up.
5. Send or post feedback to students on completed assignments soon enough for them to digest and apply your guidance in subsequent lessons. Similarly, post grades on a timely basis.
6. As an instructor, be prepared to learn new skills, such as creating instructional media and managing a learning management system (LMS).
7. When using an LMS, expect to revise your course content as needed, for example, when database interfaces change. Teaching experience will lead you to reflect about what has worked and what should be changed, so review and revise course lessons regularly. When new instructors prepare to take over a course, caution them that the previous semester's course is not fully "plug and play."
8. Gather key constituents to review the course and identify general needs to revise objectives, lessons, and delivery. Concurrently, give instructors freedom to experiment within an agreed framework. This sort of approach entails some risk, but when well balanced, will provide good bases for innovation and future assessment.

CONCLUSION

The course, Research in the Information Age, meets the Honors director's initial objective of preparing students to conduct a scholarly literature review. Lessons in the course also elicit critical thinking and self-reflection and introduce students to institutional review policies. While it does not meet all needs for students to become information literate, it is a benchmark for students as they progress toward becoming researchers. The librarian-instructors' use of student feedback promotes continuous improvement.

REFERENCES

ACRL (Association of College & Research Libraries). 2012. "Characteristics of Programs of Information Literacy That Illustrate Best Practices: A Guideline." American Library Association. Association of College & Research Libraries. Last modified January 2012. http://www.ala.org/acrl/standards/characteristics.

———. 2015. *Framework for Information Literacy for Higher Education.* American Library Association. Association of College & Research Libraries. http://acrl.ala.org/ilstandards/wp-content/uploads/2015/01/Framework-MW15-Board-Docs.pdf.

Badke, William B. 2014. *Research Strategies: Finding Your Way through the Information Fog*. Bloomington, IN: iUniverse.

Gauchat, Gordon. 2012. "Politicization of Science in the Public Sphere: A Study of Public Trust in the United States, 1974 to 2010." *American Sociological Review* 77, no. 2: 167–87. doi:10.1177/0003122412438225.

Wagstaff, Stillman, and Jesse Gant. 2015. "Learning to Do Historical Research: A Primer. What Are the Documents?" Accessed April 1. http://www.williamcronon.net/researching/documents.htm.

5

Building Bridges for Student Success

Cindy A. Gruwell,
St. Cloud State University Library

Like many academic libraries across the country, the St. Cloud State University (SCSU) library instruction (LI) program is in a state of flux as faculty librarians responsible for library instruction address and assess the changing nature of instruction in academic libraries. While the emphasis of basic library instruction focuses on first-year students who are completing their initial course work, the instruction needed for upper-division, writing-intensive, and subject-specific courses/programs requires different and more thoughtful attention. The varied information literacy (IL) skills needed for academic research are especially heightened for nursing students, who, as future health professionals, may be part of health care teams making life-and-death medical decisions. With an increased emphasis on evidence-based nursing practice (EBNP) that serves to enhance clinical decisions and methods, library instruction for nursing students has evolved from the simple "I need to find a scholarly journal article," to evidentiary findings that inform and serve as the basis for decision making in clinics, hospitals, and other health-related facilities.

As library instruction has grown into a more interactive, student-centered learning experience, so have the information literacy standards put forth by the Association of College & Research Libraries (ACRL). In October of 2013, the ACRL Board of Directors approved the "Information Literacy Competency Standards for Nursing." These standards describe the information literacy skills needed for students and practicing nurses who are continuously developing lifelong skills in the workplace and through continuing education. At its core the standards set the stage for librarians and nursing faculty to develop a curriculum that informs and advances the skills needed to understand and utilize evidence-based practices (ACRL, 2014). These skills include the ability to find and use evidence (research), best practices, and personal expertise to provide the best nursing care available. In order to meet this challenge, library and nursing faculty work together to instruct, support, and encourage nursing students to frame nursing practice questions into a clinical format that describes the *patient*, the *intervention*, an optional *comparison*, and ultimately the desired *outcome* (PICO) format and in turn seek answers that reflect the "best" information/evidence available.

Now, only two years later, ACRL has approved a *Framework for Information Literacy for Higher Education* (ACRL, 2015), which updates and provides new and innovative approaches to the construct of IL in higher education. This *Framework* will eventually coalesce with the original ACRL "Information Literacy Competency Standards for Higher Education," published in 2000. The introduction of the new *Framework* in combination with the nursing information literacy standards provides academic and health sciences librarians with a robust schema to build bridges for teaching and reinforcing students' IL skills. Unlike the previously published standards, the *Framework* promotes and expands upon threshold concepts (e.g., Information Creation as a Process, Research as Inquiry) that reflect various aspects of metaliteracy. All in all, advances in the delivery of library instruction, innovations in pedagogy, and authentic student experiences have the potential to add new dimensions to the traditional components of information literacy, thus prompting a dynamic shift that will expand to include information, visual, technology, and other literacies.

BACKGROUND

The library instruction program at SCSU has two focuses, one being the typical library instruction directed at first-year students during their liberal education course work and the second, a mix of subject-specific, writing-intensive, and graduate courses. While these instruction sessions vary in content, the overall delivery of library instruction is based on the original ACRL information literacy standards, which focus on finding, evaluating, and using information to answer questions and support research. Most importantly, the delivery of library instruction is often a reflection of the working relationships librarians have developed with teaching faculty across campus. These diverse partnerships provide the basis for customized instruction sessions, course guides, and tutorials that meet the varying research needs of SCSU students as they progress through their academic programs. The Department of Nursing Science, in particular, recognizes the need for information literacy to be embedded within appropriate classes in order to ensure that their students are prepared to continue learning beyond their university education. Ultimately, students need to have a clear understanding of how to use the research process to utilize best practices and evidence-based nursing practice skills when they enter the nursing profession.

Established in 2001 with its first cohort graduating in 2004, the nursing science program at SCSU is a fairly new and growing discipline. During the early years of the program, all nursing students were required to take IM 204 Research Strategies, a three-credit information literacy course as a prerequisite for acceptance into the nursing program. This course laid the foundation for the informatics and nursing research courses, which focus on in-depth research and exploration/application of EBNP scheduled during the students' second and fourth years in the program. However, in 2011 the program underwent substantial curriculum changes in order to meet the Minnesota State Legislature's mandate that all four-year degrees be conferred with a minimum of 120 credits. At that time the nursing program required 135 credits and in order to meet the new requirement, courses not considered essential were eliminated and several others had their credits reduced. Though the value of this course was recognized, IM 204 was a casualty of the curriculum revision.

The elimination of the information literacy course had a considerable impact on student preparation and understanding of the research process. While students participated in library instruction during the required English and other liberal education courses in their first and second years at the university, the depth of their research skills pales in comparison to the intensity of learning that former students received. Because of these changes in the nursing curriculum, library instruction has become even more critical to student success as they perform research and begin to apply their information literacy skills in clinical and other relevant settings. With the elimination of the IM 204 course, library instruction would need to bridge the information literacy gap that existed between liberal education classes and the more intense third- and fourth-year nursing informatics and research courses. In order to address this void, the librarian liaison and nursing faculty met and identified appropriate content and resources needed for the required assignments and research papers. The instruction and resources for these courses share some similarities; however, there are substantial differences, which is evident in the course descriptions. Nursing Informatics focuses on technology and information at the beginning nurse level, while the Research in Nursing Practice course emphasizes basic research concepts and the application of evidence-based practice in health care environments. Both may use databases such as CINAHL, PubMed, and Scopus; however, the research course requires a more experienced student with an advanced skill set.

In the past, instruction sessions concentrated on generating research questions presented in the PICO (patient-intervention-comparison-outcome) format, a very brief overview of levels of evidence used in evidence-based nursing practice, and health/science database searching. However, the hands-on element lapsed, and there was only a short amount of time made available for demonstrations of the CINAHL database. One-on-one consultations were offered to bridge the gap on an as-needed basis for additional support, though given the class size, scalability was sometimes an issue. The time had finally come to bridge and rebuild the instruction sessions in order to provide an appropriate amount of support needed for successful completion of the informatics and research courses.

TRANSITION

The information needs of nursing students are aligned with those of clinical medicine. Successful students need to understand and be comfortable with utilizing their knowledge, working with and manipulating data, and honing their ability to seek out information for decision making at patient point of care (Schulte, 2008). This combination of skills is learned in a variety of stages during the student's academic program. Though the Research Strategies course was dropped from the program, the students were still held accountable for learning and understanding the basic research process. This could and would prove to be challenging for many students who, through no fault of their own, lacked the formal preparation enjoyed by recent graduates. In order to bridge this gap, library instruction, subject guides, and the opportunity for one-on-one consultations would be combined to accommodate students regardless of their level of expertise. The restructured approach would include new content that clearly presented the resources and searching skills needed for finding appropriate information and resources for EBNP and informatics competencies.

MOVING TOWARD A LEARNER FOCUS

While the nursing program was undergoing its revision, the informatics and nursing research courses experienced instructor changes that took several semesters to stabilize. Due to the strong relationship with the overall department, contact with the new faculty was easily arranged. A series of meetings ensued, and excitement grew as a new collaborative effort would determine the best steps for reintegrating library instruction within the revised curriculum. During the time that the nursing faculty took to revise the content and delivery of their courses, the librarian reviewed both the ACRL "Information Literacy Competency Standards for Nursing" and the early draft of the *Framework for Information Literacy for Higher Education*. Though the *Framework* would not be finalized until February 2015, the threshold concepts had the potential to provide a fresh and robust structure for developing library instruction sessions and activities for the upcoming (2013–2014) academic year.

Restructuring the library instruction sessions challenged all parties to work together to develop opportunities to engage and frame a more consistent and relevant student experience through clearly defined learning outcomes. To this end, the ACRL "Information Literacy Competency Standards for Nursing" proved quite helpful by providing realistic and appropriate guidelines. The *Framework*, on the other hand, provided two highly relevant focal points, the first of which, Research as Inquiry, describes and defines the various aspects of research from question(s) to open and thoughtful conclusions and was clearly applicable to the instruction sessions for the nursing research course. The second, Information Creation as a Process, highlights the delivery of information including its value, format, and products, which has serious implications for the use of technology in the informatics course work. As a result of the planning sessions, the nursing faculty and liaison librarian were able to agree on four general outcomes with some slight variations for each course. The nursing informatics course, which precedes the research course, would aim for outcomes that would continue to build their information literacy skills as they

- identify health sciences databases
- utilize advanced search strategies
- evaluate the quality of information resources

This instruction anticipates the more rigorous outcomes created for the nursing research course, which is taken in the fourth year of the nursing program. Given the nature of the overall course work, students will need to know how to

- use PICO to identify and clarify questions for their research projects
- explore and find information about their topics in appropriate databases
- recognize levels of evidence
- evaluate and synthesize research from journal articles in order to answer and/or support their PICO/research questions

Discussions and activities in the revised sessions would include identifying and developing research questions, further examining and selecting appropriate health and general science information resources, and building complex search strategies. In addition, there would be a review of the general principles of evidence-based nursing practice. Additional questions and topics for discussion were anticipated; however, in order to streamline the instruction sessions, those questions/topics would be handled as they became evident during the sessions. Finally, in order to meet the goals of the sessions and allow time for activities in support of the course assignments, a full ninety minutes would be allotted with personal consultations available by appointment at a later time.

Both the nursing informatics and research courses are sizeable, with a steady enrollment of forty-five students. In the past, instruction sessions were delivered in a typical one-shot general lecture and demonstration format, or by splitting the class in two and holding concurrent or consecutive hands-on sessions. However, finding a location where all students would be able to comfortably fit could be quite challenging given the limited seats available in the library instruction classroom. Luckily, a new BYOD (Bring Your Own Device), technology-rich classroom was available. This room is designed to present students with the opportunity to sit in groups where they will be more likely to discuss their topics, seek input from their peers, and assist each other as the class moves through a variety of activities in a learner-centered environment. Each table has two monitors, one of which allows the instructor to share his or her desktop. In addition, there is a desktop computer available at each table and VGA/HDMI cables that students may use to display their work from the iPad minis they receive upon entering the nursing program or, if preferred, their personal laptops.

In order to maximize the students' time, the librarian and nursing faculty agreed to utilize customized worksheets to actively engage students in a learner-centered activity where students could demonstrate their skills and learning. These tools would also address the learning outcomes and help students jump-start the research process. This decision was based on a review of the previous library instruction content and pedagogy. Rather than assume the role of classroom lecturer, a.k.a. talking head, the instructing librarian would be better served to act as a "guide on the side" rather than the traditional role of "sage on the stage" (Kaplowitz, 2012: 8). The focus of library instruction would then shift with students taking the time and opportunity to initiate their research while building their information literacy confidence and skill set.

Several worksheets and online guides were developed to address the unique facets for both the informatics and research instruction sessions. The customized worksheets (see appendixes A and B) target the respective courses and are utilized during instruction sessions to stimulate critical thinking about topics and assist in the drafting of research questions and strategies. In addition, all findings that occur during the sessions are recorded on the worksheets and eventually shared with the nursing instructor. The second set of tools, web-based course guides (see figures 5.1 and 5.2), include informa-

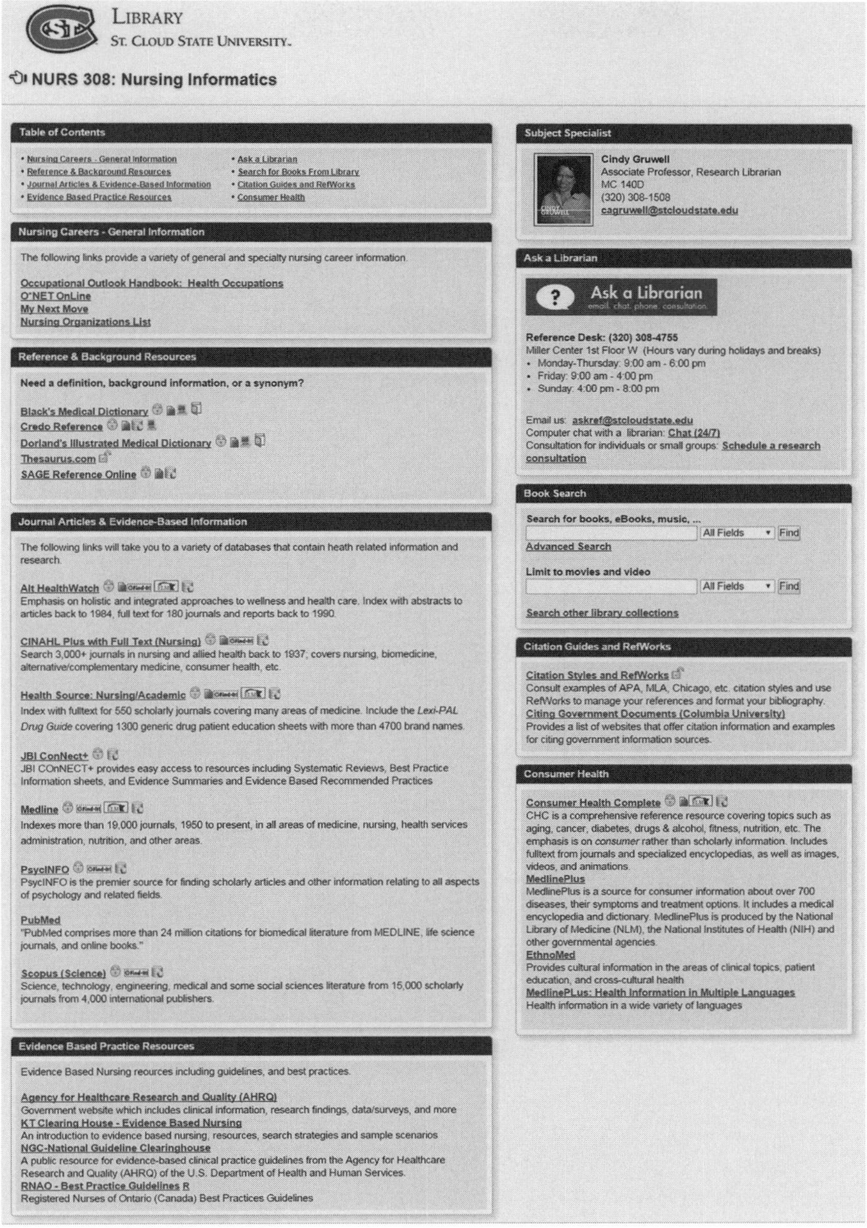

LIBRARY
ST. CLOUD STATE UNIVERSITY

NURS 308: Nursing Informatics

Table of Contents

- Nursing Careers - General Information
- Reference & Background Resources
- Journal Articles & Evidence-Based Information
- Evidence Based Practice Resources
- Ask a Librarian
- Search for Books From Library
- Citation Guides and RefWorks
- Consumer Health

Nursing Careers - General Information

The following links provide a variety of general and specialty nursing career information.

Occupational Outlook Handbook: Health Occupations
O*NET OnLine
My Next Move
Nursing Organizations List

Reference & Background Resources

Need a definition, background information, or a synonym?

Black's Medical Dictionary
Credo Reference
Dorland's Illustrated Medical Dictionary
Thesaurus.com
SAGE Reference Online

Journal Articles & Evidence-Based Information

The following links will take you to a variety of databases that contain heath related information and research.

Alt HealthWatch
Emphasis on holistic and integrated approaches to wellness and health care. Index with abstracts to articles back to 1984, full text for 180 journals and reports back to 1990.

CINAHL Plus with Full Text (Nursing)
Search 3,000+ journals in nursing and allied health back to 1937; covers nursing, biomedicine, alternative/complementary medicine, consumer health, etc.

Health Source: Nursing/Academic
Index with fulltext for 550 scholarly journals covering many areas of medicine. Include the *Lexi-PAL Drug Guide* covering 1300 generic drug patient education sheets with more than 4700 brand names.

JBI ConNect+
JBI COnNECT+ provides easy access to resources including Systematic Reviews, Best Practice Information sheets, and Evidence Summaries and Evidence Based Recommended Practices

Medline
Indexes more than 19,000 journals, 1950 to present, in all areas of medicine, nursing, health services administration, nutrition, and other areas.

PsycINFO
PsycINFO is the premier source for finding scholarly articles and other information relating to all aspects of psychology and related fields.

PubMed
"PubMed comprises more than 24 million citations for biomedical literature from MEDLINE, life science journals, and online books."

Scopus (Science)
Science, technology, engineering, medical and some social sciences literature from 15,000 scholarly journals from 4,000 international publishers.

Evidence Based Practice Resources

Evidence Based Nursing reources including guidelines, and best practices.

Agency for Healthcare Research and Quality (AHRQ)
Government website which includes clinical information, research findings, data/surveys, and more
KT Clearing House - Evidence Based Nursing
An introduction to evidence based nursing, resources, search strategies and sample scenarios
NGC-National Guideline Clearinghouse
A public resource for evidence-based clinical practice guidelines from the Agency for Healthcare Research and Quality (AHRQ) of the U.S. Department of Health and Human Services.
RNAO - Best Practice Guidelines R
Registered Nurses of Ontario (Canada) Best Practices Guidelines

Subject Specialist

Cindy Gruwell
Associate Professor, Research Librarian
MC 140D
(320) 308-1508
cagruwell@stcloudstate.edu

Ask a Librarian

Ask a Librarian
email. chat. phone. consultation.

Reference Desk: (320) 308-4755
Miller Center 1st Floor W (Hours vary during holidays and breaks)

- Monday-Thursday: 9:00 am - 6:00 pm
- Friday: 9:00 am - 4:00 pm
- Sunday: 4:00 pm - 8:00 pm

Email us: askref@stcloudstate.edu
Computer chat with a librarian: Chat (24/7)
Consultation for individuals or small groups: Schedule a research consultation

Book Search

Search for books, eBooks, music, ...
All Fields | Find
Advanced Search

Limit to movies and video
All Fields | Find

Search other library collections

Citation Guides and RefWorks

Citation Styles and RefWorks
Consult examples of APA, MLA, Chicago, etc. citation styles and use RefWorks to manage your references and format your bibliography.
Citing Government Documents (Columbia University)
Provides a list of websites that offer citation information and examples for citing government information sources.

Consumer Health

Consumer Health Complete
CHC is a comprehensive reference resource covering topics such as aging, cancer, diabetes, drugs & alcohol, fitness, nutrition, etc. The emphasis is on *consumer* rather than scholarly information. Includes fulltext from journals and specialized encyclopedias, as well as images, videos, and animations.
MedlinePlus
MedlinePlus is a source for consumer information about over 700 diseases, their symptoms and treatment options. It includes a medical encyclopedia and dictionary. MedlinePlus is produced by the National Library of Medicine (NLM), the National Institutes of Health (NIH) and other governmental agencies.
EthnoMed
Provides cultural information in the areas of clinical topics, patient education, and cross-cultural health
MedlinePLus: Health Information in Multiple Languages
Health information in a wide variety of languages

Figure 5.1. Course Guide: NURS 308 Nursing Informatics.

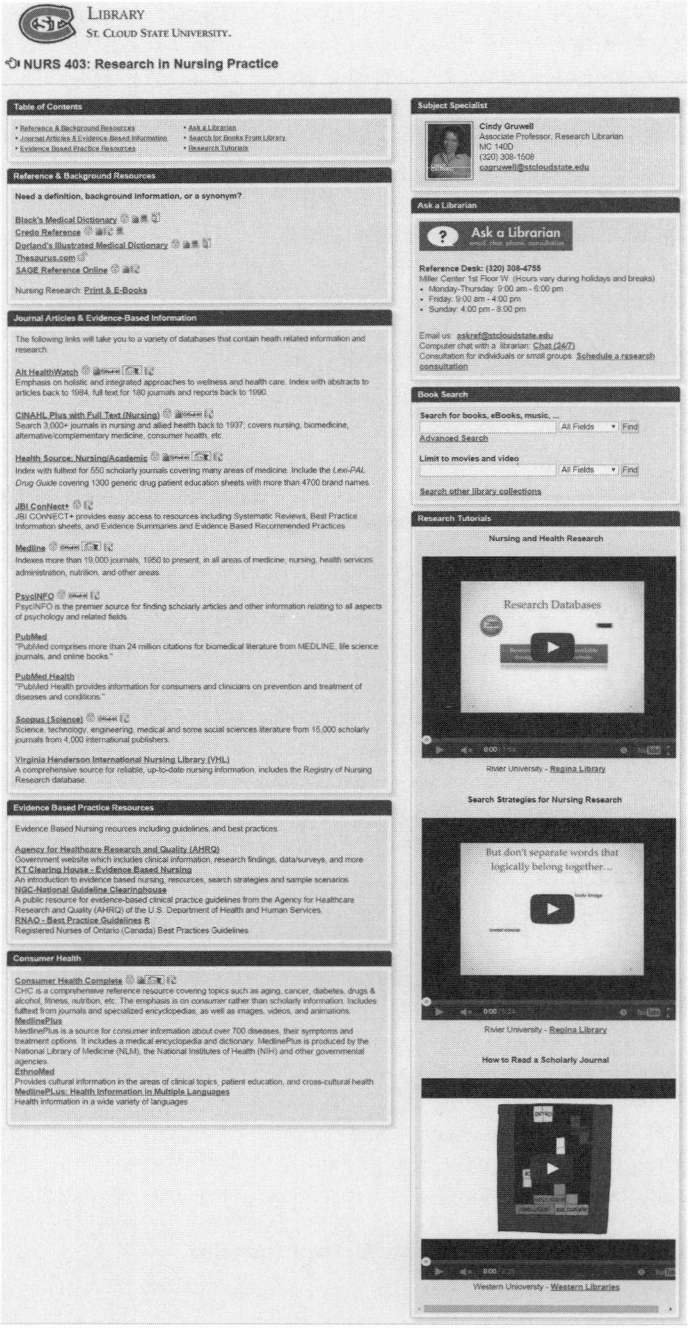
LIBRARY
ST. CLOUD STATE UNIVERSITY.
NURS 403: Research in Nursing Practice
Table of Contents
• Reference & Background Resources
• Journal Articles & Evidence Based Information
• Evidence Based Practice Resources
• Ask a Librarian
• Search for Books From Library
• Research Tutorials
Reference & Background Resources
Need a definition, background information, or a synonym?
Black's Medical Dictionary
Credo Reference
Dorland's Illustrated Medical Dictionary
Thesaurus.com
SAGE Reference Online
Nursing Research: Print & E-Books
Journal Articles & Evidence-Based Information
The following links will take you to a variety of databases that contain heath related information and research.
Alt HealthWatch
Emphasis on holistic and integrated approaches to wellness and health care. Index with abstracts to articles back to 1984, full text for 180 journals and reports back to 1990.
CINAHL Plus with Full Text (Nursing)
Search 3,000+ journals in nursing and allied health back to 1937; covers nursing, biomedicine, alternative/complementary medicine, consumer health, etc.
Health Source: Nursing/Academic
Index with fulltext for 550 scholarly journals covering many areas of medicine. Include the Lexi-PAL Drug Guide covering 1300 generic drug patient education sheets with more than 4700 brand names.
JBI ConNect+
JBI COnNECT+ provides easy access to resources including Systematic Reviews, Best Practice Information sheets, and Evidence Summaries and Evidence Based Recommended Practices
Medline
Indexes more than 19,000 journals, 1950 to present, in all areas of medicine, nursing, health services administration, nutrition, and other areas.
PsycINFO
PsycINFO is the premier source for finding scholarly articles and other information relating to all aspects of psychology and related fields.
PubMed
"PubMed comprises more than 24 million citations for biomedical literature from MEDLINE, life science journals, and online books."
PubMed Health
"PubMed Health provides information for consumers and clinicians on prevention and treatment of diseases and conditions."
Scopus (Science)
Science, technology, engineering, medical and some social sciences literature from 15,000 scholarly journals from 4,000 international publishers.
Virginia Henderson International Nursing Library (VHL)
A comprehensive source for reliable, up-to-date nursing information, includes the Registry of Nursing Research database.
Evidence Based Practice Resources
Evidence Based Nursing reources including guidelines, and best practices.
Agency for Healthcare Research and Quality (AHRQ)
Government website which includes clinical information, research findings, data/surveys, and more
KT Clearing House - Evidence Based Nursing
An introduction to evidence based nursing, resources, search strategies and sample scenarios
NGC-National Guideline Clearinghouse
A public resource for evidence-based clinical practice guidelines from the Agency for Healthcare Research and Quality (AHRQ) of the U.S. Department of Health and Human Services.
RNAO - Best Practice Guidelines R
Registered Nurses of Ontario (Canada) Best Practices Guidelines
Consumer Health
Consumer Health Complete
CHC is a comprehensive reference resource covering topics such as aging, cancer, diabetes, drugs & alcohol, fitness, nutrition, etc. The emphasis is on consumer rather than scholarly information. Includes fulltext from journals and specialized encyclopedias, as well as images, videos, and animations.
MedlinePlus
MedlinePlus is a source for consumer information about over 700 diseases, their symptoms and treatment options. It includes a medical encyclopedia and dictionary. MedlinePlus is produced by the National Library of Medicine (NLM), the National Institutes of Health (NIH) and other governmental agencies.
EthnoMed
Provides cultural information in the areas of clinical topics, patient education, and cross-cultural health
MedlinePLus: Health Information in Multiple Languages
Health information in a wide variety of languages
Subject Specialist
Cindy Gruwell
Associate Professor, Research Librarian
MC 140D
(320) 308-1508
cagruwell@stcloudstate.edu
Ask a Librarian
Ask a Librarian
Reference Desk: (320) 308-4755
Miller Center 1st Floor W (Hours vary during holidays and breaks)
• Monday-Thursday: 9:00 am - 6:00 pm
• Friday: 9:00 am - 4:00 pm
• Sunday: 4:00 pm - 8:00 pm
Email us: askref@stcloudstate.edu
Computer chat with a librarian: Chat (24/7)
Consultation for individuals or small groups: Schedule a research consultation
Book Search
Search for books, eBooks, music, ...
All Fields
Find
Advanced Search
Limit to movies and video
All Fields
Find
Search other library collections
Research Tutorials
Nursing and Health Research
Research Databases
Rivier University - Regina Library
Search Strategies for Nursing Research
But don't separate words that logically belong together...
Rivier University - Regina Library
How to Read a Scholarly Journal
Western Unioversty - Western Libraries

Figure 5.2. Course Guide: NURS 403 Research in Nursing Practice.

tion resources centered on the topics of each course. The webpages include links to subject-specific resources such as medical dictionaries, encyclopedias, journal databases, and citation guides. There are also links to external resources that address EBNP, consumer health, and career information. These guides are designed to pull together and in a sense package the primary types of information that students use during their courses.

The library instruction session was segmented and delivered in three sections with an emphasis on hands-on activities instead of lecture and demonstration. This structure presented students with the opportunity to work through the handout and search for journal articles without being pressed for time. Each segment focused on steps that supported the course's research project including defining topics, using PICO, developing research questions, and selecting search terms and strategies. The mix of presentation, demonstration, discussion, and hands-on activities ensured that the students' experience would include activities that appealed to "visual, auditory, and kinesthetic learners" (Kaplowitz, 2012: 8), all of which are integral in a learning-centered environment.

WORKING TOWARD ASSESSMENT

The assessment of SCSU's library instruction has been primarily anecdotal. In the past, evaluations were handed out at the end of each instruction session; however, they were considered cursory because there was not enough solid information gathered for true measurement. Fortunately, nursing faculty share comments regarding the quality of their students' research, resources, and ability to understand and interpret EBNP. Currently, the assessment librarian is working with all library instructors to develop a variety of tools that will help assess and quantify the library's instruction program.

One example of this is already in process. During the fall of 2014, nursing faculty requested a modular series of tutorials with accompanying quizzes for their new online RN Baccalaureate Completion Program (RN to BSN). These tutorials would familiarize students with SCSU library resources and services. In consultation with the nursing program coordinator, several ideas were explored that eventually led to the development of five specific modules and quizzes for integration into NURS 414—Role Transition to BSN, the initial course in the program. Each module covers a variety of information and/or resources available through the library. They are as follows:

1. The Basics—General Library Information
2. Nursing Research: Getting Started
3. Finding Print Books, E-books, and Video

4. Locating Journal Articles
5. Using Citation Style Guides and RefWorks

Students access the tutorials through D2L Brightspace, the university's learning management system, and are given two weeks to review the content, which includes a mix of text, images, and video. Each module has a five-question quiz that is used to assess whether students have reviewed the material.

While the modules for the tutorial took some time to develop, they were ready and easily placed in the course management system (D2L) in time for the program launch in the spring of 2015. Though early in the first semester of this new program, a quick review of the quizzes reveals that students seem to be well informed about the services available from the library and have a good sense of which resources are most appropriate for the health sciences. Further assessment and revision of the quizzes will allow for better understanding of the students' information literacy skills and prepare them for more complex research. The tutorials will also serve as an essential frame of reference for students in subsequent course work and the research phase of their program. The timing of the tutorials' inclusion was very important because it would give the library and librarian the opportunity to make a positive impression and connections with the inaugural cohort. This activity in and of itself assists in furthering the relationship and collaboration between the nursing department and faculty librarians along with the assessment of the students' information literacy skill set.

INTEGRATING THE *FRAMEWORK*

With the ACRL Board of Directors' approval of the ACRL *Framework for Information Literacy for Higher Education* in February 2015, information literacy and library instruction enters a new dimension. Such is the case with the library instruction directed at nursing students. While instruction sessions and activities noted in this chapter have changed over time, there is still room for improvement. The current instruction reflects the earliest drafts of the *Framework* with specific attention given to Research as Inquiry and Information Creation as a Process (ACRL, 2015). These particular frames, along with their knowledge practices and dispositions, cover much of the content and skills needed for evidence-based nursing practice. Questions, evaluation, and organization are but a few of the practices commonly applied to the research process. When coupled with the ability to understand the complexity of questions and methods of research, it becomes evident that the *Framework* goes well beyond the basic tenets of the research process. Instead, it approaches information literacy in a manner that requires a more in-depth and thoughtful consideration of both the knowledge and skill sets needed for multiple literacies. In many respects, the library instruction discussed in this chapter is ahead of the game. The focus on EBNP reflects some of the core concepts in the *Framework*. This is demonstrated by the practical application of individual inquiries (clinical questions), which results in engagement in the research process by finding evidence (research), evaluation, and applying the use of this knowledge in the academic and work setting. While the "Information Literacy Competency Standards for Nursing" specifically address the attributes needed for student and professional success, the new *Framework* places IL in context with everyday practice and application. As a result, nursing students actively participate in clinical settings where they utilize their information literacy skills in a variety of ways, including interacting with electronic records, developing and using best practices, and as participants in health care teams.

One of the most important questions moving forward will be how to fully incorporate the ACRL frames into current and existing student learning outcomes. What will information literacy programs look like as competencies and frames are merged? In her article regarding assessment and the new *Framework*, Megan Oakleaf states, "Librarians who design instruction quickly realize that each teaching and assessment event needs to be analyzed in the context of other teaching and assessment activities" (Oakleaf, 2014: 512). Now librarians will be drawing new maps for student learning outcomes and activities based on past and present pedagogy, information literacy competencies, and academic needs. In addition, significant attention will be placed on real-time and extensive assessment studies.

The implications for the overall SCSU information literacy/library instruction program and nursing curriculum are many. The SCSU Library Curriculum and Instruction Advisory Committee is currently developing overarching student learning outcomes (SLOs), which will inform *all* of our library instruction initiatives and credit-bearing courses. These SLOs will then need to be blended with standards for specific disciplines, such as the ACRL "Information Literacy Competency Standards for Nursing" mentioned in this chapter. Fortunately, the recent revision of SCSU's library instruction for the nursing informatics and research courses gives us a good head start.

BUILDING BRIDGES

Successful information literacy instruction and skill building may begin in the library, but it is often dependent on relationships with faculty across all disciplines and programs. The nursing science faculty have always been receptive to having library instruction embedded within their program and curriculum. The value that they place on information literacy and its relationship to research and evidence-based nursing practice is evident by their inclusion of a credit-bearing IL course during the early years of the program. Even though that course is no longer required, the nursing faculty are still committed to having their students build on their research skills acquired during their general education course work. The collaborative nature of the relationship allows library and nursing faculty to work together to achieve common goals. Like many other academic libraries, these relationships are often born out of library liaison programs and/or subject responsibilities. Regardless of how they begin, there are a few things to keep in mind as you explore opportunities to integrate library instruction and information literacy into a college/university curriculum. These include the following:

- Talking to your colleagues. You'll need to understand the current environment, past activities, and suggestions for opportunities.
- Getting to know your students better. You'll impress faculty with a good understanding of their skills and basic information literacy needs.
- Starting slow and listening carefully to departmental and individual faculty. You'll quickly pick up on where they're coming from and where they are going.
- Fostering partnerships and collaborative relationships. It will make it easier to explore ways to enhance or develop new information literacy programs and activities.
- Keeping in mind potential partnerships. Many of the best relationships result in faculty committing to actively integrating information literacy into their course curriculum.

CONCLUSION

The manner in which teaching faculty and librarians collaborate is critical to information literacy learning outcomes and student success. The relationship-building experience between the two serves as a positive example of a mutual commitment to build the information literacy skills and competencies of nursing students. The time allotted to customize library instruction is an excellent investment in our students, and as a result, these students will be well prepared to apply their skills and competencies to their course work and eventually their profession.

Now, as learning outcomes are revised and updated to reflect information literacy competencies and the ACRL *Framework for Information Literacy for Higher Education*, librarians have the opportunity to expand and guide student success across all college and university campuses. However, the implications go further than the overarching SLOs that are often developed for library instruction programs. Rather, there is the potential to effect change in both disciplines and courses that address the very specific research needs of our students and the continued preparation for their lifelong learning.

APPENDIX A

NURSING INFORMATICS
Finding Resources

Nursing Career Interest:

What do you want to learn about the specialty you are interested in:

1.
2.
3.

Search Terms:

1.
2.
3.
4.
5.

Synonyms or Related Terms:

1.
2.
3.
4.
5.

Search in CINAHL, Health Source: Nursing/Academic, Scopus, or PubMed for appropriate journal articles and note the citation information below:

Article Title:
Author (s):
Journal/Resource:
Volume, issue, page, date:
Annotation:

Article Title:
Author (s):
Journal/Resource:
Volume, issue, page, date:
Annotation:

Article Title:
Author (s):
Journal/Resource:
Volume, issue, page, date:
Annotation:

APPENDIX B

NURSING RESEARCH
Finding Resources

(P)atient:

(I)ntervention:

(C)omparison:

(O)utcome:

Research Questions:

1.

2.

3.

Search Terms:

1.

2.

3.

4.

5.

Synonyms or Related Terms:

1.

2.

3.

4.

5.

Search in CINAHL, Health Source: Nursing/Academic, Scopus, or PubMed for appropriate journal articles and note the citation information below:

Article Title:
Author (s):
Journal/Resource:
Volume, issue, page, date:
Annotation:

Article Title:
Author (s):
Journal/Resource:
Volume, issue, page, date:
Annotation:

Article Title:
Author (s):
Journal/Resource:
Volume, issue, page, date:
Annotation:

REFERENCES

ACRL (Association of College & Research Libraries). 2000. "Information Literacy Competency Standards for Higher Education." http://www.ala.org/acrl/standards/informationliteracycompetency.

———. 2014. "Information Literacy Competency Standards for Nursing." *College & Research Libraries News* 75, no. 1: 34–41.

———. 2015. *Framework for Information Literacy for Higher Education*. American Library Association. Association of College & Research Libraries. http://acrl.ala.org/ilstandards/wp-content/uploads/2015/01/Framework-MW15-Board-Docs.pdf.

Kaplowitz, Joan R. 2012. *Transforming Information Literacy Instruction Using Learner-Centered Teaching*. New York: Neal-Schuman.

Oakleaf, Megan. 2014. "A Roadmap for Assessing Student Learning Using the New Framework for Information Literacy for Higher Education." *Journal of Academic Librarianship* 40: 510–14.

Schulte, Stephanie J. 2008. "Integrating Information Literacy into an Online Undergraduate Nursing Informatics Course: The Librarian's Role in the Design and Teaching of the Course." *Medical Reference Services Quarterly* 27, no. 2 (Summer): 158–72.

II

INNOVATIVE MODELS FOR INFORMATION LITERACY INSTRUCTION

6

Right on Time

Best Practice in One-Shot Instruction

Heidi Buchanan and Beth McDonough,
Western Carolina University Library

One-shot library instruction—instruction delivered in a single face-to-face session—has become unpopular in the discourse of information literacy in higher education. While there exists some serious consideration of how to deliver one-shot instruction, the trend is to describe programs that transform, extend, or otherwise eclipse the one-shot approach with the assumption that something else—anything—is preferable. Yet, the reality is that one-shot instruction continues to be the mainstay of many information literacy programs in academic libraries. Not only is one-shot instruction what academic communities expect from libraries, but it can be highly effective—nimble, purposeful, integrated across the curriculum, and focused on relationships with teaching faculty and students. This is especially true with the promise of the new Association of College & Research Libraries (ACRL) *Framework for Information Literacy in Higher Education* (2015), which is based on six frames or foundational threshold concepts rather than a long list of standards and objectives.

One-shot library instruction is the foundation of the information literacy program at Western Carolina University (WCU). While library instruction is primarily delivered via one-shot sessions by the members of the Research and Instruction Services (RIS) department, information literacy is perceived as a shared campus-wide endeavor that is infused throughout the curriculum. RIS librarians have embraced one-shot instruction, incorporated pedagogical approaches that have been enthusiastically received by faculty and students, and strategically positioned it within the curriculum to provide support for information literacy where—and when—it is most needed.

WCU is a regional, comprehensive university in the Appalachian region of North Carolina with an enrollment of approximately 10,000 students served by a single library. It is part of the seventeen-campus University of North Carolina System. The RIS department, composed of nine librarians and one paraprofessional, operates on the liaison model: each librarian serves as the primary point of contact for specific academic departments and programs. Responsibilities for liaisons include research assistance for students and faculty and collection development—all related to the academic disciplines of their assigned departments. Along with librarians who have disciplinary subject expertise, the liaison structure also includes an undergraduate liaison, who coordinates the library's orientation to introductory composition classes and outreach to other courses and programs that do not identify exclusively with an academic department (such as first-year experience classes). Librarians at WCU are classified as faculty, meaning they undergo a similar review process as teaching faculty and earn equivalent academic rank.

ACRL's "Characteristics of Programs of Information Literacy That Illustrate Best Practices: A Guideline" (2012) has served as a guiding document for the library's instruction program over the years. This chapter describes how WCU's program aligns with those characteristics and how ACRL's new *Framework* is being incorporated into one-shot instruction sessions.

MISSION AND PLANNING

Recently, the Information Literacy Standards Committee recommended that ACRL sunset the "Information Literacy Competency Standards for Higher Education" (2000), which caused considerable consternation among academic librarians who had built their instruction programs explicitly upon those standards. Fortunately, WCU's information literacy program had been built around a more conceptual approach seeking to impart the *big ideas* of information literacy within a disciplinary context, while at the same time supporting students in acquiring the skills outlined by the ACRL standards. RIS librarians have never viewed information literacy as something that could be checked off and transferred to students by librarians in isolation; rather, it is viewed as something that builds in students over time through supported practice and the careful, strategic integration of library instruction into the curriculum. The idea of information literacy as a collaborative endeavor is reflected in WCU's information literacy program mission, which was recently revised to reflect the new *Framework*: "Our mission is to collaborate across the university to help students discover the nature of information—its value, its creation and curation processes, and its dissemination—so that they can ethically and effectively use information to create new knowledge" (Hunter Library, 2015).

Planning for the big picture of the information literacy instruction program is part of the RIS department's strategic planning process under the leadership of the department head, and program goals are aligned with the library and university strategic plans. Day-to-day coordination of the instruction program is handled by one of the subject liaisons. As coordinator of information literacy, she provides mentorship, support, and practical guidance in the areas of scheduling, using the classroom, teaching strategies, and assisting the department head in big-picture planning for the instruction program. The department works together to set and review annual goals for the library's orientation to introductory composition classes (English 101 and 202). For upper-level, subject-specific courses, liaison librarians work closely with faculty in their assigned departments and are afforded a great deal of flexibility to determine the best approaches to information literacy instruction based on the disciplines they serve.

PROGRAM ATTRIBUTES

Student learning is at the heart of WCU's information literacy program. To this end, the program emphasizes close collaboration between teaching librarians and instructors in the departments so that information literacy offerings can be customized to the needs of each course. While liaisons offer a range of instructional services to their departments, including online tutorials and research guides and presence in online courses, most instruction is provided in the form of one-shot face-to-face workshops and class sessions. The RIS department conducts approximately 250 sessions per year. More than half of these class sessions target a specific academic discipline.

One of the limitations of the liaison model is that a focus on the academic disciplines sometimes leaves students who are not yet admitted to their programs underserved. In order to consistently reach these students, the department shares responsibility for teaching information literacy sessions to introductory composition classes (English 101 and 202). These classes provide an introduction to information literacy concepts and skills and lay the groundwork for all other information literacy instruction. Presence in the introductory composition classes has traditionally been the best method for initiating contact with a large portion of WCU students in their first two years of college. Thanks to the recent hire of an undergraduate experience librarian, outreach to this segment of the student population has been greatly expanded.

The department's one-shot instruction approach is predicated upon a belief that information literacy skills should be continually reinforced throughout a course, not just in the library session and not just by the librarian. At

WCU, information literacy–related outcomes are included in each academic program's curriculum, the general studies learning outcomes, and the university's strategic plan—even if the ACRL terminology is not precisely applied. Because librarians are part of the university faculty, they take an active role in university-wide curriculum planning, and while the term *information literacy* may not be front and center of every discussion, the spirit of information literacy marries well with the shared desire among faculty that students become able users and creators of information, critical thinkers, and lifelong learners. The one-shot session is just one form of support that RIS librarians provide, and because one-shots are very flexible, they can be purposely designed around the course learning outcomes, as gleaned from assignments and syllabi for each course and positioned throughout the curriculum.

DELIVERY AND PEDAGOGY

An ideal one-shot session includes both practical skills for specific projects and more advanced concepts that students can apply to many different settings. In recent years, RIS departmental discussions have focused on redesigning pedagogy to focus on transferable skills and threshold concepts beyond the more technical "go here, click there" skills-based aspects of information use. For example, in a session focused on finding scholarly journal articles, emphasis is placed on student understanding of what scholarly information is, how it is produced, and how and why it can be used—while also teaching students how to find peer-reviewed articles. In order to incorporate more higher-order thinking skills and big ideas, RIS librarians intentionally incorporate active, cooperative, and problem-based learning in their library sessions.

RIS librarians have considerable flexibility in terms of delivery of instruction. For the introductory composition classes, the department agrees on a set of goals that include practical matters (e.g., everyone will provide a general introduction to the website) and learning outcomes (e.g., the student will be able to develop basic criteria and use that criteria for evaluating sources for their research project). These goals are applied to individual classes, and the delivery and content is customized according to the class assignments.

Each liaison librarian aligns course goals for the one-shot session with the goals of the course instructor. The planning process involves good communication with the course instructor, and we always request written copies of the syllabus and the assignments. Face-to-face meetings or phone calls are often helpful, especially when working with a course instructor for the first time, in order to make a realistic plan for the one-shot session.

In terms of classroom teaching, the department head and information literacy coordinator encourage the teaching librarians to be authentic to their own personal styles and develop their unique strengths while still maintaining good pedagogical practice. The information needs of students and faculty vary widely among academic disciplines at WCU, and librarians design their classes accordingly. Some librarians place more emphasis on introduction and presentation, but their demonstrations and direct instruction engage the participants. These librarians often employ analogies and other storytelling techniques to explain concepts. For example, comparing search refinements in shopping websites to library databases or describing the construction of a peanut butter and jelly sandwich to illustrate AND and OR in Boolean searching (this particular example is featured, along with others, on the library's YouTube channel [https://www.youtube.com/user/wcuhunterlibrary]).

Many librarians also use inquiry-based methods—prompting students to respond to questions (in writing, in pairs, or out loud). For example, "What is the one thing you want to accomplish in this session?" or "Describe your struggles and successes during your last library research project" (see the "Reflections on Library Experiences" example in the "*Framework* in Action" section of this chapter). Other librarians design library instruction that emphasizes activities and discussion—with little or no introduction and demonstration. The workshop model—where students spend much of the time on their own projects with support from both librarians and instructors of record—is also very popular. (See the appendix for an example of a structured workshop that incorporates class discussion, authentic assessment, and follow-up from the librarian.) In each of these settings, regardless of the librarian's approach, students are active participants and are encouraged to think and share rather than follow along as a librarian navigates through a specific resource.

It can be daunting to teach big ideas, such as threshold concepts, in a fifty- to ninety-minute session. RIS librarians are encouraged to set a realistic plan in collaboration with the course instructor. It is tempting for librarians to try to convey everything they know about information literacy in one session, but that task is hardly possible, and it takes more than simply conveying material for students to learn. Librarians spend years developing information expertise, and expecting undergraduate students to mimic that expertise after fifty minutes of instruction is not reasonable. RIS libranrians strive to set realistic goals for information literacy sessions, prioritize those goals, and forgive ourselves if all the goals are not met. Emphasis is placed on engaging students with meaningful, relevant content rather than trying to *cover* large amounts of material that is unlikely to be remembered and used (Buchanan and McDonough, 2014). The RIS librarians recognize that one-shot instruction is just one component of the overall research and instruction program and realize that there are other teaching opportunities, such as one-on-one assistance, online research guides, and collaboration with teaching faculty on research assignment design.

SETTING

RIS librarians teach one-shot sessions in other academic buildings, at remote locations, and increasingly via online conference software. The primary venue for instruction is the library's electronic classroom, which has recently been redesigned to facilitate active and collaborative teaching and learning and to accommodate growing class sizes (see figure 6.1). Flexibility is a hallmark of the instruction program, so all furniture is easy to move according to the design of the class session.

Figure 6.1. Active learning classroom.

OUTREACH TO FACULTY

In order to reach out to faculty and let them know about the library's one-shot instruction services, visibility is key. Library liaisons engage in outreach by communicating their instructional services, including one-shot sessions, to their departments; participating in departmental meetings; and through newsletters, e-mail, and individual contacts. Often, casual conversation—in hallways, after meetings, or chance encounters at local restaurants—has been the most successful strategy for initiating relationships with faculty. In addition to attending new student and new faculty orientations, library faculty have a strong presence in university academics, including curriculum and strategic planning committees, as library faculty. Some RIS librarians partner with teaching faculty to conduct research about teaching and learning within the disciplines and to publish and present their findings. These are fruitful settings for conversations about information literacy and ways that the library can collaborate and provide support, including library instruction.

TIMING OF INSTRUCTION

For teaching faculty, the appeal of one-shot library instruction is its capacity to provide targeted library support for students at their points of need, that is, when students are at a critical stage of a research assignment. Faculty often want to schedule library instruction too early in the semester, before students can appreciate the value of more customized instruction. RIS librarians are encouraged to negotiate the timing of library instruction with teaching faculty by reviewing the syllabi to identify the best timing for what the department terms "a librarian intervention," scheduled after the students have had the chance to think about their topics and explore (and even struggle) on their own for a while. It's more meaningful for students to discuss the evaluation of resources, for example, after they have already found a few resources and may have some questions about their relevance.

RIS librarians are proactive about scheduling one-shot sessions, targeting instructors of research-intensive classes to offer instructional support. Also, librarians discourage faculty from bringing students to the library without a specific purpose in mind or because "it is good for them to see the library." These are important characteristics of the department's one-shot model, which distinguish WCU's program from scattershot approaches that have earned one-shot instruction a poor reputation. One-shot library instructions can and should be closely tied to the curriculum, the goals for the class, and the timing of the research assignment.

ASSESSMENT

RIS librarians use a combination of assessment techniques to evaluate their teaching, the program as a whole, and how one-shot instruction fits into the overall academic curriculum.

Classroom Teaching Assessments

Formal assessment of library instruction is built into the department's annual evaluation process by design. As a department, by consensus, RIS librarians adopted an observation instrument that is aligned with the teaching observation instrument that is used campus-wide, which emphasizes pedagogical content knowledge (Shulman, 1986). Twice each year, librarians who have faculty status are observed while teaching—once by a peer teaching librarian, once by the department head. RIS librarians also solicit formal feedback from teaching faculty about the librarian's services, including instruction. These evaluations are submitted to the department head, de-identified, and shared with the librarian as part of the overall annual review.

In addition to more formal assessment, some RIS librarians make use of classroom assessment techniques (CATs) (Angelo and Cross, 1993). CATs are simple, informal, formative assessments that also function as vehicles for active learning. Examples include the "minute paper," which prompts the student to respond briefly to a two-question prompt, which is followed by discussion or a "think-pair-share" activity, which guides students to brainstorm a topic, discuss with another student, and then share with the class. These simple assessments are well suited to one-shot instruction because they engage students and offer the librarian an idea of what students know and what remains fuzzy, so that instructional approaches can be modified on the fly to target the needs of the students at hand.

Program-Level Data

On a programmatic level, the RIS department keeps data about each course that is offered: the date, course (section, title), the instructor of record, the librarian, the number of students, the location, and so forth. These data are useful for reporting to ACRL, the Department of Education, and other agencies, but more importantly, they provide a good snapshot of the overall instructional program along with justifications for budget and grant proposals. Success is also gauged by seeing that over the years, the same faculty request us again—and recommend us to their colleagues. Typically, a successful librarian's instruction statistics will increase over time as these partnerships

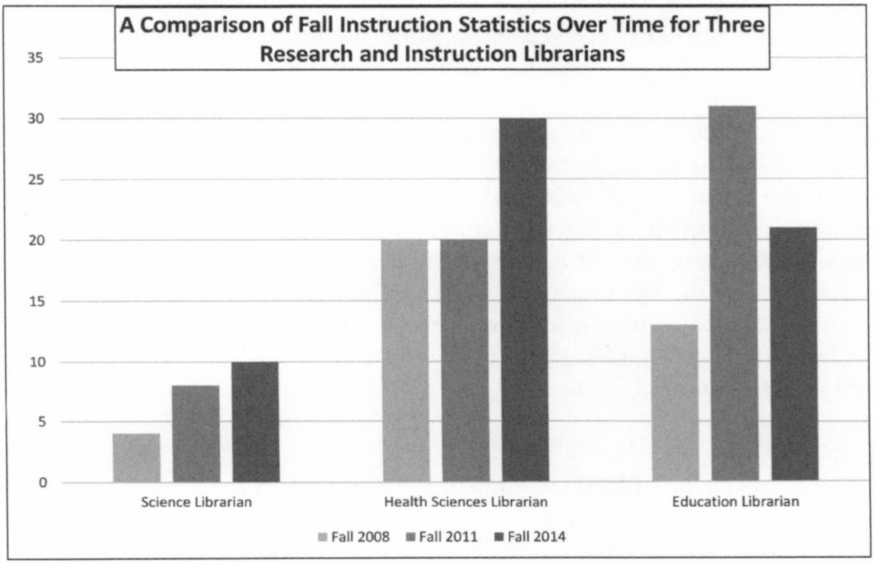

Figure 6.2. A comparison of fall instruction statistics over time for three research and instruction librarians.

evolve (see figure 6.2). Sometimes, RIS librarians find themselves needing to reevaluate their workload. In these situations, the librarians might work with the department head to scale back on other responsibilities such as committee assignments or introductory composition sessions, or they look for ways to strategically reduce the number of sessions they conduct each semester.

Curriculum Mapping

Effectiveness of library instruction is not measured simply by the quantity of sessions offered; instead, RIS librarians work to integrate one-shot sessions into the courses that are most in need of information literacy instruction. These efforts are made more strategic through curriculum mapping, which is used as a method of assessing instructional offerings. In the curriculum mapping process, librarians can take the data about the classes they have taught in the past and see how they align with requirements and progressions (the curriculum) for academic programs and departments. For example, one RIS librarian piloted curriculum mapping for a specific program at WCU, then published her findings in the New Review of Academic Librarianship, together with three other case studies of curriculum mapping from librarians at other institutions (Buchanan et al., 2015). Curriculum maps were used to see whether students received information literacy instruction consistently, appropriately, and in a sequence that made sense. Since the initial pilot, several other librarians in the department have begun the curriculum mapping process in order to identify opportunities to build on previous instruction sessions and identify places in the curriculum where library instruction is needed. The curriculum map itself is a useful visual of these gaps and opportunities and provides a basis for conversations with faculty and administrators in the departments. It also provides a way for very busy librarians (like the education and health science librarians in figure 6.2) to identify ways to spread the teaching workload more evenly throughout the academic year—or to focus more on courses with a heavier research component and scale back on other sessions.

PROFESSIONAL DEVELOPMENT

Mentorship and Training

The information literacy coordinator serves as a mentor and trainer for all librarians who teach. In this role, she provides training and support for engaging students, building relationships with faculty, and various instructional and presentation techniques. Training sessions often take place in departmental meetings but also occur one-on-one. Because everyone in the department has a role providing instruction, the department head also serves as a formal mentor and provides formal feedback to librarians regarding their teaching.

Professional Learning Community

The department serves as a community of practice and for the past several years has set aside monthly time for shared collegial inquiry in the form of a "Teaching Circle," an informal learning community where librarians share stories from their classroom experiences and ideas, as well as literature about teaching information literacy. The Teaching Circle serves as a safe environment for librarians to discuss and reflect upon concerns and problems and as a place for librarians to support and learn from one another.

Beyond the Library

RIS librarians take advantage of the university's teaching center, the Coulter Faculty Commons, for teaching and instructional design support. The Faculty Commons offers workshops, conferences, and online training to help faculty develop as teachers. Administration provides some financial support so that librarians can participate in webinars, conferences, and immersion programs offered by state and national library organizations.

FRAMEWORK IN ACTION

The new ACRL *Framework for Information Literacy in Higher Education* incorporates threshold concepts that were identified through a Delphi study (Townsend, Brunetti, and Hofer, 2011) and consists of six frames:

- Authority Is Constructed and Contextual
- Information Creation as a Process
- Information Has Value
- Research as Inquiry
- Scholarship as Conversation
- Searching as Strategic Exploration (ACRL, 2015)

The big ideas, process-based approach that our department has taken toward information literacy instruction has provided us with a head start toward integrating the new *Framework*. Overall the *Framework* aligns with our approach to information literacy instruction because the framework is a "cluster of interconnected core concepts" rather than a long list of intended outcomes (ACRL, 2015). Most concepts are familiar—others are ripe for exploration. There are many instructional scenarios that RIS librarians have experimented with that lead to rich discussion with students and address multiple frames. Here are a few examples.

Start Where They Are

Allowing students to start searching their topics using any method they wish—not limiting to library or a single database—opens up an opportunity for discourse in multiple frames. Many students inevitably start with a search of the open web, which opens up the conversation about the breadth of information available on the open web as well as its limits. This approach also touches upon Research as Inquiry and Information Creation as a Process. *Wikipedia* is a wonderful conversation starter to address several of the frames because, for a novice beginning the research process, *Wikipedia* provides background knowledge, terminology, and often references to scholarly and professional information sources. A glimpse behind the scenes at the *Wikipedia* discussion pages is a great demonstration of how authority is constructed and scholarship is conversation.

RELEVANT FRAMES

- Authority Is Constructed and Contextual
- Information Creation as Process
- Scholarship as Conversation

Behind-the-Scenes Tour

The RIS librarians rarely accept requests for tours unless there is a close curricular tie for the library as place, such as in a university experience class. Such requests are instead treated as an opening for discussion about more relevant information literacy instruction. Librarians often use the physical setting of the library as a piece of a library session, especially if the students need to be comfortable finding physical materials in the building. It is possible to make a library tour meaningful and purposeful. For example, when asked each semester to come to speak to a course, Introduction to the English Major, about careers in librarianship, the library instructor suggested a behind-the-scenes tour as an alternative. The students divided into groups and toured different units of the library: circulation/interlibrary loan, reference, technical services, and digital projects. At each location, each group would meet a librarian in that unit; students were instructed to ask the librarians a list of questions including *What does your department do? What project are you working on now? Why did you decide to become a librarian? Where did you go to graduate school?* Additional, more customized, questions were provided for each unit. For example, students would ask the acquisitions and electronic resources librarians: *How does the licensing process work?* and *How much does* Nature *cost*? The answers are always real eye-openers to information creation and the value of information. The tour allowed those who were interested in librarianship as a career to learn about different career paths, graduate schools, and so forth, but everyone was exposed to the real people and the process behind the resources and services in the library.

RELEVANT FRAMES

- Information Has Value
- Information Creation as a Process

Reflections on Library Experiences

Starting with an appropriate prompt for a one-minute paper or think-pair-share allows students to reflect and share about their personal experiences and problems encountered in secondary research (Buchanan and McDonough, 2014). It helps students to understand that others share the same problems as they do as well as to hear of each other's successes. The subsequent discussions are sure to include problems with accessing full text. This opens the door to a natural and relevant conversation about the cost of information, pay walls, and so forth. This conversation is especially useful in clearing up misconceptions about access to library subscriptions on campus versus off campus and practical details about resources such as Google Scholar. A think-pair-share can also be used to generate discussion about how students have paid for information in everyday life (smartphone data plans, Netflix subscriptions, iTunes accounts).

RELEVANT FRAMES

- Information Has Value
- Information Creation as a Process

Starting at the End

A bibliography from an article, book chapter, or website can serve as a basis for several activities. For example, in a history class, the librarian can teach students how to identify parts of a citation, briefly demonstrate how to track the original source, and then have students practice finding the full text for two or three citations (for undergraduates, these can be preselected by the librarian). As time allows, students can be guided to identify the different types of sources used by the scholar and/or examine how the citations were used in the text (e.g., Were they quoted directly? Is the cited work about the exact same topic as the article or did the author use it to support just one aspect of the paper?).

Another variation on this theme is to ask the students to identify the expertise of the authors. These exercises combine the very practical skills of identifying parts of a citation with more conceptual ideas such as how experts use other experts in their own work. It also allows students to explore the nuts and bolts of library resources. These activities are worth spending the majority of

RELEVANT FRAMES

- Authority Is Constructed and Contextual
- Information Creation as a Process
- Research as Inquiry
- Scholarship as Conversation
- Searching as Strategic Exploration

a fifty-minute session because of their relevance to multiple frameworks and potential to enhance student understanding of academic scholarship.

Structured Workshop

This is an excellent way to lead students through strategies for finding information while still allowing them to bring their own knowledge and approach to the process. The appendix of this chapter is a handout one of the librarians used with an introductory English class to prompt students to create their own research guide. An exercise like this works best when the students already have their topic and have done some preliminary searching. This activity is not busywork—the students have the freedom and flexibility to search for information about their individual topics and create a guide that they can return to—written in their own language. Having the students explore on their own helps generate student-driven questions and discussion, which can be peppered throughout the class session. Structured workshops also allow ample time for the librarian to observe the student, to gather formative information, uncover misperceptions, and better understand what the students need to be successful. The instructions in the handout can be easily adapted to any assignment or scenario.

You also have the option of collecting the handouts at the end of class (ask the students to put their names on them). Use them to assess the session by

RELEVANT FRAME

- Searching as Strategic Exploration (Revise prompts to include any of the frames.)

gauging the students' progress and provide follow-up by adding suggestions and search tips to each paper before returning them to the students (via the course instructor). If you plan to collect the papers, be sure you let the students know you are planning to do so when you introduce the agenda at the beginning of class.

CONCLUSION

It is rare to hear the term *best practice* paired with the term *one-shot library instruction*. But for many academic libraries, where such instruction is the primary vehicle for information literacy, best practice should be the goal. The one-shot approach has the capacity to be versatile, strategic, built upon collaborative relationships with teaching faculty, and best of all, effective.

Here are some takeaways for one-shot success:

- Be visible and build relationships with teaching faculty.
- Strike a balance to provide support and build on the strengths of individual teaching librarians.
- Try new things, reflect, revise, and try again.
- Recognize that your one-shot session is part of a bigger picture. Students will build on the skills in class, and your many library services, from research guides to individual research assistance, provide additional support.
- Talk about the big ideas—and how to teach them—with other librarians and with teaching faculty.

APPENDIX

Structured Workshop Handout, Annotated

Your Name: ______________

1. **Your topic (be as detailed as possible):**
   [The students write for a few minutes while the librarian roams the room, getting an idea of each topic.]

2. **Describe one high-quality source that you have already found about your topic (for example, an informational webpage from the Centers from Disease Control):**
   [The librarian can meet the students where they are--and acknowledge the work that they have already done.]

3. How did you decide that it was a quality source? List at least three criteria:

[*Good opportunity for a class discussion. Students can discuss in smaller groups first, then write some of their criteria on the board. If the students don't mention topic of scholarly/peer reviewed, the librarian can add it to the criteria and explain the peer review process.]*

*

*

*

4. Try to find one scholarly article or book about your topic. You can use any of the library resources to do this. Try a couple different ones. When you find one that is relevant, save it or email it to yourself. If you find a call number for a book that is in the library, go get it!

[*The librarian can provide brief instructions for how to find library resources, how to search, how to limit. This task allows students to explore various options.*]

5. Write down the databases, search terms, or other resources that were helpful for you today so you won't forget!

[*While students are working on their own, the librarian and course instructor mill about the room to answer questions, brainstorm search strategies, and make suggestions of specific resources. At the end of the session, the librarian can address some frequently asked questions for the entire group*].

REFERENCES

ACRL (Association of College and Research Libraries). 2000. "Information Literacy Competency Standards for Higher Education." American Library Association. Association of College and Research Libraries. http://www.ala.org/acrl/standards/informationliteracycompetency.

ACRL (Association of College & Research Libraries). 2012. "Characteristics of Programs of Information Literacy That Illustrate Best Practices: A Guideline." American Library Association. Association of College & Research Libraries. Last modified January 2012. http://www.ala.org/acrl/standards/characteristics.

———. 2015. *Framework for Information Literacy for Higher Education*. American Library Association. Association of College & Research Libraries. http://acrl.ala.org/ilstandards/wp-content/uploads/2015/01/Framework-MW15-Board-Docs.pdf.

Angelo, Thomas A., and K. Patricia Cross. 1993. *Classroom Assessment Techniques: A Handbook for College Teachers*. San Francisco: Jossey-Bass.

Buchanan, Heidi E., and Beth A. McDonough. 2014. *The One-Shot Library Instruction Survival Guide*. Chicago: ALA Editions.

Buchanan, Heidi, Katy Kavanagh Webb, Amy Harris Houk, and Catherine Tingelstad. 2015. "Curriculum Mapping in Academic Libraries." *New Review of Academic Librarianship* 21, no. 1: 94–111.

Hunter Library. 2015. "Library Instruction & Information Literacy." Western Carolina University. Accessed May 22. http://researchguides.wcu.edu/libraryinstruction.

Shulman, Lee S. 1986. "Those Who Understand: Knowledge Growth in Teaching." *Educational Researcher* 15, no. 2: 4–14.

Townsend, Lori, Korey Brunetti, and Amy R. Hofer. 2011. "Threshold Concepts and Information Literacy." *portal: Libraries and the Academy* 11, no. 3: 853–69. *Project Muse.*

7

The Role of the Flipped Classroom in Information Literacy Programs

Sara Arnold-Garza,
Albert S. Cook Library, Towson University

This chapter describes the information literacy opportunities and context at Towson University, including observations about implementing the flipped classroom for library instruction at this institution. Although the flipped teaching structure has been used for several years in classrooms at all levels, it has only more recently been employed by librarians for information literacy instruction (Gibes and James, 2015). This classroom model exemplifies many of the "Characteristics of Programs of Information Literacy That Illustrate Best Practices: A Guideline" (2012) from the Association of College & Research Libraries (ACRL's best practices) and deserves a place in the teaching repertoire of instruction librarians. Its structure offers flexibility and adaptation necessary for diverse and dynamic teaching environments, and also encourages a reflective, collaborative pedagogical style, which benefits learners.

THE CONTEXT: THE TOWSON SEMINAR COURSE AND BEYOND

At Towson University, all freshmen see a librarian during the Towson Seminar, a class focused on introducing college-level rigor and requiring a research paper assignment (Towson University, 2015). Typically, the seminar integrates two to four library instruction sessions staged over the course of a semester to support the research paper process and, ultimately, the use of evidence to make an argument using academic research tools and practices. Since all freshmen take the seminar, librarians share responsibility for the sessions, often teaching out of their usual subject areas. Some seminar topics include digital society, the policy and practice of education and teaching, religion and politics, African American literature, and automobiles in the United States. Regardless of the content of any particular seminar, freshmen have the chance to write a paper based on evidence from scholarly and other sources, which may be a new exercise for them. In this course, librarians address concepts like these:

- Developing or narrowing a topic idea
- Using reference sources to understand background information
- Critically analyzing web sources
- Differentiating sources across the spectrum from popular to scholarly
- Choosing discipline-appropriate research sources
- Developing a research strategy based on Boolean search and other database-specific tools
- Integrating sources appropriately into an argument
- Avoiding plagiarism and using citation styles

It is not typical that all of these topics can be fully covered in the limited time that the librarian-instructor may get with students during the semester.

Library instruction does not end after the Towson Seminar. Additionally, librarians at Towson University teach course-integrated sessions to students in subject liaison areas. At this level, students' exposure to library instruction will depend on their major, the classes they select, and classroom instructors' use of library partners. These sessions are usually limited to one-shot instruction, and they likely address a more specific aspect of the research process related to the course and the assignment. For example, course-integrated sessions may focus on using a specialized resource like U.S. Census data in government-oriented courses, working with primary sources in the history disciplines, or accessing tests and measures in the social sciences.

THE PURPOSE: INSTRUCTION OBJECTIVES

The primary aim for library instruction is to prepare students to be able to complete their assignments. This focus helps classroom instructors see value in using class time for library instruction, especially when the quality of student work is improved by the library instruction session. It will also influence student perception of the usefulness of the library and library resources. By making the research process easier for students, they will be receptive to librarian suggestions and willing to return for other assignments.

In the bigger picture, library instruction is also intended to craft learning experiences that will impact lifelong critical thinking skills and enthusiasm for learning. These outcomes are much more satisfying for students (and for the instructor), but they take more time to develop, often an entire college career. In order to achieve these outcomes, the immediate goals of an assignment and course must be used as building blocks to greater understanding about information and research.

In the Towson Seminar, students have variable skill levels and understanding of the research concepts their professors expect. At this point, they need instruction and guidance on the full extent of information literacy skills and concepts. Since this is an impossible task, focusing on the objectives most relevant to the assignment and those that the professor emphasizes are the best strategies for planning a manageable scope of objectives.

The flipped classroom is one way to make the most of the limited time librarians typically get with students who seem to need more instruction than there is time to include. By using this teaching model, which transposes the traditional settings for conceptual learning and practical application, students more often get both the specific skills that will help them be successful with assignments and the satisfaction that comes from critical discussion and engagement with concepts.

THE PLANNING: LOGISTICS OF THE FLIPPED CLASSROOM

Planning for a flipped classroom experience is similar in many ways to planning for other library instruction. Here are some general steps to follow:

- Gather information about the course and students.
- Determine the goals for instruction.
- Create an experience that meets the goals.
- Get buy-in from, and include the classroom instructor in, as much of this planning as possible.

There are some differences in planning for the flipped classroom, though. The following is an example of the planning process used with a Towson Seminar course.

Gather Information

Typically, the librarian asks the classroom instructor for a copy of the syllabus and the research assignments students are completing. Assignments could include selecting a source (encyclopedia entry, scholarly article) and writing a reflection, creating an annotated bibliography, or writing a lengthy research paper, among other assignments. It can sometimes be difficult to get a written description of an assignment, especially before or at the start of a semester. In these cases, it's important to plan ahead based on what you know and then ask the classroom instructor to fill in gaps about the assignment as necessary. Often, this process helps classroom instructors understand what role the librarian can play as a support for student learning in their course.

Determine Goals

Depending on the assignment and what the instructor covers during regular class time, the next step is selecting learning objectives for the sessions. It's important to articulate a specific skill or concept to teach students and the research activity or ability that students will achieve as a result. The sessions may look like this:

- *Session 1*—students will learn techniques for brainstorming on topics in order to narrow or develop their chosen topic appropriately for the assignment; students will understand differences between scholarly and popular sources in order to select sources most appropriate for their assignment.
- *Session 2*—students will create search strategies based on the topic development process in order to locate relevant sources; students will identify and practice using academic databases in order to find sources that support their assignment.
- *Session 3*—students will develop a working definition of academic integrity in order to behave ethically during the research process; students will access citation guides and tools in order to create well-formatted citations for their assignment.

Structure the Learning Experience

The next step is to determine if any of the learning objectives can be supported through exposure to a preclass video. For example, in order to spend the most class time applying evaluation criteria to scholarly and popular sources, consider introducing students to the criteria before class through a video. Doing so will avoid lengthy explanation of each criterion during your limited time together, and students can be asked to quickly begin evaluating sample materials in pairs and sharing their observations, for example.

Collect or create the video materials that you want to expose students to before a class session, based on the activities you plan to engage students with during class. These materials should be short and to the point, since opportunity for extended discussion comes during this in-person session. Librarians can create customized materials for their sessions, but many libraries, including Towson, have produced videos and tutorials that can also be relied on for this purpose and can be reused over time. Students should receive explicit instructions for completion of these materials, including a short accompanying quiz. The quiz will alert the librarian-instructor to any concepts a student may not have grasped well from the prematerial, allowing follow-up on the most important points from the videos, and will convey a sense of accountability for completion of the prevideos. See figures 7.1 and 7.2 for sample preassignment screenshots that use a Google Form.

In class, students engage in activities planned to specifically confront the concepts that the preassignment introduced. For example, if students viewed a video demonstrating how to move from a research question to a well-built database search strategy, you may ask them to help build a search from a sample research question. Then, they can attempt to do this for their own research questions, alone or in pairs. The repetition of the process helps students practice and allows them to encounter the challenges that are a normal part of research. The interactive approach encourages students to ask for and offer help while they learn to identify the important concepts in their research question and how to make use of an academic database.

Collaborate with Classroom Instructors

Collaboration starts at the information-gathering stage and continues throughout the process. When scheduling library instruction, the classroom faculty should be notified that students will be expected to complete a brief preassignment to prepare for the library session. If they confirm that they will be able to accommodate this assignment in the workload of the semester, and that they will include it in the syllabus and on the course management system, the librarian-instructor should provide a timeline of when preassignment materials will be available and when each one will be due, so that classroom faculty can anticipate the inclusion of these components. To encourage student participation, it is best if classroom faculty give credit for completion of the assignment and include it in the syllabus's list of assignments. In addition to planning for the preassignment logistics, the librarian-instructor should work with the classroom faculty to make sure that the learning objectives identified are appropriate. This is an opportunity to invite input from classroom faculty about how to meet the research needs of their students.

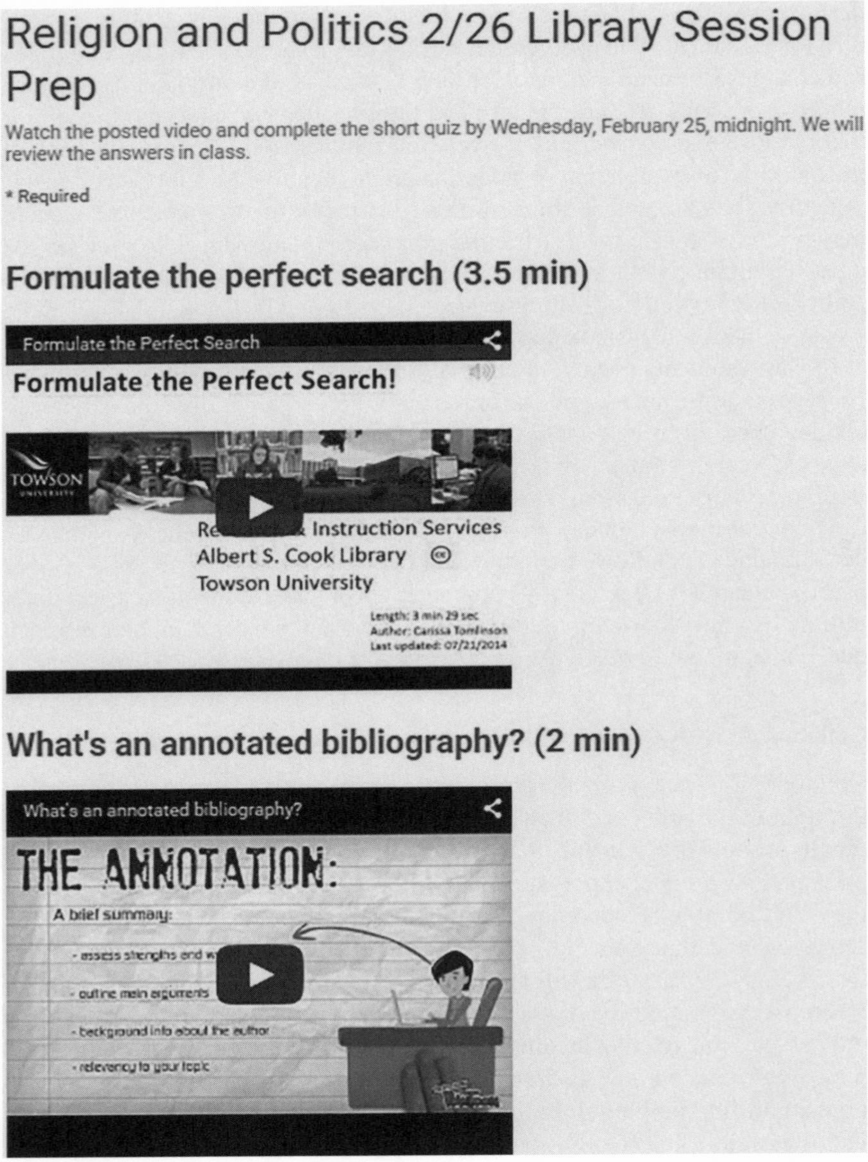
Religion and Politics 2/26 Library Session Prep
Watch the posted video and complete the short quiz by Wednesday, February 25, midnight. We will review the answers in class.
* Required
Formulate the perfect search (3.5 min)
Formulate the Perfect Search
Formulate the Perfect Search!
TOWSON
Instruction Services
Albert S. Cook Library
Towson University
Length: 3 min 29 sec
Author: Carissa Tomlinson
Last updated: 07/21/2014
What's an annotated bibliography? (2 min)
What's an annotated bibliography?
THE ANNOTATION:
A brief summary:
- outline main arguments
- background info about the author
- relevancy to your topic

Figure 7.1. Google Form preassignment videos.

What is your full name? *

What are the key concepts in the topic [recruitment of male nurses]? *

What are the key concepts in the research question [What are "faith-based initiatives" and how do such programs fit in with or violate the 1st Amendment separation of church and state?]? *

What are the key concepts in your own topic/research question/thesis statement? *

What are the 2 main ingredients in an annotated bibliography? *

Describe at least 2 things you can include or discuss in an annotation. *

Describe at least 2 ways your annotated bibliography may be useful to you as a writer and researcher. *

Figure 7.2. Google Form preassignment quiz.

Alternative Ideas

In addition to the activities already outlined, there are likely to be options that may work better in varying library and classroom environments. For example, a preassignment can take the form of an interactive tutorial, or other media, depending on the instructional technologies available. Additionally, asking students to write a brief reflection or to submit questions for clarification could achieve the same goals as a short quiz. Some flipped classroom components that work for one teaching environment may not be appropriate for others. Since the flipped classroom is not a prescriptive label, instruction librarians can experiment with preassignment materials and in-class activities and determine which activities work best in particular settings.

THE RESULTS: ASSESSMENT ACTIVITIES

During a pilot phase in 2013, flipped Towson Seminar participants completed student, faculty, and librarian questionnaires to share what they thought of the experience. Students overwhelmingly agreed that the preassignment component and the in-class activities worked together to support their learning. Of course, student perception is not necessarily an accurate depiction of their actual learning. Comparing student work samples from flipped classes to traditional library instruction sessions could provide a controlled understanding of the real learning outcomes from this practice. Faculty feedback indicated that they also felt the practice improved the student work product, though actual student work was not evaluated during this pilot. Librarian feedback provided a more complex picture about the use of the flipped classroom, which has helped Towson University librarians refine their flipped instruction practice. One of the most important findings was that planning with intention and instruction tailored to the specific needs of the assignment, students, faculty, and environment leads to more success. There is not a single formula that can be adopted for all instructional scenarios.

Even without a specialized assessment procedure for flipped teaching, gathering feedback from students as an ongoing activity for all instruction, flipped or not, may provide useful insight on what they found helpful or confusing and what could be improved. For example, specific student comments could help improve how the librarian-instructor distributes time, designs a worksheet, or structures activities. Conversely, student feedback can highlight what content or approaches students appreciate, which can be included or emphasized in future sessions.

THE CHARACTERISTICS: ACRL'S BEST PRACTICES AND THE FLIPPED CLASSROOM

The flipped classroom shines when compared to the characteristics described in the various categories of ACRL's best practices document for information literacy. Following is a description of some of the ways that the flipped classroom can address selected characteristics. Practitioners may find many more opportunities to exemplify ACRL's best practices when using the flipped classroom, depending on their own program and its features.

The flipped classroom "accommodates the level of the program, department, and institution" (ACRL, 2012: 356) by the flexible nature of the model. It can be employed uniformly across a specific set of courses, or it can be modified to suit the student learning needs and academic style of a course. The extent of accommodation depends on the time and resources available for instructional design in the library, which is a very real challenge instruction librarians may face.

Many institutions face cuts that challenge growth and experimentation in the classroom. As instruction librarians grow more successful with integrating information literacy into the curriculum and demonstrate the value of library instruction to faculty, they must face questions of sustainability. Our abilities to expand information literacy are limited, and the flipped classroom "addresses and prioritizes human, technological, and financial resources (both current and projected), taking into account administrative and institutional support" (ACRL, 2012: 356). The following discussion addresses these elements of sustainability individually.

Although the number of librarians available for instruction may not grow, the flipped classroom model increases the capacity of one-on-one interaction for problem solving in the classroom. Rather than spending large amounts of time lecturing to an entire classroom, a librarian-instructor can get students working immediately and can spend time interacting with individual students as they encounter difficulty or develop questions. This one-on-one support is most available when in-class activities are planned in such a way that individuals and small groups can drive their own work and seek direct assistance as needed from a library instructor in the room. Human resources in the library classroom are enhanced by the use of this model.

The flipped classroom may appear to be dependent on the use of technological resources, but it actually does not require a high level of technical skill or equipment. The model takes advantage of tools that allow for flexible content delivery and interaction. Tools can take the form of free web platforms and content created at other institutions for those with a lack of technological resources. For campuses with well-equipped and supported technological resources, creation of original content and use of technology in and out of the classroom setting can be incorporated. For example, tutorial creation software like Adobe Captivate (http://www.adobe.com/products/captivate.html) provides lots of functionality but comes with a price. Less fully featured web-based tools for screen capture, like Jing (http://www.techsmith.com/jing.html) are free and may be completely sufficient for most needs. Additionally, many libraries make their content available for use by other institutions, which can supplement the resources available for instruction.

By making use of existing resources, the flipped classroom does not require new purchases or financial commitments. Technology for preclass assignments has been addressed above. In class, active learning can take many forms, perhaps using paper and pencil to create mind maps of a topic and associated research questions, or iPads for each student to contribute to a collaborative online space that includes web links and photographs, depending on what is available. Administrative support is easiest to get when using the resources already at one's disposal, even at a time when course redesign and innovative teaching and learning are priorities. Support can come in a variety of forms, and although financial support is often a sticking point, administrators can also provide the policies, trust, advocacy, and collaborative opportunities that make programs sustainable (Noe, 2013).

The flipped classroom does not benefit from the use of technology for technology's sake. Instead, in its best form it "incorporates and uses relevant and appropriate information technology and other media resources to support pedagogy" (ACRL, 2012: 357). Online video and interactive tutorials offer an opportunity to transform what may have previously been lecture to material reviewed outside of class, preparing learners for encountering practical experiences in class. If this can be accomplished with an available technology tool, it should be employed. Learning should not be made more complicated by the need to learn a specialized tool—only enriched by the use of it.

Planning for a flipped classroom "encourages librarian, faculty, and administrator collaboration at the outset" (ACRL, 2012: 356) because it is simply not possible to implement without extensive collaboration between librarians and faculty and without support for teaching transformation from administrators. Working with faculty to plan for the flip, including creating learning outcomes appropriate to the learners and the assignments, communicating with students about the expectations for this model, and engaging faculty as participant instructors in the information literacy classroom, is vital to its success. Students will participate and benefit from library instruction only if they perceive that their regular instructor is supportive and engaged as well. This is especially true if the flipped model diverges from what they are used to in their regular classroom. This change in activity can be a difficult adjustment for students, so instructor support is absolutely necessary. Because collaborative planning is required for the success of a flipped library session, classroom instructors are likely to be more engaged with these sessions than the ones planned without as much of their input. These instructors are likely to be receptive to communication that focuses on student work and outcomes (Noe, 2013).

Preassignments and in-class activities "emphasize learner-centered learning" (ACRL, 2012: 357) in a variety of ways. Students are provided with independent learning opportunities and peer-learning opportunities in a flipped classroom. Since students complete preassignments on their own, they can choose when and how to engage with the content. Students who quickly understand the material may choose to complete the preassignment and arrive to class without questions about the material. Students who find the preassignment challenging can review it as many times as they like before class, and may arrive with a need for clarification on many points. Most students will fall somewhere on a spectrum between these extremes. The preassignment quiz (or feedback mechanism of some kind) can help the librarian-instructor shape the learning experience based on the student needs demonstrated. For example, if several students have difficulty articulating the correct answer to a preclass quiz question, the librarian can use this to shape the lesson content, creating a practical experience that engages students on the points the assessment highlighted. A preassignment "promotes critical thinking, reflection, and recursive learning" (ACRL, 2012: 357) in addition to allowing students to determine the support they receive by asking directly for help or to be spurred by feedback mechanisms that a librarian-instructor builds into an activity. The learner-centered experience also ensures that a student "endeavors to work collaboratively with others and support each other's learning development" (ACRL, 2012: 358). By creating in-class activities where peers depend on each other to accomplish goals, like a team-based citation creation competition, students can help reduce the gaps in skills among learners.

An important feature of the flipped classroom is that students take responsibility for their learning. It "focuses on enhancing student learning and skill development for lifelong learning" and similarly, "prepares students for independent lifelong learning" (ACRL, 2012: 358) by encouraging students to become accustomed to driving their own learning experience. Preassignments provide an opportunity for students to prepare themselves for the classroom. If they neglect the preassignment, students suffer the consequence of observing their more prepared peers in the classroom. This emphasis on self-dependence recurs during the classroom activity, when students are expected to engage with material to problem solve or accomplish some goal, rather than passively listen as an instructor talks. Using active learning shifts control from the instructor to the student, building the student's independent research skills (Noe, 2013). Students in a flipped classroom become aware of the control and power they possess when it comes to their own education, if this realization has not come to them before. Activities that also "include learner-, peer-, and self-evaluation" (ACRL, 2012: 358) extend the process of independent learning and peer-learning opportunities to the assessment phase by supporting information transfer and metacognition about the activities. Self- and peer assessments, like classroom peer review of paper drafts, or directed reflection, provide information about what a student knows, and also allow the student to participate in this observation so he or she can reflect on the learning process and objectives.

Flipped classroom activity is most useful to students when it "works within the context of the course content, and other learning experiences, to achieve information literacy outcomes" (ACRL, 2012: 357). For example, preassignments and assessments could ask students to reflect on concepts of information literacy in the context of their course, with research topics and source examples matched to the discipline. Context becomes even more important for in-class activities, because practical application is built on the specifics of an assignment, course, or discipline. Classroom interaction provides an opportunity for the librarian to model how the same method or process for doing research may be adapted by student researchers, depending on the assignment need. Due to the modular nature of preassignments and active learning experiences, the same concepts can be adapted depending on the course. Examining a sample annotated bibliography with citations of material similar to what students will be expected to use can help students transfer their abstract conception of the purpose of an annotated bibliography to the practical experience of creating and using them during the research process.

One of the most appealing features of the flipped classroom is that it "supports diverse approaches to teaching and learning" (ACRL, 2012: 357). Regardless of an instructor's style of approaching material, the basic model of a preassignment with assessment and in-class practical application can accommodate it. Librarians with a creative streak can infuse entertainment into preassignments, but simplicity will also get the job done. Instructors who are talented in engaging whole classes in conversation can plan for this type of activity. For those with less confidence in this area, small-group work or activities led by students can be used.

The flexibility described above applies to student work as well. Activities can "take into account diverse teaching and learning styles" (ACRL, 2012: 357) by allowing students to engage with content and demonstrate their learning in a variety of ways. For example, activities could be based on discussion, writing, demonstration, multimedia, or even games. Although some students may typically prefer to read and write, other students may appreciate activities that also allow them to speak/listen and perform for their peers. Offering an array of acceptable options for demonstrating understanding is a way to "acknowledge differences in learning and teaching styles in the outcome measures" (ACRL, 2012: 358) and can be refreshing for students and instructors, who may become fatigued or even hampered by the repetition of traditional or uniform course work. This approach also exemplifies Universal Design for Learning principles, which some have advocated as a useful strategy for meeting diverse learning needs and improving teaching effectiveness (Zhong, 2012).

The modular and flexible nature of the flipped classroom makes it a useful tool for a variety of library instruction environments. As highlighted by ACRL's best practices, it offers opportunities in sustainability, the use of technology, independent learning, peer learning, diverse teaching and learning styles, and collaborative connection. With flipped classroom success, a library instruction program can "contribute to information literacy's advancement by sharing information, methods and plans with peers and stakeholders both within and outside of the institution" (ACRL, 2012: 358).

THE WARNING: FLIPPING IS NOT ALWAYS BEST

The flipped classroom, like any instruction method, should be used when appropriate. There may be many circumstances that call for other strategies or structures for a learning experience. This can only be determined by carefully considering an instruction scenario and its features. The following questions can help to reveal barriers to using the flipped classroom:

- Can the planned learning objectives be addressed with a preassignment plus active learning structure formula, or is something else needed?
- Is the classroom instructor willing to allow the use of the flipped session and also able to collaborate in the flipped classroom planning?
- Will you be able to communicate the expectations of the flipped classroom to students?
- Are there specific circumstances that will prevent this model from being successful?

In some cases, a librarian may not have the time or ability to adequately plan a preassignment that matches the desired learning objectives. Or, students may be too accustomed to a strong culture of classroom lecture in a particular course. Upper-level classes might not require exposure to new material before a library session, nor expect very structured activities during the session in order to be useful. These are just a few examples of the many situations that are not best suited to a successful flipped classroom experience.

At times, a librarian may decide that the flipped classroom is a good match for a particular class and then encounter problems during the implementation. These situations cannot be avoided, just like any teaching mishaps. But they can possibly be remedied if the potential problems are anticipated. Consider these questions:

- What if students don't complete the preassignment?
- What if students don't participate in the active learning component?
- What if the technology tools don't work like you planned?

As with all instruction, having a backup plan in place for reconfiguring when things don't go as planned can salvage a difficult situation. Flexibility is probably the most universal teaching tool.

THE TAKEAWAYS: LEARNING FROM EXPERIENCE

Here are some important lessons gleaned from trial and error with flipping the library instruction classroom:

- It's not a time saver—planning for the flipped classroom takes as much time (or more!) than planning for any other instruction. Assuming otherwise is a mistake.
- Do check students' knowledge before class—any kind of assessment tool that will provide you with an understanding of student comprehension of the preassignment material is important for planning active learning. Using this assessment also means your instruction is automatically more learner centered.
- Do plan highly structured class time—in order to make sure you are truly making the most of the flipped classroom model, students should be directed to engage with concepts introduced in preassignment material. This engagement does not happen by accident; planned activities should guide them through the experience.
- Do practice letting go of control—if you are used to showing and telling students everything they need to know to be successful at library research, letting go of the lecture format will be hard. Designate practice

time so that you know you can limit your time speaking and students can focus on the activity.

- Don't worry about the technology—only use the tools that you are comfortable with and are necessary for the experience. There is no reason to make it high tech or complicated, and doing so will likely cause problems.
- Do focus on the pedagogy and the fundamentals—you can keep your instruction simple and accessible by being clear about what the learning objectives are and why you are doing what you are doing. If your instruction planning seems to be getting muddy, remind yourself of your goals for the session and the reasons you have chosen to flip.
- Do consider opportunities and challenges—the flipped classroom may not be the best option for every class. If the arguments against it outnumber the arguments for it, think about alternatives.
- Do try it and tweak it—you won't know all the benefits and pitfalls of using the flipped classroom in your teaching environment until you try it. Take advantage of the learning experience and build on what you think you can do better next time.

CONCLUSION

The role of the academic library on campus is continuing to change, just as change in higher education is ongoing. Today's best practices will likely evolve, and experimenting with pedagogical techniques like the flipped classroom both instigates and chases the process of change. For example, as instruction librarians consider and use the ACRL *Framework for Information Literacy for Higher Education* (2015), new models for library instruction will be adopted. This time of review and reflection on library instruction activities is a great opportunity to consider integrating the flipped classroom and other innovative models into the information literacy instruction repertoire.

Experimenting with library instruction makes our work fun and helps us improve our practice. The flipped classroom provides the chance to meet the instruction goals of making the most of limited time with students to help them be successful in their assignments and to eventually become adept at research. It also illustrates many of ACRL's best practices, making a library instruction program stronger. As librarians continue to experiment with this method, and many others, they should be guided by reflection on the needs of students in order to keep pace with the changing academic environment.

REFERENCES

ACRL (Association of College & Research Libraries). 2012. "Characteristics of Programs of Information Literacy That Illustrate Best Practices: A Guideline." *College & Research Libraries News* 73, no. 6 (June): 355–59. http://crln.acrl.org/content/73/6/355.full.pdf+html.

———. 2015. *Framework for Information Literacy for Higher Education*. American Library Association. Association of College & Research Libraries. http://acrl.ala.org/ilstandards/wp-content/uploads/2015/01/Framework-MW15-Board-Docs.pdf.

Gibes, Elizabeth Andrejasich, and Heather James. 2015. "Is Flipping Enough? A Mixed Approach to Introductory Information Literacy Instruction." *College & Research Libraries News* 76, no. 1 (January): 10–13. http://crln.acrl.org/content/76/1/10.full.

Noe, Nancy. 2013. *Creating and Maintaining an Information Literacy Instruction Program in the Twenty-First Century*. Oxford, UK: Chandos.

Towson University. 2015. "University Core Curriculum Requirements." Accessed January 7. http://catalog.towson.edu/undergraduate/university-curriculum/university-core-curriculum-requirements/.

Zhong, Ying. 2012. "Universal Design for Learning (UDL) in Library Instruction." *College & Undergraduate Libraries* 19, no. 1 (March): 33–45. doi:10.1080/10691316.2012.652549.

III

BRANCHING OUT: TEACHING SPECIAL LITERACIES

8

Visual Literacy

Benjamin R. Harris,
Elizabeth Huth Coates Library, Trinity University

In higher education and beyond, images have become crucial to our methods of meaning making, teaching and learning, and problem solving. The changes brought about by increased access to information online have introduced challenges to finding accurate, authoritative written text and have influenced searching methods for images as well. Just as students must find, evaluate, and use written texts in their academic work, they are often called upon to complete the same types of activities using images. And this extends into their nonacademic lives as well, where most texts are varying combinations of visual and verbal components. While there are differences in the reading and uses of images as opposed to written texts, research involving both words and images call upon many of the same skills and critical faculties.

CONTEXT/BACKGROUND

Trinity University is a private liberal arts and sciences institution in San Antonio, Texas. The Elizabeth Huth Coates Library supports the work of approximately 2,500 students, 250 teachers, and over 400 staff members. Trinity offers a long-standing Seminar and Writing Workshop program for first-year students, a core curriculum requirement for undergraduate majors across twenty-five academic departments, and several graduate degree programs. The mission of the Coates Library is to ensure that students in classes across disciplines have opportunities to develop and enhance their information literacy skills. Twelve faculty librarians and a number of crucial classified staff members lead these efforts in a library that has been proactive in such areas as open access and alternative models for managing access to journal subscriptions, as well as its robust information literacy program. In 2007, the Coates Library received the Association of College & Research Library's Excellence in Academic Libraries Award.

With several changes in administrative structure in 2002, the library made information literacy a main focus of its teaching, learning, outreach, and assessment activities. In 2007, Trinity's administration and faculty adopted information literacy as the topic for the campus Quality Enhancement Plan (QEP), a program required by the Southern Association of Colleges and Schools (SACS) to enhance and assess a focused educational initiative at each institution receiving SACS accreditation. The Trinity QEP was centered on five learning outcomes for students, based on the ACRL's "Information Literacy Competency Standards for Higher Education." Through instruction and assignments, students would learn (1) to understand when information was needed and the kinds of information sources available to meet the need; (2) to access and (3) evaluate information and information sources; and (4) to use information ethically as they (5) create new information products. Through workshops for faculty, course creation and revision grants, assessment development activities, and other programming, information literacy learning outcomes and assessment measures were integrated across the curriculum. In 2013 at the end of the five-year program, SACS deemed Trinity's information literacy QEP a successful project to enhance student learning.

As the QEP ended, the presence of information literacy across the curriculum was confirmed—above and beyond all programming and assessment associated with the QEP itself—by the continuation of information literacy as a goal of the campus in the university's curriculum documentation. More recently, information literacy learning outcomes have been specifically stated as embedded components in a number of other requirements included in the curriculum. For example, all classes that meet the curriculum's "Global Awareness" requirement must include a significant information literacy learning experience.

Many courses across the Trinity curriculum blend the location, evaluation, and ethical use of images and texts in the creation of new information. For the purposes of this chapter, three classes suggest the opportunities associated with including information literacy related to images in assignments and instruction. The first two examples are drawn from classes designed for first-year students, while the third example is offered as part of the major curriculum in the Art Department (and may also be taken for a core curriculum credit). Each of these examples has been selected, in part, due to its potential for being adapted and applied across different types of courses and learning situations.

EXAMPLE ONE: FIRST-YEAR SEMINAR—"FRANKENSTEIN, AND BEYOND"

"Frankenstein, and Beyond" is a First-Year Seminar course designed to engage students in discussions that draw from an initial reading of Mary Shelley's classic work. Students consider the scientific implications of the text, as well as responses, critiques, and adaptations of the Frankenstein mythology from various disciplinary perspectives (e.g., religion, art, history). Aside from its topical focus and to meet the requirements of all courses in the First-Year Seminar program, the instructor has established learning outcomes, instruction, and assignments to improve students' critical reading abilities, writing, oral presentation skills, and information literacy development.

Students receive library instruction at two points in the course. The first session focuses on finding textual sources for a specific assignment and is scheduled during the fourth week of the semester. At week six, students receive a new assignment to (1) select an image from those posted at the course website, (2) find background information on the image, and (3) conduct research to explore the narrative of the image. As part of their research, students are expected to find information on the artist and his or her intentions in creating the image, as well as any background information on the figure(s) or event(s) depicted.

During the first iteration of this class, computer-filled library instruction spaces were at a premium. In response, the librarian used the regular course classroom, equipped with a computer and projection equipment. The librarian distributed several pieces of green paper at the launch of the session, and students were asked to make notes about the process and sources they might use independently after the session. This strategy was intentional. While we may be tempted to give students prefabricated handouts, the act of putting pen to paper helps to maintain student attention and engagement. The use of green paper also has purpose. Called "green sheets" in this case, as an alternative to the typical "research guide" or "log," the colored paper suggests growth and vitality and helps to distinguish these pages from others that students may collect or use as part of the class. This strategy was utilized again when the course was taught in future semesters.

The first challenge that students must face in completing the assignment is the identification of the images they have selected for the project. While a number of images are posted at the course website, none of these include identifying information. An image used in class to illustrate the use of allegory and classical mythology in art—*The Vision of Aeneas in the Elysian Fields* by Sebastiano Conca—was selected for the librarian to model a process for identifying an image (see figure 8.1). Searching for information on this image is particularly challenging and gives the class an opportunity to explore some of the difficulties involved in identifying images online, where extensive documentation does not always accompany an image.

At one time, the best way to locate information about specific images using the Internet was to use a resource that specialized in "reverse searching." TinEye, Idee, and BYO Image Search are several examples. While these tools still have value in terms of specific search functionality, Google's image search now includes this option and allows the researcher to find an image and then locate an identical or related image. In the case of the Conca example used in class, questions arose about the authenticity of the image. Several similar images attributed to the same artist with the same title are available online. The librarian asks students to consider the various methods that can be used to confirm that a particular version of the image was the "original" or

Figure 8.1. ***The Vision of Aeneas in the Elysian Fields*, circa 1735–1740, by Sebastiano Conca, Italian, 1680–1764. *Source: Oil on canvas, 48 x 68½ inches, SN168. Collection of The John and Mable Ringling Museum of Art, the State Art Museum of Florida, Florida State University***

authentic work (with verifying this at the museum, institute, or owner of the work as the best and most authoritative way to identify the image).

After determining the title and artist of the work, students must draw from their previous information literacy session to suggest information sources that might answer questions about the background of the artist, the purpose of the artwork in question, and the narrative presented in the image. For the work by Conca, the class looks at reference sources focused on art to learn more about the artist. To discover the context of the image, students identify books in the library and Internet sites that would help explore the Elysian Fields and its place in Vergil's *Aeneid.* As the class explores this example, the librarian asks students to record each question and some of the search strategies used on their green sheets. Ideally, by the end of the session, each student has created a map or guideline for exploring his or her selected image that combines the strategies and sources included in the first information literacy session as well as the one focused on images. For assessment purposes, the librarian quickly reviews each green sheet at the end of class and offers suggestions where appropriate.

Approved in 2011, the ACRL's "Visual Literacy Competency Standards for Higher Education" offers a means for connecting our goals as information literacy educators with visual learning outcomes. The assignment for this course aligns with outcomes from Standards One to Four in this document. Specifically, this assignment asks students to articulate the "ways images can be used to communicate data and information" and also helps them to see that "existing images can be modified or repurposed to produce new visual content" (Standard One, Performance Indicator Two, Learning Outcomes d and e). Students must also select "the most appropriate sources for and retrieval systems for finding and accessing needed images" (Standard Two) and must make "judgments about the reliability and accuracy of image sources" (Standard Four, Performance Indicator Four). Most importantly, the student must perform a number of activities as he or she "interprets and analyzes the meaning of images and visual data" to meet the needs of the assignment (Standard Three).

The assignment and instruction session also align with the suggestions detailed in the ACRL's "Characteristics of Programs of Information Literacy That Illustrate Best Practices" (2012) document. Category Seven of the Characteristics on pedagogy is particularly applicable here. The process students are introduced to and then practice for this assignment "contextualizes information literacy within ongoing coursework" and "builds on learners' existing knowledge" by asking them to use skills acquired in the location of text-focused sources to find information about images. Further, modifications made to the course due to the classroom situation are suitable for the type and location of the instruction. Lastly, the development and use of the innovative "green sheets" may be particularly relevant to students in future courses as they plan and execute the research process.

Student work in this course also aligns with learning outcomes described in the ACRL *Framework for Information Literacy for Higher Education*. The first frame, Authority Is Constructed and Contextual, shifts away from the laundry-list process of determining the value of sources and instead, the researcher is expected to contextualize evaluation criteria in relation to specific projects (ACRL, 2015). This assignment teaches students that, while information about an image may seem correct, referring to multiple sources ensures a higher probability of accuracy. In fact, it may be the only way to determine accuracy, so keeping an open mind about information as it is discovered and then comparing the information with other sources when possible helps to foster a skeptical stance when researchers encounter new information. As an added benefit, the diligence and effort of the researcher are reinforced by the ability to compare and contrast sources and possibly qualify their use depending on the goal of the research. This shift in the way we think about the evaluation of sources in relation to authority is more complex than former models and recognizes that evaluative criteria can and should adapt to the information-seeking situation.

EXAMPLE TWO: "WRITING WORKSHOP"

During their first year, Trinity students are required to take a seminar such as "Frankenstein, and Beyond" as well as a first-year writing course. ENGL 1302: Writing Workshop is intended to help students acclimate to academic writing situations and often will focus on improving students' persuasive writing abilities. However, this is not a requirement. While some classes may concentrate on writing arguments, others may focus on writing research papers, literary analysis, and even poetry. Still, the shared goal of these classes is to give students experiences that will help them to move away from exam-centered writing instruction (often a focus in their high school writing classes) and adapt to writing situations that are more complex and varied across disciplines.

Most Writing Workshop sections assign an essay that requires students to draft an analysis of a text to build on students' previous writing experiences while also making sure that they understand the difference between summary and analysis. To make this distinction clear, the class described here asks students to write two different essays in which they first summarize a text and then analyze its features. The summary is expected to be concise but comprehensive, and the analysis should build on the summary by focusing on specific features of the text or argument. Ideally, the reader of the essay will gain greater insight into the text in question.

The summary/analysis essays are assigned early in the course. For the first essay, students summarize and analyze a written text with an eye for the ways an author has used the author's own character (ethos), his or her reasoning (logos), or the reader's emotions (pathos) to persuade. Texts for summary and analysis are assigned to groups of writers, and after conducting a critical reading of the chapter or article, members have an opportunity to discuss their ideas about the text before completing their individual essays. In the second essay, students must locate a printed book that incorporates images. They must select a chapter, offer a summary of that chapter, and then they must analyze the way the text uses images to help persuade the reader. As in the first essay, writers are asked to consider the ways that images included in the text help to establish the author's credibility or authority, reinforce the author's reasoning, or influence the reader's emotions.

Students are often the first to question the requirement that they use traditional, printed books for the assignment. It would, in fact, be much more manageable for students to choose a web text or another source that is more easily accessible and would most likely include the integration of words and images. However, one of the reasons for requiring students to use printed books was to make certain that first-year students had gained experience in using the library's online catalog and also had located a book in the library. A survey of students conducted in 2013 (as part of the library's presemester summer reading and research assignment) showed that more than 50 percent of the incoming class did not remember ever locating a book in this manner.

In preparation for the information literacy instruction session, the librarian selects several texts that integrate images in varying ways. Aside from offering examples of books using images to persuade the reader through the uses of ethos, pathos, and logos, examples also include texts that either focus on the image as its subject or include images as evidence for information provided in the text. For example, the book *Little Rock Girl 1957: How a Photograph Changed the Fight for Integration* by Shelley Tougas (2012) focuses on the familiar image of Elizabeth Eckford being taunted by a crowd of white onlookers as she attempted to attend a newly integrated Arkansas school in 1957 (see figure 8.2). The information included in this book dissects and analyzes the different components and figures in the image. In another example, Toni Morrison's *Remember: The Journey to School Integration* (2004), the image is one of many that are used as visual inspiration for the author's fictional narrative.

Figure 8.2. Image of Elizabeth Eckford attempting to attend classes in Little Rock, Arkansas (1957). ***Source: permission for use provided by Will Counts/Indiana University Archives***

During the instruction session, the librarian divides students into the same groups that worked together to complete the first summary/analysis essay. While this grouping is not required by the teacher of the course, it is useful for the librarian to depend on students' experiences in working together prior to the session to facilitate a more efficient and effective collaborative discussion during the library session. The librarian offers the groups several sample topics and a brief introduction to the library's online catalog. After conducting online searches in the catalog, the librarian directs students to the descriptive information about the text and, in particular, points out information in the catalog record related to a book's use of illustrations. In addition, students are encouraged to browse the physical location of books they find in the catalog to see if other titles are particularly relevant to their search.

Each student is then charged to find at least one book on the group's topic that includes images appropriate for the summary/analysis assignment. After locating the item in the catalog, students find the physical item in the library and return to the instruction space. Together, group members review the selection of books and then evaluate the "best" option for the assignment and identify (1) if the image in the example helped to persuade the reader through ethos, logos, or pathos and (2) whether the image was used as the focus of the written text or as an enhancement of the text. A group member then reports these findings on the "best" option for the rest of the class. The assessment of this instruction session focuses on these reports, as well as each student's ability to find a viable option for the assignment.

An assignment asking students to summarize and analyze a visual text meets a number of learning outcomes in the ACRL "Visual Literacy Competency Standards" (2011). Standard Three is particularly relevant here, as the work of writing the paper will require students to interpret and analyze the meanings of images. The instruction session, specifically, focuses on helping students to achieve several additional outcomes as a student "recognizes the role of textual information in providing access to image content, and identifies types of textual information and metadata typically associated with images" (Standard Two, Performance Indicator Two). In addition, students must "evaluate textual information accompanying images" (Standard Four, Performance Indicator Three) and this may begin the process where they "evaluate the effectiveness and reliability of images" in context (Standard Four, Performance Indicator One).

As with the First-Year Seminar example, this assignment aligns with the ACRL "Characteristics of Programs of Information Literacy That Illustrate Best Practices" (2012) in its use of specific pedagogical strategies to enhance student learning. Students are asked to collaborate to achieve the desired learning outcomes of the course. In addition, the assignment is designed to promote critical thinking and recursive learning, as students must draw upon their experiences in the previous summary/analysis essay in developing their arguments for the second paper.

While not directly related to the visual literacy component of the assignment or instruction session, the teaching and learning situation provided in this class aligns with the sixth frame in the ACRL *Framework*—Searching as Strategic Exploration (2015). Students must explore the print collections to find a suitable text for the assignment, and through this process and the discussion that follows, students will have an opportunity to experience serendipitous searching and retrieval. While they may not have experienced the value or benefits of serendipitous searching in the same ways that faculty researchers tend to think of it, the activities involved in targeting a specific text and then using that location to browse for other texts before considering possible options mirrors the same kinds of activities that students conduct online but tend not to apply to research involving print.

EXAMPLE THREE: "SCULPTURE (CLAY)"

Art history courses often include research assignments and information literacy instruction as a part of their curricula. At Trinity, applied arts courses include information literacy instruction and assignments even more often than the art history sections. "Sculpture (Clay)" is an applied arts course offered in Trinity's Art/Art History Department that may count as either a requirement for sculpture students or as a "creative expression" course for nonmajors. Therefore, students enrolled in the class may or may not have a background or experience in studying and creating artwork. The assignment described here is intended to support both experienced and novice artists and was later adapted for similar courses focusing on carving and relief sculpture, as well as an interdisciplinary course on the intersection of chemistry and art production.

The professor for this class collaborated with the librarian to develop the assignment based on two needs. First, the instructor felt that students were challenged to verbalize their goals in the creation of sculpture and were then challenged to critique the work of others. Second, the instructor felt that students' understanding of current trends, issues, techniques, and aesthetics for contemporary sculpture was limited. The assignment offers students an opportunity to explore the works of artists in a particular medium and to develop reference points and a vocabulary for discussing their own creations.

The assignment requires students to select an artist working in a medium selected by the professor (ceramics, architecture, land art, etc.). Students must find (1) biographical information on the artist, (2) an artist's statement, (3) information about the artist's chosen materials and methods, and (4) a minimum of ten images of the artist's work. Sources and images must all be cited in MLA style. Students must use their collected resources to create a PowerPoint presentation that answers several questions about the value of the artist's work to the student's understanding of art and creation (see figure 8.3 for a slide from a sample presentation).

Two assignment requirements deserve special mention. First, students must select "high-quality" images to include in their presentations. As we know, images found on the Internet may already be compromised in terms of color and their representation of other characteristics of an artwork. Also, low-quality images may be further corrupted if the student must make size adjustments or modifications when creating a slide. As a second requirement, students must draw from a minimum of five different information sources to create the presentation. In an assignment such as this, it would be possible for students to depend on one or two sources and replicate chunks of text and images to create the presentation. Instead, the instructor and librarian

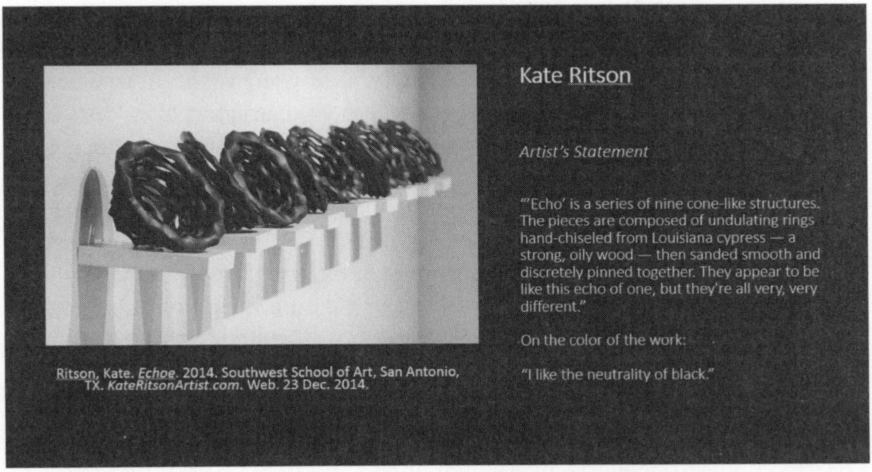

Figure 8.3. Sample slide used as an example in class showing an image with citation and an artist's statement for a sculpture by artist Kate Ritson. Photographer: Ansen Seale. *Source: permission for use provided by Kate Ritson*

ask students to synthesize information from a variety of sources in a very conscious way by drawing from a minimum of five textual and five image-related resources.

The information literacy instruction session begins with the assignment description and explanation, offered not by the course instructor but by the librarian. This shift in roles indicates the role of the librarian as an authority as well as a partner in the class. After students receive instructions and have an opportunity to ask questions, they receive time to browse a suggested website or conduct Internet searches to locate an artist for the presentation. The librarian then offers suggestions and instruction to help students find the information and images necessary to complete this assignment.

Special consideration is given to finding images of artworks. The library's licensed Artstor database offers images of art but also includes high-quality images as well as information about the artwork that may be helpful when creating citations. In addition, Artstor's functionality allows students to create "detail" images. Students can select an image in Artstor and focus on one part or component of the image and create a detail that can be used to highlight a specific part of the work. More importantly, the discussion of Artstor is ideal for introducing the issue of licensing of images for use by students in an educational context.

The research guide for the course includes a variety of additional online search engines. While Google's image search is a standard resource for an assignment such as this, it can also be helpful to use Instagram or Flickr to locate "amateur" photographs of artworks that give an unusual or distinctive perspective of a visual text that is not often seen in published images. In relation to these resources, students are made aware of the copyright issues involved with locating and reproducing images available on the Internet.

Lastly, before receiving considerable "lab time" to work (with support from both instructors), the librarian reviews the use of MLA citation style for citing sources, specifically those formats that are most helpful when citing images. MLA citation style is particularly well suited to this assignment, since it includes a number of different models for citing visual texts rather than citing the locations of visual texts (as in APA style) or treating images in a very different manner from cited textual works (as in Chicago style). In early iterations of the class, instruction on citation was reserved for late in the class period, after students had already begun to collect sources. However, resequencing this part of the instruction session ensured that students were aware of the citation requirements for a visual text and could collect the necessary information at the same time that they located the image.

To assess students' final presentations, the instructor uses a rubric incorporating criteria focused on both the course content learning outcomes and the information literacy learning outcomes for the assignment. The librarian receives a copy of these rubrics and has access to the final presentations. Since both the instructor and librarian have access to students' completed products, the two are able to discuss the results of the assignment and the instruction session before teaching the class in future semesters.

The learning outcomes for the assignment and the instruction session align with a number of the ACRL "Visual Literacy Competency Standards" (2011). Due to the concentration on the citation of images and the location of sources to find appropriate images, students have an opportunity to develop their understanding concerning the "ethical, legal, social, and economic issues surrounding the creation and use of images and visual media" (Standard Seven). This consciousness is particularly important for artists who may one day feel the impact of these issues, but it should also be useful to other students as they locate, evaluate, and use images in their academic, personal, or professional lives.

This assignment also offers the librarian and faculty member an ideal opportunity to collaborate, a key component of the ACRL Characteristics (2012). The librarian and faculty member develop and execute the assignment together, and the librarian takes on the role of course instructor by introducing and explaining the assignment to students. This blending and sharing of common classroom roles fosters greater communication between the two teachers and enhances the alignment of information literacy with course/disciplinary content. This collaboration occurs throughout the process, from planning and delivering instruction to the assessment of students' learning, and ultimately involves further collaboration when the assignment is revised for subsequent courses.

The learning opportunities associated with this assignment also relate to two of the six frames in the ACRL *Framework* (2015). First, as students locate images, they are asked to focus on the quality of these visual texts. Image quality can differ between electronic and print sources, but for art images specifically, the presentation of images online can be particularly problematic. The shade of red used in a specific ceramic sculpture, for instance, may appear differently when viewing the sculpture as opposed to viewing an image of the work. While the quality of the color of red can be controlled in a printed image in a book, for example, the color may look different in various online images of the same ceramic sculpture. As students consider the ways that the format of publication or presentation of an image can change the properties of the image, this may offer one of the best examples of the importance of the Information Creation as a Process frame—that the creation, format, and (re)presentation of texts is a process and should be a conscious component in researchers' evaluative methods.

In addition, the discussion on copyright and intellectual property of images as well as citation guidelines for visual texts is highly relevant to students pursuing a career in the arts. This situation can help to personalize the third component of the *Framework*, Information Has Value. The discussion on the value of information is so often carried out in the abstract, featuring unnamed or faceless constituencies. In this case, the importance of these issues can be applied to the students' own present and future work as creators of visual texts, reinforcing in a very personal way the need to give credit to creators and sources of information, to understand the purpose of intellectual property and copyright guidelines, and to manage the use of these sources in an ethical manner.

CONCLUSION: ADVICE FOR THE READER

While the examples provided in this chapter are intended to inspire adaptation and revision as they are applied across different courses and contexts, there are other efforts the reader can make to integrate visual literacy learning with information literacy instruction:

- Review the ACRL "Visual Literacy Competency Standards for Higher Education" and refer to the ACRL/IRIG Visual Literacy Bibliography (https://www.zotero.org/groups/acrl_irig_visual_literacy_bibliography). The substantial work invested in these resources offers librarians and others a strong starting point for thinking about the ways that visual and information literacy teaching and learning can be aligned in the curriculum and in the classroom.

- Educate yourself on the types of images and visual texts that are a part of the research and classes on your campus. In particular, consider the ways that visuals play a part in the data of research, above and beyond artistic considerations. For example, how are images located, selected, used, and created in the studies of meteorology or astronomy? Are image-focused assignments relevant to classes in sociology and anthropology? While some disciplines are obviously concerned and involved with visual literacy learning, students studying in disciplines outside of the arts and humanities can benefit greatly from the alignment of visual and information literacy instruction. As a starting point to broaden one's perspective on the uses of images across academic disciplines, see *Visual Practices across the University* (Elkins, 2007) and *Using Visual Evidence* (Howells and Matson, 2009).
- Explore opportunities to associate visual and information literacy instruction with faculty partners. Consider starting small and then communicate the results of these collaborations to others. As always, allow collaborators across campus to communicate these results.
- Look to courses with presentation assignments as an opportunity to integrate visual literacy learning with information literacy. Even in courses or disciplines where images are not a primary topic, visual texts will almost always be included, either to present information or enhance the visual appeal of the speaker's message. These discussions should go above and beyond good practices for creating presentation slides to consider the appropriateness of the image, the richness of the image in building a narrative component into presentations, and the ethics of selecting and using images.
- Lastly, as professionals, examine your own uses of images and visual texts as part of your professional and scholarly practice. Just as our developed information literacy has an impact on our ability to teach it, the same holds true regarding our visual literacy skills.

REFERENCES

ACRL (Association of College & Research Libraries). 2011. "ACRL Visual Literacy Competency Standards for Higher Education." American Library Association.

Association of College & Research Libraries. http://www.ala.org/acrl/standards/visualliteracy.

———. 2012. "Characteristics of Programs of Information Literacy That Illustrate Best Practices: A Guideline." American Library Association. Association of College & Research Libraries, Best Practices Initiative Institute for Information Literacy. http://www.ala.org/acrl/standards/characteristics.

———. 2015. *Framework for Information Literacy for Higher Education.* Final Draft. American Library Association. Association of College & Research Libraries. http://acrl.ala.org/ilstandards/wp-content/uploads/2015/01/Framework-MW15-Board-Docs.pdf.

Elkins, James, ed. 2007. *Visual Practices across the University.* Munich, Germany: Wilhelm Fink Verlag.

Howells, Richard, and Robert W. Matson. 2009. *Using Visual Evidence.* Maidenhead, UK: Open University Press/McGraw-Hill.

Morrison, Toni. 2004. *Remember: The Journey to School Integration.* Boston: Houghton Mifflin.

Tougas, Shelley. 2012. *Little Rock Girl 1957: How a Photograph Changed the Fight for Integration.* Mankato, MN: Compass Point Books.

9

Information and Scientific Literacy Support

Aligning Instruction with Standards and Frames to Prepare Students for Research and Lifelong Learning

Michele R. Tennant, Mary E. Edwards, Hannah F. Norton, and Sara Russell Gonzalez,
University of Florida Libraries

This chapter focuses on information literacy instruction targeted to University of Florida (UF) science students, in the contexts of the ACRL "Information Literacy Competency Standards for Higher Education" (ACRL, 2000) and the new *Framework for Information Literacy for Higher Education* (ACRL, 2015). UF is a comprehensive land-grant, sea-grant, and space-grant institution, with approximately 50,000 students, including over 30,000 undergraduates. Biology and health science are among the most popular undergraduate majors, with over fifty falling into the STEM (science, technology, engineering, and mathematics) and health disciplines (University of Florida, 2015). UF's sixteen colleges and many institutes and centers are served by the George A. Smathers Libraries, including the Health Science Center Library (HSCL) and Marston Science Library (MSL). HSCL librarians work with students, faculty, clinicians, and administrators at the Academic Health Center (AHC), composed of six health-related colleges (Dentistry, Medicine, Nursing, Pharmacy, Public Health and Health Professions, and Veterinary Medicine), a hospital complex, a veterinary hospital, and associated health-related research centers and institutes. MSL librarians work with students, faculty, and administrators in agriculture, environmental science, biology, chemistry, physics, engineering, mathematics, and statistics. At both libraries, liaison librarians provide instruction and develop workshops, collaborate on faculty projects, offer personalized reference and consultation services, and provide collection management for assigned academic units.

INFORMATION LITERACY FOR UNDERGRADUATE GENETICS STUDENTS

Since 1996, a librarian has partnered with a professor to provide students in undergraduate genetics (PCB3063) with authentic scientific experience (Tennant et al., 2012). Students learn to use the online tools and resources used by practicing geneticists and bioinformaticists to find, evaluate, and synthesize scientific information in a rigorous and ethical manner. Although the focus of the course is to provide students with a thorough grounding in genetics, a generous amount of class time is devoted to information literacy instruction and activities encompassing scientific communication, collaboration, and data and visual literacy. The course predates the creation of the ACRL standards, but course goals and assignments in the course align well with them, and recent course changes have been made keeping the standards in mind. This section of this chapter will focus on that alignment, and how the more conceptual nature of the new *Framework* may guide instruction in areas still difficult for students to understand or incorporate into their mindsets.

The 120 students in the course are required to complete a class term project, worth 25 percent of their course grade. Students are individually assigned a specific genetic disorder to research and determine the "story of the gene," including how the gene works, what happens biologically to cause disease when mutated, what experiments scientists used to understand the gene, and whether those experiments and data interpretations were appropriate. In recent years, the final project work product has been a group-created poster presented at a formal session in the HSCL.

Students attend two library instruction sessions to help them learn to gather, evaluate, and synthesize the required information. The first session concentrates on online resources, including Online Mendelian Inheritance in Man (OMIM), PubMed, and sequence databases such as GenBank and RefSeq, focusing on concepts (curated versus noncurated databases, controlled versus noncontrolled vocabularies, information for researchers versus clinicians, developing effective search strategies) rather than on the mechanics and technical aspects of database interfaces. The second session covers the concept of science building on preexisting science; the ethics of citing the literature; and tools such as the National Center for Biotechnology Information's (NCBI) Gene, SNP (single nucleotide polymorphism), and Structure databases; and clinical tools such as GeneReviews and the Genetic Testing Registry. Student learning is individually assessed three times during the semester through incremental homework assignments that require students to successfully use these databases to search for their uniquely assigned gene and genetic disorder and evaluate their retrieved information. Students are later assigned to groups of four, and choose one of their assigned genes to present on their posters. Students work collaboratively to create their posters, and defend their work at the formal poster session held in the HSCL.

Due to the emphasis on information resource instruction, there are ample opportunities to tie the project to the current standards, particularly Standards One and Two (see table 9.1). During the two library instructional sessions, students learn to determine which questions must be answered in order to successfully complete the term project (Performance Indicator 1.1); which resources will answer which questions, and which resources serve which audience—researcher, clinician, patient (1.2); what data (sequence, structure, literature, etc.) might best meet a particular information need (1.2); what information is available at or online through UF and what might need to be ordered or gathered via interview with a local expert (1.3); and after initial inquiry, which information gaps still exist and how to refine the searches to address them (1.4). In the second assessment of the semester, students choose the five articles that will be most useful to use and cite in their final posters, and provide cogent written arguments as to why these are the "best" sources (1.4, 3.1, 3.2). This evaluative component facilitates an understanding of whether the initial question asked (and search strategy employed) requires revision (3.7).

A primary component of the poster project is for students to determine what experimental evidence exists for the information found in the primary literature, whether the method of investigation was appropriate, and whether the information is reliable (2.1). Because of the emphasis on database instruction, it is not surprising that students learn to develop effective search strategies in numerous literature and fact-based tools, explore multiple search systems, and learn to refine searches as needed (2.2–2.4). Because students must use both data and the literature to understand their topic and must include visual representations (charts, tables, figures, photographs) in their poster, they learn to use tools for information extraction, as well as organization (2.5). Not only do students need to clearly present information in the graphic content of the poster, designing the overall layout of the poster is an exercise in visual literacy as students learn how to balance text and graphics to best present complex scientific information.

Through the use of an assigned journal's house style, students learn the components of citations; the differences between types of sources; formatting and labeling of figures, tables, and their legends; and how to create the required bibliography (2.5), as well as the legal and ethical uses of information (5.1 and 5.2). The discussion of GeneTests and the Genetic Testing Registry provides a case study regarding gatekeepers and changing access to informa-

Table 9.1. Class Learning Activities Mapped to the ACRL "Information Literacy Competency Standards for Higher Education" (ACRL, 2000)

Performance Indicator	*Instructional Activity*
Standard One: "The information literate student determines the nature and extent of the information needed."	
1.1 ". . . defines and articulates the need for information."	Homework searching activity Research proposal
1.2 ". . . identifies a variety of types and formats of potential sources for information."	Homework searching activity using multiple databases Introduction of information portal
1.3 ". . . considers the costs and benefits of acquiring the needed information."	Poster project
1.4 ". . . reevaluates the nature and extent of the information need."	Homework searching activity
Standard Two: "The information literate student accesses needed information effectively and efficiently."	
2.1 ". . . selects the most appropriate investigative methods or information retrieval systems for accessing the needed information."	Poster project Research proposal
2.2 ". . . constructs and implements effectively-designed search strategies."	Poster project Abstract-writing assignment Letter to a researcher CV and biosketch assignment Research proposal
2.3 ". . . retrieves information online or in person using a variety of methods."	Poster project Abstract-writing assignment Letter to a researcher CV and biosketch assignment Research proposal Introduction of information portal
2.4 ". . . refines the search strategy if necessary."	Poster project
2.5 ". . . extracts, records, and manages the information and its sources."	Poster project Bibliography creation Annotated bibliography
Standard Three: "The information literate student evaluates information and its sources critically and incorporates selected information into his or her knowledge base and value system."	
3.1 ". . . summarizes the main ideas to be extracted from the information gathered."	Choose "best" articles and justify
3.2 ". . . articulates and applies initial criteria for evaluating both the information and its sources."	Choose "best" articles and justify
3.3 ". . . synthesizes main ideas to construct new concepts."	Poster project

Performance Indicator	Instructional Activity
3.5 ". . . determines whether the new knowledge has an impact on the individual's value system and takes steps to reconcile differences."	Peer discussion and debate
3.6 ". . . validates understanding and interpretation of the information through discourse with other individuals, subject-area experts, and/or practitioners."	Poster presentation Research proposal Peer discussion and debate
3.7 ". . . determines whether the initial query should be revised."	Choose "best" articles and justify
Standard Four: "The information literate student, individually or as a member of a group, uses information effectively to accomplish a specific purpose."	
4.1 ". . . applies new and prior information to the planning and creation of a particular product or performance."	Data visualization Research proposal
4.3 ". . . communicates the product or performance effectively to others."	Poster presentation Data visualization Oral presentation Research proposal
Standard Five: "The information literate student understands many of the economic, legal, and social issues surrounding the use of information and accesses and uses information ethically and legally."	
5.1 ". . . understands many of the ethical, legal and socio-economic issues surrounding information and information technology."	Bibliography creation
5.2 ". . . follows laws, regulations, institutional policies, and etiquette related to the access and use of information resources."	Bibliography creation Letter to a researcher Research proposal

tion. When GeneTests first appeared on the web, only medical professionals and librarians were allowed password access. Such resources are now freely open to the public.

The abilities to usefully synthesize information (3.3) and use it for a specific purpose (Standard Four) are crucial to student success. Students use their existing knowledge of genetics (gained through lecture and their textbook) with what they have discovered through the primary literature and data to construct new, more complex knowledge of genetics requiring them to evaluate and apply what they have learned. It is at this point in the project that genetics and information literacy are most integrated.

In modern science, it is essential that students have the communication skills to participate in discourse and to accurately and convincingly convey the results of their investigations (3.6, 4.3). Students must be able to effectively communicate to their teammates what they have learned about their individually assigned genetic disorder—this discussion forms the basis for the team decision as to which of the four assigned disorders to use for their poster presentation. Through this discourse, students gain experience in discussing their genes using the specific language of genetics, and develop a persuasive argument based on evidence. Finally, the poster presentation itself, which is made to professor, librarian, teaching assistants, classmates, and invited guests (researchers, clinicians, educators, family), provides students with the experience of formal defense of their ideas and knowledge in an authentic environment, the scientific poster session.

While the current standards match well with the intent of the project, particularly searching, evaluating, synthesizing, and appropriately crediting information, the new *Framework* promises to move beyond these skills to encompass others essential for modern scientific and clinical inquiry. The Scholarship as Conversation and Research as Inquiry frames have great potential to help students understand the "messiness of research." Students are often frustrated by the primary literature and factual data presented in tools such as GenBank, as information presented from different studies may not agree. Science builds on previous research, and sometimes researchers get different answers to the same questions. Students must develop the skills to help them decide which studies have the most credence, the underlying reason that students are required to investigate and evaluate the experimental evidence—"How do the scientists know what they know?" While Performance Indicator 3.4 aligns with these needs, grounding students in the *Framework*'s concepts of Research as Inquiry and Scholarship as Conversation may be more persuasive in making students comfortable with scientific messiness and with their role in deciphering that mess.

Science, particularly biomedical science, is increasingly collaborative, multidisciplinary, and translational. The Research as Inquiry and Scholarship as Conversation frames also have potential to expand students' thinking to recognize that divergent perspectives and skill-diverse teams move science forward. Persistence, adaptability, and flexibility are key to success in science, as is collaboration. PCB3063 provides students with the opportunity to work collaboratively, and exit surveys indicate that the group work provides a positive learning experience for most students (Tennant et al., 2012). Using frames to highlight the importance of collaboration and communities of science may facilitate this aspect of the project.

The "art and science" of searching may be another area in which using the more conceptual *Framework* may be a more successful approach. Students are presented with a number of databases and other online resources and a variety of searching options (keyword versus controlled vocabulary, field searching, limiting to main point). Many are confounded by the array of choices and ask why they have to make so many decisions when they could just "type stuff into the PubMed search box" or "google it." Although students are introduced to the rationale underlying these choices, an emphasis on the strategic nature of searching may help them better appreciate why multiple options exist, and how to use them to develop search strategies that best meet their information needs.

Over the next year, the librarian and the professor will determine which aspects of instruction would most benefit from *Framework* incorporation and reevaluate their instructional methods. The librarian's sessions are currently delivered through lecture with some hands-on searching examples that students replicate. The advent of the more conceptual and thematic *Framework* seems an apropos time to redesign the information literacy instruction to follow the "flipped classroom" format (Bishop and Verleger, 2013), in which class time could be spent on discussion of concepts and collaborative/interactive learning activities guided by the *Framework*.

DISCOVERING RESEARCH AND COMMUNICATING SCIENCE

In 2006, the UF MSL developed its first three-credit course to teach undergraduate students the expertise they need to begin conducting research succesfully early in their education. Students are focused upon gaining the required subject material expertise to begin research projects but often lack the knowledge and skills classes normally neglect, such as abstract and grant writing, searching for scholarly literature, data management, and presentation skills. Named "Discovering Research and Communicating Science," this course provides undergraduate students with these ancillary research skills to successfully transition from student to researcher early in their academic career.

In addition to traditional library skills, the course also includes guest lecturers who speak about their own research, National Science Foundation (NSF) program officers, basic statistics, and experience with oral and poster presentations. This class is offered approximately once a year and taught by a team of librarians, with at least one having previous experience as a research scientist. Johnson and Gonzalez (2010) provide more detail about the original curriculum and motivation for the assignments. This section of this chapter will focus on the most recent offering that modified the curriculum to include a greater emphasis on ethical issues and data-intensive skills, reflecting their rise in importance to research.

The course is listed with the UF Honors Program and typically twenty to twenty-four undergraduates enroll. They are predominantly in their first two years and their interests lean heavily toward the health sciences. To highlight the importance of collaboration in research, the first class includes a CoLAB (Collaborating with Strangers) session (de Farber, 2013) to allow students to meet each other and discover their interests. The curriculum is structured to build familiarity with the scientific research process and scholarly communication, culminating in a team project that presents a research proposal designed for a hypothetical summer project. Groups choose research areas early on and then use these to guide their choice of readings and decide which scientists and research programs to investigate. Instructors emphasize that the research does not need to be scientifically valid since that can be a difficult requirement for new freshmen.

Students are required to write a total of ten abstracts throughout the semester, based upon readings that they select from peer-reviewed journals correlating to their proposal topic. A guest instructor presents an introduction to scholarly communication and the major components of a journal article abstract. Then, once a week, students choose a peer-reviewed research article and write their own abstract, restricted to a 250-word limit. They must also include a citation to the article using APA (American Psychological Association) format. The assignment has several objectives. The first one is that students successfully use an article database to locate a peer-reviewed article. Students quickly grasp the concept of peer review but struggle to distinguish standard research articles from commentaries and review articles. Another objective is for the students to develop a familiarity with literature relevant to their area of interest, including key terms and methodology, to prepare them for writing the longer research proposal at the end of the semester. The word limit and APA format are deceptively difficult requirements since they demand clarity of language and close attention to detail. The APA format also provides strong encouragement for the students to begin using reference management software. This assignment meets ACRL Standard Two, specifically Performance Indicators 2.2 and 2.3. In order to successfully write an abstract, students need to search and locate a peer-reviewed article using the appropriate scientific database. It can be challenging for nascent researchers to choose effective keywords and select articles that are both understandable and a reasonable length. Students must also either download the electronic version or locate the paper article. By the end of the semester, students are familiar with multiple research databases and have searched and retrieved at least ten peer-reviewed articles.

Once students have selected an area of research for their project, they identify a researcher in that field, ideally one that is offering a research project for undergraduates. Students are tasked with composing a letter to that researcher, introducing themselves, and expressing interest in the research project. The goals of this assignment are to encourage students to explore relevant scientists and learn how to write a concise professional letter, including using the correct salutation and avoiding slang. This letter requires students to identify keywords that successfully locate a researcher using a search engine or research profile system. Similar to the abstract assignment, this satisfies Standard One (1.2 and 1.3). The requirement to use formal, professional language in the letter meets Standard Five (5.2). Students report that, after this assignment, they feel much more confident about successfully communicating with researchers.

Data management and visualization are increasingly important topics in scientific research and, over the years, their coverage has been expanded to an entire week of the semester. After students learn about locating datasets, metadata, and data management, they are required to locate a dataset, being careful that they understand each field. Students pick a visualization type to represent their data and produce a graph that visualizes a trend or feature. Along with the plot, students submit a data citation and paragraph describing the dataset and explain the visualization. The major objective is for the student to explore different types of visualization and realize that the purpose of a graph is to highlight trends. Students also gain experience searching for open datasets and creating a citation to that dataset. This assignment focuses on achieving Standard Four: students download and manipulate data (4.1) and then visualize it to communicate meaning, keeping in mind best practices for graphic design (4.3).

The next assignment is to create a curriculum vitae (CV) and biosketch for an accomplished researcher, plus create a CV for themselves using provided templates. Students must identify a researcher relevant to their research topic and find enough professional details to fill out the templates. In preparation for this assignment, the class discusses author disambiguation and research profiles online, such as VIVO, ORCID, and Mendeley. The overall goal for this assignment is to encourage students to start developing their CV, understand author identifiers, and understand differences between a CV, résumé, and biosketch. This assignment correlates with Standard Two, specifically Performance Indicators 2.2 and 2.3, to identify search keywords and locate information about a relevant researcher.

The annotated bibliography assignment is a bridge between the ten abstracts each student wrote and the literature review that is a component in the research proposal. Students use the research articles they read for the abstracts and write a one- to two-paragraph summary that describes, evaluates, and explains how each article relates to the topic. Each summary must also contain an APA-formatted citation. Students may select other peer-reviewed articles if their topic has changed, but the objective is for the students to then be able to use the annotated bibliography to easily write the literature review. Along with teaching various databases, instructors show students how to use reference software to manage and export citations into an APA-formatted bibliography (2.5).

The capstone project of the semester is a group research proposal along with an oral presentation. The research proposal requires students to follow the template for the NSF graduate student fellowship, synthesizing many of the previous assignments and class lectures. Elements of their proposal include a cover sheet, abstract, literature review, proposed research, budget, timeline, bibliography, and CVs for each of the group members. Page limits are strictly enforced, and students are encouraged to be as realistic as possible with their research methodology and budget. Ideally, this proposal has developed over the semester, with the abstract assignments leading to the annotated bibliography then the literature review.

Developing this research proposal draws upon all five of the ACRL information literacy standards. Students must identify a research topic (1.1) and develop a search strategy that identifies the key papers and researchers for their topic (2.2, 2.3). One of the most difficult aspects of the proposal for students new to a topic is developing the research methodology, so the instructors encourage them to use methodologies specified in the literature or interview researchers to discover what they recommend (2.1, 3.6). Groups must also use a citation management system to produce their bibliography (2.5). As students write the proposal (4.1, 4.3), they are encouraged to consider if their research conforms to the university policy regarding human and animal subjects and to follow strict attribution guidelines for citations and images (5.2).

The ability to present research in compelling ways—to funding agencies, to colleagues, and to potential lab partners—is an essential skill for scientists. The final class activity is a ten-minute oral group presentation about their research proposal. Presentations must include an introduction to the topic, a description of the problem, the importance of the research to the field, proposed methods and analysis plan, resources needed, and a project timeline. Students must also provide constructive feedback for each group, using an evaluation template. The grading rubric not only considers the content but also the quality of the presentation, including oral presentation skills and whether each group member participated equally in the presentation (4.3).

Examining this class in light of the new ACRL *Framework* suggests that it strongly correlates with several of the major concepts. The first module in the course is devoted to understanding scholarly communication and how it fits within the research method. This supports the Scholarship as Conversation frame, with the goal that students can identify key researchers in their topic of interest and map out the major research developments over time. This is followed by intensive instruction of the major scientific databases and data repositories. This module, along with the requirement to locate literature for the majority of assignments, correlates to the Searching as Strategic Exploration frame. One of the course objectives is to raise awareness of the importance of research integrity through understanding responsible conduct of research and insisting upon proper attribution. The research proposal embraces the concept of Research as Inquiry. Students must successfully formulate a research question and gather background information to identify an appropriate methodology. They are encouraged to contact experts in their topic, including faculty and experienced students.

The course curriculum is currently under revision for fall 2015, and this process allows an opportunity to ensure that the major concepts that comprise the new ACRL *Framework* are being addressed. One frame that should be explored more fully is Information Has Value. It is partly covered through the course's emphasis upon attribution and activities that examine various methods of scientific communication, including informal networking through blogs and e-print repositories. However, these topics are approached from a research ethics angle rather than the idea that information is a commodity and possesses socioeconomic value.

SEX AND GENDER DIFFERENCES IN HEALTH

In addition to the comprehensive courses described above, HSCL librarians have also integrated information literacy into instruction sessions within other departments' courses and some of the library's time-limited, externally funded projects. One such project that featured instruction was the Women's Health and Sex/Gender Differences Outreach Project (Edwards et al., 2014). With funding in 2013 and 2014 from the National Institutes of Health (NIH) Office of Research on Women's Health and National Library of Medicine, librarians at the HSCL engaged in a multipart outreach effort to increase awareness of the need for sex and gender differences research both in the basic and clinical sciences, and to enhance the visibility of existing research at UF. The librarian team expected that introducing students to these concepts and resources early in their careers would increase their awareness of the importance of sex differences across research and patient care, as well as pique the interest of some students in future research in this area. As part of this project, HSCL librarians offered eighteen instruction sessions in ten courses or programs to over 800 students in both the basic sciences and health professions. Two new opportunities for instruction came about because of this project: instruction to undergraduates in the health disparities minor and to high school students in the STEM Summer Immersion Program.

One librarian provided instruction for students in two courses within the health disparities minor: “Women’s Health and Well Being” and “Introduction to Health Disparities.” This minor is designed to raise students’ awareness of health disparities, encourage critical thinking about the assumptions that shape medical research and clinical practice, and add diversity to the health professions workforce. In both courses, the librarian introduced the concept of sex and gender differences research and walked students through the Women’s Health Resources Portal (http://womenshealthresources.nlm.nih.gov/), a primary information source for this topic at the time. Students learned about the different types of information contained in the portal (funding priorities, consumer health information, primary literature, and clinical trial information) and examples of when each would be useful.

Two librarians provided instruction for two groups of high school students involved in the STEM Summer Immersion Program run through the UF Center for Precollegiate Education & Training (CPET). CPET focuses on promoting excellence in science, math, and technology at the secondary education level through a variety of outreach activities to both students and teachers. While other instructional activities in the funded project focused on UF students, the team also wanted to include “pipeline students” who would eventually matriculate to universities including UF. In these sessions, high school students from rural areas of Florida were introduced to the need for research in sex/gender differences in health, regulations and policies relating to research in sex/gender differences, and the Women’s Health Resources Portal. Numerous examples of specific conditions and disorders that differ in men and women were also included in the presentation to provide concrete illustrations supporting the need for research in this area. After the introductory presentation, the students spent the last forty-five minutes of the session on a group discussion activity. Students were broken into groups of two to four and prompted to share with their group members examples of sex and gender differences topics with which they were familiar or had heard about in the media. Once the groups had time to discuss a chosen topic, they summarized their discussions for the entire class. The facilitators did not restrict the discussion when topics shifted toward more social or psychosocial issues of gender and sex differences. Instead, facilitators were able to both relate the “off-topic” discussions back to influences on health and to help students see how social science issues can be related to health and vice versa. Both of these sessions were very interactive as the students enthusiastically participated in the discussion, questioning each other and expanding on the topics presented.

These examples of instruction related to sex and gender differences and women's health align with several of the standards, performance indicators, and outcomes in the ACRL standards—specifically, components of Standards One through Three. The lecture presentations in the undergraduate and CPET sessions included information about policies, resources, tools, and sources of information related to sex and gender differences and women's health. This content supports performance indicators from Standards One and Two. The Women's Health Resources Portal, a major highlight of the lecture presentations, provides access to various health information resources from the NIH including ClinicalTrials.gov (a registry of clinical trials), MedlinePlus (consumer health information), preformulated PubMed searches (retrieving research articles), and consumer health information from specific institutes within NIH. This provides a ready-made example of information targeting different audiences with varying purposes and through varying formats (1.2). The instructors' emphasis on navigating and searching this resource demonstrates how to effectively access the information it contains (2.3).

The discussion portion of the CPET session focused on supporting the learners as they constructed new knowledge for themselves based on information shared during the lecture and previous information and experiences. In assisting the learners with constructing new knowledge through their own questioning and conversation, the instructors incorporated outcomes of Performance Indicator 1.1. Through discussion with their peers, students were able to fit new information into their existing knowledge and beliefs; CPET instructors (other than the librarians) and parent facilitators/guides also participated in the conversation. This broad-ranging conversation demonstrates students' work to shape their understanding and interpretation of the topic through discussion (3.6). Ultimately, the students were well-positioned to determine whether the new knowledge presented by the librarians and ideas raised by their peers diverged from their value system, and how to respond to the differences (3.5).

In looking toward the future at how the team can better teach information literacy through sex/gender differences sessions and other one-shot sessions in health science curricula, it is useful to consider how these topics fit within the new *Framework*. The Scholarship as Conversation frame is especially apt in introducing sex/gender differences research. Looking at differences in health between men and women, beyond the obvious reproductive differences, is a part of the scholarly conversation that has been silent, or at least muted, up until recently. Teaching students about sex/gender differences research provides an opportunity to discuss scholarship as a conversation that is not finished and that includes changes in perspective over time. In future discussions of this topic, librarians could further emphasize that students can be contributors to this scholarly conversation. The Research as Inquiry frame also connects naturally with this type of session. In the CPET discussion, students were asked to identify the type of questions they would be interested in pursuing within this topic area. In future discussions, librarians could ask students to perform preliminary searches to determine where their questions fit within existing research and knowledge. Finally, the Authority Is Constructed and Contextual frame applies to the introduction of specific information resources in these sessions. While the team generally focuses on the authoritative sources recommended to students (e.g., the Women's Health Resources Portal)—in the future, librarians could discuss the nuances of authority and where it comes from. Although time constraints are a limiting factor in one-shot sessions of this type, the *Framework* suggests some small changes in emphasis that could more holistically present the research, scholarship, and information landscape. Overall, the team aspires to consistently use the *Framework* to guide information literacy instruction in one-shot sessions. While these sessions typically focus on the hows of using specific tools or accomplishing specific tasks, using the *Framework* as a guide for instructional design would lead to a more conceptual take on these topics, leading students to think about the whys of their interactions with information.

LESSONS LEARNED

The process of writing this chapter and intentionally aligning course components to the ACRL standards has provided the UF team with insights for planning future instructional sessions. While not all sessions align well with the more rigid concepts described in the standards, as librarians move to the *Framework* approach, its flexibility can facilitate alignment with national recommendations for information literacy. In addition to the benefits of including the standards and *Framework* in planning, the following lessons have been learned:

- Information literacy training aligned with the ACRL standards can be successfully applied in academic courses in which librarians have been integrated, credit-bearing classes developed and taught by librarians, and one-shot guest lectures.
- STEM information literacy instruction benefits from authentic assignments, such as those related to scientific communication, collaboration, and discipline-specific resources.
- The conceptual nature of the *Framework* may facilitate the development of instruction and discussion that address the "whys" of information literacy, as well as the "hows."

- These "whys" can move learners beyond low-level cognitive processes such as remembering and understanding to more sophisticated processes including analyzing, evaluating, and creating, better preparing them for a future of lifelong learning.
- The conceptual nature of the Framework also lends itself to being used in the flipped classroom, where active and collaborative learning and discussion are key.
- Whether incorporating information literacy into courses through the standards, the *Framework*, or a combination of the two, close collaboration with academic teaching faculty (instructor of record, guest lecturers, and others) is essential to integrate domain knowledge and information literacy and lends credence to the library component.

ACKNOWLEDGMENT

This project has been funded in part with federal funds from the National Library of Medicine, National Institutes of Health, under contract #HHSN-316-2012-00028-W.

REFERENCES

ACRL (Association of College & Research Libraries). 2000. "Information Literacy Competency Standards for Higher Education." American Library Association. Association of College & Research Libraries. http://www.ala.org/acrl/standards/informationliteracycompetency.

———. 2015. *Framework for Information Literacy for Higher Education*. American Library Association. Association of College & Research Libraries. http://acrl.ala.org/ilstandards/wp-content/uploads/2015/01/Framework-MW15-Board-Docs.pdf.

Bishop, Jacob Lowell, and Matthew A. Verleger. 2013. "The Flipped Classroom: A Survey of the Research." 120th ASEE Annual Conference and Exposition, American Society of Engineering Education. http://www.asee.org/public/conferences/20/papers/6219/view.

de Farber, Bess. 2013. "Initial Steps to Create the CoLAB Planning Series: Workshops Designed to Spark Collaborations and Creativity through Revealing and Leveraging Community Assets." University of Florida Institutional Repository. http://ufdc.ufl.edu/IR00003505/00002.

Edwards, Mary E., Hannah F. Norton, Nancy Schaefer, and Michele R. Tennant. 2014. "Facilitating Collaboration and Research in Sex and Gender Differences and Women's Health: Year One Experiences." *Medical Reference Services Quarterly* 33, no. 4 (October): 408–27.

Johnson, Margeaux, and Sara Gonzalez. 2010. "Creating a Credit IL Course for Science Students." In *Best Practices for Credit-Bearing Information Literacy Courses*, edited by Christopher V. Hollister, 93–108. Washington, DC: Association of College & Research Libraries.

Tennant, Michele R., Mary E. Edwards, and Michael M. Miyamoto. 2012. "Redesigning a Library-Based Genetics Class Research Project through Instructional Theory and Authentic Experience." *Journal of the Medical Library Association* 100, no. 2 (April): 90–97.

University of Florida. 2015. "Enrollment." Accessed March 26. http://www.ir.ufl.edu/factbook/enroll.htm.

10

Diving into Data

Developing Data Fluency for Librarians

Scott Martin and Jo Angela Oehrli,
University of Michigan Library

As data services continue to emerge as a growth area for academic research libraries, many librarians are finding themselves in need of a skill upgrade in order to support research data at a level of excellence consistent with other library services. With the full support of its administrators, the University of Michigan (UM) Library has implemented a three-stage professional development program to develop readiness for data services within the organization. The first stage consists of a two-part workshop series presenting basic data concepts around data structures, storage, security, and sharing. These workshops build a shared understanding and vocabulary among librarians across the institution as a foundation for more specialized training. The second stage employs a workflow developed by UM librarians, the Deep Dive into Data, which provides a self-directed, iterative, nonlinear method for exploring the data landscape around a particular research discipline. Deep Dive workshops apply this workflow to an example discipline through in-class exercises and discussion, providing librarians with an expert-mediated means to build their familiarity with the tool before applying it to their own work. The ongoing third stage addresses specific topics in research data that are broadly applicable across disciplines. Some of these workshops explore cross-disciplinary data techniques that librarians may encounter or recommend to researchers, such as text mining. Others connect librarians to services provided elsewhere on campus, such as data storage, by inviting colleagues from those providers to brief library staff on the basics of the service and how to make an effective referral. Another type expands traditional public services skills, such as reference interviews, into the data services realm by providing an overview of current best practices and reports from individual librarians who have been piloting these services. Feedback gathered from participants at each stage has informed planning for subsequent offerings.

GETTING STARTED

Like many other large academic libraries, the University of Michigan Library has been considering how to respond to the needs of researchers around managing, disseminating, and curating their research data. The library had launched several initiatives in research data support, including participation in the DataCite service for Digital Object Identifier (DOI) assignment, support for ORCID identifiers for disambiguation of researcher names, and exploratory programs in data management plan consultation and data archiving, all under the auspices of its new Research Data Services group. As these efforts unfolded they highlighted clear needs, both among library staff and the wider campus community, for increased education about data concepts. In response, a meeting was called in the summer of 2013 to bring together librarians from the Research unit, who were primarily tasked with liaison duties to specific schools and departments, with librarians from the Learning and Teaching unit, as well as from data-relevant programs of the Collections and Publishing units, to form a Data Education Working Group (DEWG) whose charge was to create library programming specifically to address the educational needs we had observed.

As a part of this initial meeting, the director for Research Data Services outlined a vision for life cycle-oriented data education. This education would begin with in-reach to librarians, to prepare them to engage productively with researchers as data services providers, and eventually expand in scope to include outreach to our campus service population. Discussion during this and subsequent meetings refined the in-reach portion of the effort to a two-part approach. First, there would be training aimed at establishing a baseline level of general data literacy among librarians. This would set the stage for a second phase, in which librarians would receive more specific training in resources, techniques, and approaches rooted in the context of specific disciplines.

GENERAL DATA LITERACY

The UM Library's approach to general data literacy started with an examination of existing options, focusing largely on MANTRA research data management training (http://datalib.edina.ac.uk/mantra/) and its associated do-it-yourself training kit for librarians. While there was much value in these materials, the decision was made not to simply suggest them to our librarians as "background reading" prior to in-house workshops, for a number of reasons. First, the existing approaches lacked practical information: the materials discussing storage, for example, provided copious testimonials from researchers about the value of good backup practices, but less information about how to create an effective data storage plan. Second, the available materials were more heavily biased toward STEM examples and applications than we preferred, given our mandate to develop materials for the entire UM Library system. Finally, the existing programs, as structured, demanded more time commitment than could reasonably be expected from our librarians.

Rather than implement MANTRA, the UM librarians elected to create an in-house "Research Data Concepts for Librarians" training, which would distill some of the more basic and practical information into a more accessible form. The objective was to create a common institutional vocabulary of data concepts as a basis on which to build contextual data education later, and to provide librarians with some practical information on best practices for their own data management needs. A small subgroup, composed of volunteer staff with some experience in working with research data, divided the training into two 2-hour workshops. Each workshop was taught by two librarians and covered two thematic modules, using lecture, discussion, and in-class exercises.

The first workshop, "Working with Data," focused on topics related to the creation, documentation, and storage of data. The session began with a module discussing basic concepts in data management and design (best practices in file-naming conventions, open versus proprietary file formats, relational database concepts, metadata), illustrating these concepts with a data design exercise for a hypothetical circulation-data project. The second module continued with an overview of best practices in data storage and security, such as physical versus online options for storage, planning backup procedures, proper data disposal, and basic information about encryption, and spurred discussion with an interactive exploration of some of the available data storage options for University of Michigan researchers.

The second workshop, "Sharing and Preserving Data," discussed data publishing, data citation, and data management planning. Its first module explained the differences between data repositories and data journals (using a "repository safari" exercise to explore the variety of repositories currently available in various disciplines) and discussed data citation practices and catalogs of published datasets, while the second module gave a brief overview of the Office of Science and Technology Policy (OSTP) memo and its potential impact on federally funded research, outlined the basic elements of a data management plan (DMP), and previewed a UM Library project to assess the existing DMP practices at the College of Engineering.

The DEWG debuted this introductory training during the fall semester of 2013, offering two sessions of the first workshop on consecutive days in October, and two sessions of the second workshop in November. One session was offered in the morning and one in the afternoon, to provide maximum scheduling flexibility for staff who wished to attend. An additional session of each workshop was held in January 2014. Over sixty librarians attended at least one session of this training, with approximately half attending a session of both of the workshops.

The DEWG solicited feedback from attendees using an online survey and received twenty-three responses. About 80 percent of respondents indicated that the level of the material presented was "just right"; none reported that it was "too advanced." Twenty percent of respondents reported that the workshop material was relevant to questions they'd received from researchers; 71 percent reported that the material was relevant to questions that had arisen in their own work with data. Attendees were also polled about their perceived ability to provide data management services. When asked whether they were comfortable talking with researchers about data management issues, only 15 percent responded "yes," while another 71 percent responded "somewhat," and 14 percent responded "no." A related question about preparedness to provide research data management support found no respondents answering "very prepared"; 67 percent indicated that they felt "somewhat prepared," 14 percent reported that they felt "not prepared," and 19 percent reported that the question was not applicable, presumably because their duties did not involve liaising with research communities. These responses indicated that while the initial offering was useful, more education would be needed before library staff felt ready to support a new set of research data services.

DEEP DIVE INTO DATA

Following the basic instruction in data concepts, a larger subgroup of the Data Education Working Group was charged to plan contextual educational offerings focused on exploring data in particular disciplinary contexts. One obvious strategy would be to offer workshops that introduced participants to the data landscape of a particular discipline: ecology, psychology, and so forth. On reflection, however, there were some drawbacks to this approach. First, the sheer scope of the disciplines served by the University of Michigan Library prevented any sort of comprehensive coverage. Moreover, the librarians most likely to benefit from any particular discipline-based session were also likely to be the librarians the DEWG would want to recruit to teach such a session, and the divergence of data cultures between disciplines meant that most librarians were likely to derive substantially less practical benefit from attending sessions outside their disciplines.

Our solution to this dilemma was to develop and teach a methodology that individual-subject librarians could use in a self-directed exploration of their own disciplines. This method, which we named the Deep Dive into Data, consisted of several categories of exploration, corresponding to common features of a particular data landscape: data requirements of stakeholders (such as journals and funding agencies); data repositories; metadata standards; subject-specific data literature; and disciplinary data culture. Librarians could begin their exploration in any of these categories, using knowledge about their discipline's data culture that they had already gleaned from other sources (conversations with researchers, conversations with professional colleagues, readings in research data topics, etc.), and proceed in a nonlinear fashion through the categories as they uncovered additional information. Exploration of a data repository, for example, might reveal a frequently used metadata standard, which was originally published in a journal devoted to data issues in the discipline, whose most recent issue might contain an article examining researcher attitudes toward data sharing. See appendix A for the detailed Deep Dive workflow document, written in collaboration with a Council on Library and Information Resources (CLIR) Data Curation fellow, who at that time was embedded with the UM Library.

In order to teach the Deep Dive methodology, we returned to the idea of subject-focused workshops but with a modified approach in teaching them. Rather than simply deliver factual information about the data landscape of a particular discipline, these workshops investigated sample disciplines interactively using the Deep Dive methodology as a means to illustrate how it could be applied. Attendees performed an in-class exercise for each category, under the direction of the subject liaison librarian for that discipline, and shared their results in group discussion. Teaching the methodology in this way provided two key benefits. First, since participants could not be expected to come into the workshop with prior knowledge of the discipline on which to build their investigations, the DEWG developed exercises that could uncover features of a data landscape from scratch. To investigate stakeholder requirements, for example, participants had to identify top-ranking journals in the discipline by using the Journal Citation Reports rankings and explore their data deposit requirements (if any). Disciplinary data repositories, likewise, were identified using online repository directories such as OpenDOAR, Databib, and re3data, which provided browsable subject categories. These approaches then enriched the methodology as suggested tactics to augment librarians' existing knowledge of data in their disciplines. Second, leading librarians, through an exploration of a foreign discipline, successfully built their confidence with the methodology, which would facilitate its application to investigation of their "home" discipline(s).

The Data Education Working Group offered a number of Deep Dive into Data workshops during the winter semester of 2014. Originally, we planned for two workshops to serve as paradigms for disciplinary groups: an Ecology workshop to model a STEM Deep Dive, and a Psychology workshop to model a social sciences Deep Dive. The Psychology session drew thirty-one attendees and included subject liaisons from arts, humanities, and STEM disciplines as well as nonliaison library staff. The Ecology session, by comparison, drew fifteen attendees, largely from the Science/Engineering/Data Services cluster within the library's Research unit. The DEWG subsequently offered a Deep Dive into Clinical Data workshop, as a means to explore some of the sensitive-data and intellectual property issues more commonly found in medical research environments, as well as a workshop presenting the Deep Dive workflow in the abstract, without a paradigmatic subject to serve as an example (and necessitating, therefore, a lecture-based presentation rather than one integrating exercises and discussion). These drew eight and twenty-five attendees, respectively, with the attendees at the Clinical Data workshop coming exclusively from the Health Sciences and Science/Engineering/Data Services groups. These attendance numbers suggest that while interest in data issues among librarians is broad, the contextual framing of presentation can significantly affect attendance: sessions advertised as STEM-related drew substantially fewer attendees, especially from non-STEM disciplines, than materials based on the same content but advertised using non-STEM-specific language.

ADVANCED DATA WORKSHOPS

The third stage of the UM Library's educational effort emerged during planning sessions for the Deep Dive workshops, as the need for more in-depth education on specific data-related topics that transcended the boundaries of any individual discipline became evident. The DEWG conceptualized this third stage as Advanced Data workshops: an open-ended series designed to focus on one tool, strategy, task, or type of data and explore it in detail through presentations, active learning strategies, and guest lectures. The DEWG generated topics for these sessions via the feedback surveys from the previous workshops, conversations with colleagues (within the workshops and in other informal settings), and proposals from DEWG members. Once the list of topics had been assembled, the DEWG met to describe each possible workshop more fully, to brainstorm with possible UM librarians or campus instructors who could teach each workshop, and to assign a coordinator from the group who would be responsible for the logistics of the workshop (scheduling rooms, publicity, working with instructors to develop workshop content, etc.). In some cases, librarians from the DEWG both coordinated and taught the workshop.

The titles of the proposed Advanced Data workshops for fall 2014 were as follows:

- Data Storage
- Qualitative Data
- Data Reference Interview
- Strategies 101: Teaching Data Concepts
- DMPTool
- Data Interviews with Faculty
- Text Mining
- Grants Data Sources
- International Data
- Data Citation
- Legal and Ethical Concepts in Data

To facilitate so many workshops, we soon realized that it would be difficult to coordinate instructor availability and room availability with the campus academic calendar and with sufficient preparation time. The plan was to schedule all the workshops so that only one of the workshops would be held in any given week, necessitating the use of a shared calendar to avoid clustering the workshops. While it might have been possible to create workshops that were curricular and progressive—each workshop building on knowledge gained from prior workshops—the logistics of scheduling the workshops and coordinating library instructor availability seemed too difficult to coordinate the instruction on a more curricular level.

The Data Education Working Group was able to ask both UM librarians and another campus instructor to teach the workshops, signifying a great commitment by the library to collaborate and provide staffing for lifelong learning and professional development to grow the library's capacity to meet data services needs across campus. The library reached out to a data storage specialist in the IT department of the College of Literature, Sciences, and the Arts to present the Data Storage workshop. One librarian graciously agreed to teach more than one workshop. Members of the DEWG often coordinated more than one workshop throughout the semester and planned their assigned workshops simultaneously. Descriptions of individual workshops and librarians who served as instructors can be found in table 10.1. Workshops used various strategies to convey each concept, tool, or strategy including presentation, group discussion, role playing, scenario building, inquiry-based learning, and think/pair/share activities.

Table 10.1. Advanced Data Workshops

Name	*Description*	*Instructor*
Data Storage	A specialist from LSA IT will give us a librarian-centric overview of the services provided by campus IT units and selected outside vendors. Topics include: pros and cons of particular services; moving large volumes of data between storage solutions; access for off-campus collaborators; and moving data from "working" storage into repositories.	IT Specialist in the College of Literature, Science, and the Arts
Qualitative Data	(No description available at time of publication)	Government Information, Law & Political Science Librarian
Data Reference Interview	Effective reference interviews often uncover researchers' needs for more and different kinds of information, including research data. In this workshop, you will learn to ask productive questions and respond effectively to data-related information needs. Resources for locating data and for incorporating data literacy concepts will also be presented. All library staff, particularly liaison librarians, are encouraged to attend. Please come prepared to participate in interactive components of the workshop. Time for questions and discussion will be included.	Spatial & Numeric Data Librarian; Librarian for History & American Culture
Strategies 101: Teaching Data Concepts	Join several librarians to discuss the following questions regarding teaching data concepts. * What data concepts might we teach? * How might we teach these data concepts? This workshop is designed to address all disciplines and domains. During the workshop, attendees will engage with these 2 questions by discussing instructional issues, looking at models of possible instruction, and thinking about how the strategies discussed could be integrated into their own work.	Chemistry Librarian; Government Information, Law & Political Science Librarian; Research Data Services Manager; Learning Librarian; University Library Associate
DMPTool	(No description available at time of publication)	Physics & Astronomy Librarian

Data Interviews with Faculty	A librarian will describe her experience creating a data curation profile. She will then highlight interview questions from the Data Curation Profile Toolkit that can be applied to data interviews with faculty. The profile describes data needs for a structural geology and neotectonics research project; however, the session will be geared to all disciplines.	Earth & Environmental Sciences and Natural Resources and Environment Librarian
Text Mining	This workshop will give a basic introduction to text mining and discuss its applications in the humanities, sciences, and social sciences. The workshop will also explore ways to gather and prepare sources for text mining and include a demonstration of relevant tools. All library staff, particularly liaison librarians, are encouraged to attend.	Bioinformationist; Electronic Resources Officer; Librarian for English Language and Literature; Librarian for Romance Languages & Literatures and Comparative Literature; Instructional Technology Librarian
Grants Data Sources	Learn about the grant activity in your department by using resources available at the University of Michigan. In this session we will review a number of databases including U-M's SAW, or Sponsored Awards on the Web, ProQuest's Pivot, and the Foundation Directory on the Web to identify the kinds of information available. We will also briefly review Michigan Experts [database].	Grants and Foundations Librarian
International Data	Disciplines across the academy are increasingly seeking and publishing data sets whose scope transcends the English-speaking West. Working with these data presents particular challenges, which the presenters will describe. In the course of this workshop, they'll discuss: strategies for locating data at various demographic levels; types of data publishers; common challenges in working with international data sources; and techniques for identifying NGO and other international funding sources in departmental grant information.	International Government Information and Public Policy Librarian; Librarian for Near Eastern and Religious Studies
Data Citation	(No description available at time of publication)	DataCite Implementation Team
Legal and Ethical Concepts in Data	(No description available at time of publication)	Research and Data Informationist

Of the eleven workshops that the DEWG planned to offer in fall 2014, seven were ultimately offered. The four workshops that could not be completed were the Qualitative Data workshop, the Data Citation workshop, the DMPTool workshop, and the Legal and Ethical Concepts in Data workshop. Instructors were willing to teach all of these workshops, but the DMPTool workshop was delayed until the university deployed the newest version of the tool (and shelved it altogether following the university's decision not to support it institutionally), and scheduling difficulties ultimately prevented the others being offered during fall semester. The original plan was to offer repeat sessions of all workshops in the following winter semester, but attendance patterns for the workshops suggested that the DEWG should repeat only the three workshops that fostered the most interest (Data Reference Interview, Strategies 101: Teaching Data Concepts, and Data Storage). This approach freed up staff effort, which could then be dedicated to revisiting the planned workshops that were not offered in the fall, as well as planning and offering new workshops; these efforts are ongoing.

ASSESSMENT

Several strategies were used to assess our overall data education efforts. Attendance records were compiled from the individual sessions into a deduplicated master list of attendees, which gave some demographic information about the audience. Feedback was solicited following each of the individual workshops, using a standard survey form in Qualtrics delivered to attendees via e-mail. The DEWG also used the master list of attendees to distribute a broader survey about incorporation of the data education material into librarians' regular duties.

As of the end of 2014, a total of 128 library staff had attended at least one of the data education workshops (see table 10.2). This represents approximately 26.5 percent of the library's total staff count (as of mid-November 2014). A handful of the attendees listed, however, had left the library by the time data analysis began, so this number is a slight overrepresentation of the coverage of current staff. Unsurprisingly, a large percentage of attendees came from the library's Research unit, which includes most of the subject liaison librarians; these librarians are most likely to receive requests or perceive a need for research data services among the researchers they serve, and as such are likely to be more motivated to advance their skills in that area. We also achieved our highest unit-level coverage of staff among the Research librarians, with 80 percent of the unit staff attending one or more workshops. By head count, the next-most-represented area of the library was

Table 10.2. Workshop Attendance by Library Unit

Library Unit	*# of attendees*	*% of attendees*	*% of unit staff*
Collections	25	19.5	22.9
Health Sciences	12	9.4	41.4
Learning & Teaching	12	9.4	22.2
Library IT	5	3.9	9.4
Operations	4	3.1	4.8
Publishing	2	1.6	5.6
Research	56	43.8	80.0
Other	12	9.4	N/A
Total	**128**	**100**	**26.6**

the Collections unit; the next-highest-coverage unit was the Health Sciences Library. The DEWG's greatest concern from this analysis was the relatively sparse coverage of the library Information Technology unit, an area in which we would expect substantial interest in research data issues. Offerings to date may have been deemed either too basic or too public service focused to address the specific needs of the more infrastructure-oriented staff in that unit, although it's not possible to rule out problems of communication or staff concerns about work-scheduling priorities. Meetings will be arranged with managers in the unit to explore these issues.

DEWG members asked participants in the Deep Dive and Advanced Data Training workshops for their feedback on the workshops' content, ratings of their comfort with research data, and suggestions for additional workshops (see appendix B for a sample survey). In general, participants rated the content level of the workshops "just right" compared to their existing knowledge, with scattered responses of "too basic" and no responses of "too advanced." When asked whether the information was relevant to data questions received from researchers, respondents answered "yes" four times more often than "no"; when asked whether the information was relevant to data questions arising from their own work with data, "yes" responses were six times more frequent than "no" responses.

When attendees were asked about their comfort with providing data services, however, the results were less encouraging. Over half (54 percent) of the respondents answered "somewhat" when asked if they were comfortable talking about data issues with researchers, with 17.4 percent responding "no." When asked how prepared they felt to provide research data management support, only 3 percent responded "very"; over a quarter (27.6 percent) responded "not prepared," with the remainder answering "somewhat." Moreover, the responses to these questions did not show any temporal trend to indicate that comfort with data issues increased as the educational program proceeded.

As registration for these workshops is voluntary, the continuing indications of discomfort with providing research data services may reflect a self-selecting population of librarians who attend because they are uncomfortable with data concepts, and who may therefore stop attending once they start to feel comfortable. Contrary to this hypothesis, the attendance data clearly show that individual librarians have a fairly strong tendency to attend multiple sessions (128 attending staffers represent 371 individual attendances), and therefore presumably have submitted multiple feedback responses. A more likely scenario is that while they find the workshops to date valuable, attendees still perceive a gap between their current skills and the skills they need to confidently provide data services to their researchers. Reviewing the free-text answers to the question "Which topics should be addressed by future workshops?" suggests that data management plans remain a prime area of need for further education. While the plan was for DMP education from the beginning of the process, institutional uncertainty about support for DMPTool delayed and ultimately scuttled this offering; the library has, however, explored DMP consulting in the meantime via individual pilot projects, and those experiences will be translated into educational offerings in the months to come.

In mid-November 2014, an additional survey was sent to all the current library employees who had attended at least one data education session. In total, of 114 e-mails sent, there were thirty-five responses received, for a 30.7 percent response rate. The largest set of respondents was from the library's Research unit, with Collections, Learning and Teaching, and Health Sciences making up the bulk of the remainder. When asked about the workshops they had attended, about two-thirds of the respondents reported that they had attended one or more of the Deep Dive into Data workshops, but only six respondents indicated that they had used the method to explore their own disciplines, and three of those six had served as instructors for Deep Dive workshops. (As the Deep Dive materials are freely available to library staff, an affirmative response to the attendance question was not required to view the usage question.) This suggests that while they may find the method valuable, few librarians have felt enough urgency around exploration of subject data landscapes to prioritize this exploration above other projects and duties. Another contributing factor was that only the subject liaison librarians have formally assigned research communities to support, but attendance at the Deep Dive workshops was not limited to that population; it would be natural to expect nonliaison librarians to feel less urgency about conducting a Deep Dive in the absence of a specific project that requires greater familiarity with a specific subject's data landscape. Respondents' answers to the question

"How have you applied what you learned in these workshops to your work?" support these conclusions: of the eighteen respondents who gave an answer to this question, half reported that they had applied the content in some fashion, and many of the remainder indicated that they expected to use the information in the future or had no service communities to which the content could be applied.

Respondents were asked whether they had conversed with researchers about data needs; depending on their response, they were asked either what needs had been expressed or observed, or what the library could do to help facilitate those conversations. There were twenty-nine responses to this portion of the survey. A third of the respondents answered "yes" to the first inquiry; the observed researcher needs that they reported included storage and/or preservation of datasets, metadata assistance, data management training, data sharing, and assistance in handling sensitive data. The respondents who answered "no" to the first question suggested conversation-facilitating activities ranging from "a checklist of things to cover with researchers when talking about data" to "conversations about how to best approach and market to faculty" to "I'll let you know."

LESSONS LEARNED

At this stage in data education efforts, we have amassed enough data and experience to make some generalizations about the process:

- Based on both the survey feedback and informal conversations with colleagues, this staged approach works well as a library-wide strategy for data education: it provides an entry point for staff with less familiarity with data concepts while quickly moving into areas that can effectively engage more experienced staff. We cannot, however, rule out the possibility that the attendees effectively self-select for workshops that match their perceived skill level and interests; the relatively low levels of attendance by Library Information Technology staff provide some support for this hypothesis.
- Library interest in data education is both broad and deep: attendees were drawn from every unit of the UM Library, not just those tasked directly to research support, and represented approximately a quarter of the current staff.
- Proper time allocation was crucial to the success of the program. Planning and implementing workshops that use a variety of teaching methods can be time intensive. In addition, it can be helpful to have multiple

instructors, which may add other difficult time components in coordinating schedules. Finally, providing professional development workshops during the fall semester when many other library activities may take place, including more information literacy sessions, can strain librarian and space scheduling.

- The DEWG recruited a variety of library colleagues and campus partners to present and/or teach during these sessions. This helped distribute the effort outside of the DEWG members while highlighting the existence of a broad-based community of practice within the library.
- Use of an assortment of instructional methods in the workshops, ranging from presentation style to role-playing, helped to sustain librarian interest. Workshop length was tailored to suit both content and methods: sessions using active learning strategies usually were eighty to ninety minutes in length, while presentation-style sessions usually ran sixty minutes (including time for questions).
- While the Deep Dive method is perceived as valuable, that value alone is not a sufficient motivator for librarians to independently put it to use; other duties are apparently perceived as having a higher priority at present. DEWG members are exploring ideas for a library-wide data event with a report-out component, which might spur additional use of the method.
- Additional education, even when positively received, does not always translate into increased readiness for service, particularly when a service need (in this case, data management plan consulting) that staff perceive to be significant has not yet been addressed by the educational program.

CONCLUSION

Our educational efforts in this area are far from complete. The work to date has established a firm foundation for research data support; the next challenge is to build on it. DEWG members are currently planning several activities in this area. First, the Advanced Data Training series continues, with new workshops (Metadata for Research Data, Introduction to Visualization) and previous successes scheduled for winter semester of 2015. A formal announcement of library-wide research data services is expected later in 2015, and an important role for the Data Education Working Group is in offering more targeted skill-building education in support of these services. A sustainable plan is being developed for making this education available both to new library staff and to existing staff whose changing duties may create new needs for education. Finally, DEWG members will need to look beyond the library to the on-campus research communities we support and develop educational offerings targeted to their needs.

ACKNOWLEDGMENTS

Thanks to RDS director Jen Green, for kicking off this whole effort; CLIR Data Curation fellows Katherine Akers, Natsuko Nicholls, and Fe Sferdean, for their dedicated contributions; Jen Brown, for assistance in analyzing the assessment data; and our DEWG colleagues: Jake Carlson, Marisa Conte, Leena Lalwani, and Alexa Pearce.

APPENDIX A: DEEP DIVE INTO DATA WORKFLOW

Katherine Akers, Scott Martin, Jo Angela Oehrli

GOAL

The goal of this workflow is to become familiar with the research data management landscape of a particular discipline or area of study. Finding answers to the following questions will provide you with relevant information that you can share with researchers in your department(s).

ADVICE

This workflow is iterative. Expect to keep circling back to look at different resource categories as you explore the landscape. Not all resource categories will be relevant to all disciplines.

FIND AN ENTRY POINT AND DIG DEEPER

The research data management landscape of a particular discipline may be a complex web of funding agency requirements, data policies of academic societies and/or journals, subject-specific data repositories, metadata standards, and disciplinary best practices. How can you start exploring this landscape?

I. Data Requirements of Stakeholders

While exploring the research data management landscape of a particular discipline, search for data policies and requirements from these stakeholders:

A. Journals

- What journals do your faculty publish in most frequently?
- Do these journals have data sharing/access policies?
- Do these journals require specific metadata or other data documentation?
- Do these journals recommend/require specific data repositories?
- Do these journals accept datasets as supplementary materials?
- Do these journals have temporal access policies (e.g., data must be available for X years, option for an embargo)?
- Are there data journals or journals that accept data papers in your discipline? Do these journals recommend/require specific data repositories?

B. Funders

- Who is funding the research in your department(s)?
- Do these organizations have data sharing/access policies?
- Do these organizations require data management plans as components of grant proposals?
- Do these organizations have requirements for secure storage of sensitive data?
- Do these organizations have temporal access policies (e.g., data must be available for X years, option for an embargo)?

C. Societies

- What academic societies are most prominent within your discipline?
- Do those societies (or their publications) have data sharing/access policies, guidelines, or standards?

D. Institutes or Local Organizations

- Do local research organizations (e.g., U-M departments and programs, regional research organizations) have data sharing/access policies?
- Do local research organizations provide or recommend specific data repositories?

II. Data Repositories

A. Identify Relevant Data Repositories

- What data repositories have already surfaced in your explorations?
- Search or browse data repository directories to identify other relevant data repositories. What did you find?
  - OpenDOAR (http://www.opendoar.org/)
  - Databib (http://databib.org/)
  - re3data (http://www.re3data.org/)
  - Open Access Directory (http://oad.simmons.edu/oadwiki/Data_repositories)
- Search Thomson Reuters' Data Citation Index to identify other relevant data repositories. What did you find?

B. Describe Relevant Data Repositories

- Use the Data Repository Description Tool to describe the data repositories you found (in terms of their subject focus, data deposit and access options, deposit fees, persistent identifiers assigned to datasets, etc.).
- Examine these data repositories more deeply to learn about their metadata requirements, preservation plans, etc.

III. Metadata Standard

- Does your discipline use common metadata standards or data documentation practices?
- Are there tools available for assisting with metadata creation?

IV. Subject-Specific Data Literature

- Have people written about data sharing or research data management in your discipline (e.g., journal articles, blog posts)?

V. Subject-Specific Culture of Data Sharing

- What have your explorations told you about the culture of data sharing in your discipline?
- What are some barriers to data sharing in your discipline (e.g., sensitive data, intellectual property concerns, no relevant data repositories)? [Note: Keep in mind that if your search fails to reveal data repositories that are relevant to your discipline, your institutional repository or

general-purpose repositories such as FigShare (http://figshare.com/) can be alternative options.]

PUT IT ALL TOGETHER AND SHARE THE INFORMATION

Now that you have a deeper understanding of the research data management landscape for your discipline or area of study, what can you do with this information? How can you share this information with your researchers and members of the library community?

I. Research Guides

- Consider creating a Research Guide containing this information, either as a stand-alone guide or incorporated into a more general subject guide.

II. Instruction/Education

- How could this information be included in instructional sessions or education provided to students?

III. Outreach

- How could you share this information with researchers in your department(s) (e.g., departmental/faculty meetings, research symposia, one-on-one conversations)?
- How could you share this information with other librarians (e.g., internal special interest groups, conference presentations)?

APPENDIX B: SAMPLE WORKSHOP ASSESSMENT SURVEY

Sample Workshop Assessment Survey

Library Unit:

How did the information presented in this workshop compare with your level of knowledge about research data?

Too basic

Just right

Too advanced

Was the information presented in this workshop relevant to questions you've received from researchers?

Yes

No

Not applicable

Was the information presented in this workshop relevant to questions you've had about your own work with data?

Yes

No

Not applicable

Do you feel comfortable talking with researchers about research data management issues?

Yes

Somewhat

No

How prepared do you feel to provide research data management support?

Very prepared

Somewhat prepared

Not prepared

Not applicable

What data topics should be addressed by future librarian-focused workshops?

Is there anything else you'd like to add?

11

Teaching Spatial Literacy

Location, Distance, and Scale

Eva Dodsworth,
University of Waterloo Library
Larry Laliberté,
University of Alberta Library

In recent years there has been a significant increase in the use of maps and visualizations in education, research, media, and in online applications. Communicating with spatial references has become a popular process for sharing facts, discovering patterns, and for finding solutions to problems. Maps are used daily for obtaining information about the weather, trending facts in media, and for driving directions. Maps and GIS technology are used to calculate distances, speed traveled, and places visited. The regular uses of mapping technology have increased users' spatial skills, helping them develop spatial thinking and geospatial literacy. Although for some it may be considered a social and organizational tool, spatial literacy is the fundamental ability to visualize and interpret location, distance, direction, relationships, movement, and change through space (Sinton, 2011), a skill so essential in higher education and in many organizations and corporations.

The objectives of higher education do not include curriculum-wide spatial training; as a result, libraries often step in, providing faculty and students with lectures and workshops, or embedding GIS technology into individual courses. However, very few librarians have these skills themselves. Some library science programs do offer GIS or spatial literacy courses and workshops. For those who did not have the opportunity to take them, postdegree classes are also available through library organizations.

Spatial literacy is also a growing component in higher education. Examining and understanding the world immediately in front and beyond our view requires us to understand the numerous spatial literacy concepts noted above, but more critically, to see that they are all the spatial properties of location, distance, direction, size, shape, connectivity, overlap, dimensionality, and hierarchy and are all encompassed by scale, arguably the cornerstones of spatial literacy.

While not explicitly outlined in the ACRL *Framework* (2015), spatial literacy, or geoliteracy, can be expressed within the six frames. Scholarship Is a Conversation is clear as spatial conversations unfold every day, from obtaining directions to the thousands of spatial visualizations generated by governments, media organizations, academia, not-for-profits, and community groups. Authority Is Constructed and Contextual as spatial literacy is used to discern the authority behind these map or online visualizations. Issues range from the image's shape as determined by projection (why does it look that way), to its extent (why is it showing this area and not that one), to who created the final product, and where it was published. These questions allow users to examine all the evidence through the spatial lens as they rely on the map interfaces to tell the story quickly and effectively.

Searching as Exploration is a perfect spatial metaphor as users rely on searching mapping interfaces to locate where they are, where they are going, but also to explore along the way. Furthermore, tagging information with spatial attributes (latitude, longitude, addresses, and place-names) opens up the ability to both search and explore the spatial relationships between information that cannot be discerned in traditional searching methods. While a powerful method is connecting information based on its precise location, its distance from other items and the scale at which the information is presented reinforces how critical these spatial literacy concepts are in creating a "spatial habit of mind" (Kim and Bednarz, 2013). Information Has Value can therefore be tied to the information available about the map or geospatial data (metadata). Through descriptive metadata, you can not only discover the provenance of the data but also the accuracy, currency, and temporal stamp or span. Metadata and its associated licensing can act as a guide to the intellectual property of the data, its copyright information, and whether it is open access or in the public domain. Finally, metadata provides the framework to speak to the importance of proper attribution and citation of the geospatial dataset.

Research as Inquiry and spatial literacy form a combination of complex narratives. Essentially every map or visualization on one side of an issue will often have its mirror on the other side, which opens up the door for debate. However, in order to open up the door, spatial literacy is an important key both metaphorically and figuratively. It is important to note that this is not just a modern debate relegated to online platforms, but rather it is one that has been going on cartographically over the past 500 years where a map was not only judged on its accuracy and effective use of symbols, but also as a way to understand how mapping practices and their cartographic outputs have been in the service of the state and as an expression of exploitation and ongoing colonial control. Format as a Process highlights the transition of printed maps to the "born digital" data available today. What were once stored and only available in university map libraries have now become digitized and derived into widely available GIS datasets. This chapter will highlight personal experiences in teaching at two ends of the scale spectrum from the in-person "one-shot" class to a full-semester online course that teaches geospatial literacy concepts to students. Course objectives, preparation, and course content will be shared in the context of ACRL's best practices.

ONE-SHOT CLASSES

In most cases, librarians' interaction with students will either be a full class or a portion of it, and often at the beginning of the semester. With such limited time, it is important that the instructor grab the attention of the class immediately in order to pack a punch without being overwhelming. There is a need to balance spatial literacy with data literacy, as in most cases the aim of the class is to show students where they can find geospatial data, how they can access it, while providing cautionary tales of integrating data in GIS. These points will be detailed in the following sections entitled "You Are Here," which is a conversational exploration of scale and situating the class within it; "The Mercator versus Peters Parable," which details how all maps and spatial visualizations are inherently distorted, and as such caution should be exercised; and finally, "Behind the Scenes," which emphasizes the critical importance of metadata in order to determine a geospatial dataset's value for use in research.

"You Are Here"

As stated in the ACRL *Framework for Information Literacy for Higher Education* (2015), many librarians engage with the campus community via the one-shot information literacy session, and if you were to add up the session types, one-shots would greatly outnumber all the other session types. However, they would not in terms of total hours, as while they are numerous, they are often in the half hour to fifty-minute range, and in many cases situated in places when the faculty member teaching the full course is away. Regardless of length, these sessions are often easier to "elevator pitch" to faculty (especially newer faculty) to get spatial literacy onto the syllabus as part of the introduction sessions.

One-shots offer a great opportunity to highlight Scholarship Is a Conversation by employing a conversational style that weaves location, distance, and scale into the positional experience of the students in the room. Traditionally, scale served as an equation that reflected the numerical difference between reality and the reduced mapped reflection that was held in the hands. With the advent of computer mapping and GIS, changes in scale occur on the fly as users perform multiple iterations of geospatial data visualizations. Scale also integrates within the daily lives of individuals as they inhabit the locale with their physical movements and unique habitation, or scale acts as a virtually expansive concept, exemplified by the numerous social networks that are tethered across the globe allowing anyone to cohabitate within various online communities. Scale also serves as a way to bridge spatial literacy concepts embedded both within the printed maps, and GIS data, as well as everyone's daily lives, because scale is not only a core concept of geography, along with distance and location, but it is arguably the most recognizable concept, and as such it serves as a starting point for introducing spatial literacy in the brief amount of time afforded by the one-shot.

Enhancing the students' situational awareness can be done by noting that each individual in the room occupies an exact location and that there exists a very distinct pattern and numerous connections that interact between each precise location and those around them. Instructors can emphasize this by asking the following opening question:

> In addition to arriving to the campus, there is a more detailed manner in how you arrived to the classroom. Everyone occupying a unique position, your chair, had to navigate to the building to get to this room; some of you may have accessed the building from various doors and used the stairs or an elevator; some of you may have stopped for coffee, were running late or were early. Yet here we all are, in a room that is within a building that is itself one of many buildings on campus.

Such a statement to the class facilitates a better understanding of scale by increasing both the distances and locations relative to the room that everyone is occupying and by highlighting the fact that everyone had to navigate through various trajectories in order to arrive to the room and to their seats by increasing scale and expanding connections and locations.

An instructor can continue to increase the scale question by asking students how they arrived on campus (drive, walk, cycle, take transit), and ask from which parts of the city (south, east, west, north) did their journey begin. This line of questioning highlights that while everyone has something spatially in common (they all arrived on campus), the manner on how they arrived and from where they originated is varied, all because the scale was increased. Furthermore, the concept of pattern can be reinforced by asking questions relating to who takes the same route every day, and if not, does it vary much from day to day. These open-ended questions highlight location (origin and destination), distance and direction, and pattern, all of which are aligned and nested within the concept of scale.

So far the discussion has been carried out at a large scale (individuals in their chair to where they live in the city), yet the line of questioning can be nudged into the small scale realm by asking the students where they are originally from and how did they get to where they currently live. Did they take a train, fly, drive, or perhaps they have always lived close by. By changing the scale, the distances increase and so it alters the connections as the pattern becomes more diffuse. This is the same process that occurs when making decisions about the scale of a traditional printed map or an online geospatial visualization.

Finally, the questions relating to scale can be wrapped up and brought full circle by overlaying administrative boundaries to highlight that some individuals are from the city, or from another state or province, and others from another country. At this point, the line of questioning has reached its physical spatial extent and reflects the concept that the most common attribute of the classroom is that on a large scale students occupy a chair in a room on campus within a city, and shifting to a small scale, the city is within a state/province in a country on a continent on the earth. Of course, Earth occupies an interconnected location with its moon and other planets at various distances from the sun.

The main takeaway from the questions relating to scale is that since everyone is a spatial being, he or she innately understands how location, distances, and relationships change as scale is altered. The issues arise, however, when they want to visualize any of these interactions across a particular scale; at such a time, they then have to utilize various tools and methods in order to abstract reality into a representation or visualization of it. To do this, it's important to understand other spatial literacy concepts to produce accurate (as can be in an abstraction of reality) representations (projections) by utilizing symbols to represent locations, distances, connections, and patterns. For example, anyone can symbolize a chair at the scale of a classroom and represent the viewable attributes of an individual occupying the chair. However, this cannot be done at the scale of the campus. After all, mapmaking is about effective communication through the utilization of symbols. Symbols serve as signs that guide and make sense of the abstraction of reality, which is in a constant flux as you move between local, regional, national, and global levels. Moving from the personal to the communal helps one to understand that place is not only a location within a hierarchy of space, but that it is also constructed by experience (Tuan, 1977). When focused on representations of reality, either printed or digitally visualized, it becomes important to show that, as people move from the local to the global, projection becomes critical; not only are they abstracting reality through symbols and signs, at these larger geographical extents, they are also distorting areas and angles.

The Mercator versus Peters Parable

How all maps are distortions of reality can best be highlighted by comparing and contrasting the Mercator projection and the Peters projection. Essentially, no map or visualization can represent the earth accurately, and when the earth's features are projected onto a flat surface, either a paper map or computer screen, distortions are inevitable. Minimizing the distortions is achieved by selecting an appropriate map projection, which is a mathematical transformation that will preserve some aspects of the spherical earth on a flat surface at the expense of others (Dodsworth and Laliberté, 2014).

In one corner, there is the Mercator projection, which has been in use for over 400 years, and in the other corner there is the Peters projection, which made its debut in the 1970s. The Mercator projection maintains the shape of earth's landmasses. However, the only area of true scale is along the equator and as such, the size of the landmasses becomes erroneously enlarged as you move north and south as seen in figure 11.1.

The Peters projection, announced in 1973, set out to replace perceived outdated projections like Mercator, as they were seen as the embodiment of Europe's geographical conception of the world in an age of colonialism, and as such diminished the midlatitudes zones or areas where many third world nations were located (Sriskandarajah, 2003). As a result, the Peters projection maintains a landmass's area at the expense of its angle; the end result is a map projection that dramatically stretches continents north and south as seen in figure 11.2.

The outcome of this parable of contrasting these two distortions is that in the end, neither the Mercator nor the Peters projections should be used to depict the world, but they do serve as a cautionary tale of the issues involved when using map projections especially in an online environment where global visualizations are the "de jure" and their abstractions and inherent distortions can only be questioned with a sound grounding in spatial literacy concepts. Finally, by comparing and contrasting these two projections as well as the cartographic controversy that followed the publication of the Peters projection, students can see that scholarship is constantly in flux and worldviews change and rearrange territorial space, and that this is currently happening at the moment, and as a result individuals need to curate a spatial habit of mind in order to understand these changes.

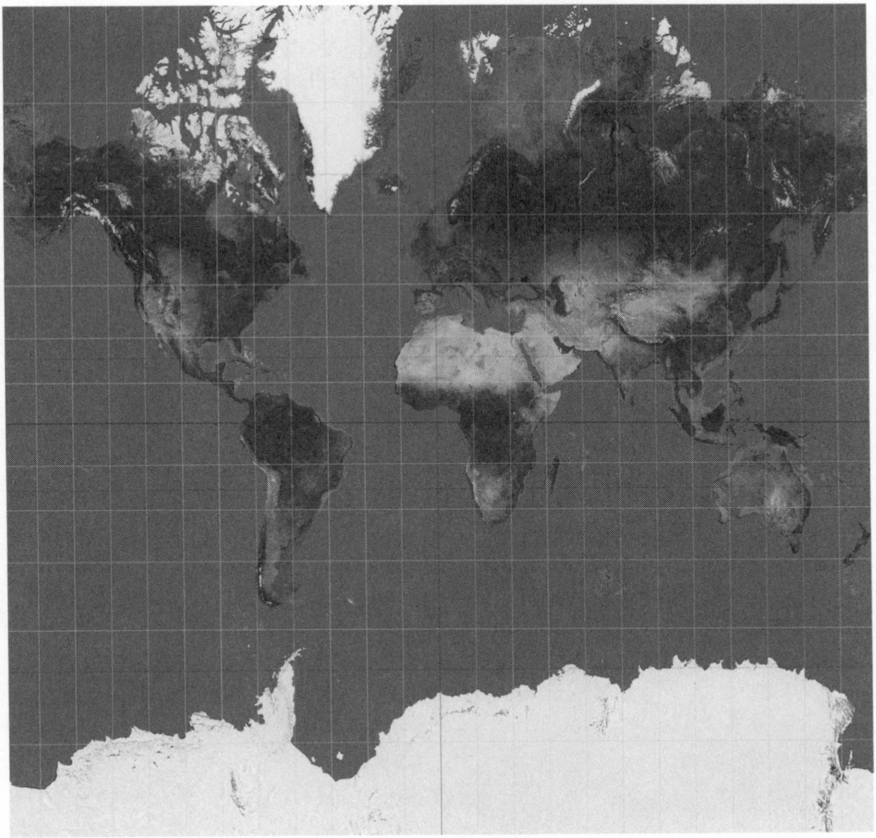

Figure 11.1. Mercator projection. ***Source:*** **Wikipedia.** ***2015. "Mercator projection." http://en.wikipedia.org/wiki/Mercator_projection***

Behind the Scenes

Metadata has a very simple definition, "the data about the data," but at the same time, it has a great deficit in terms of understanding both how critical it is to discovering data and how detailed it can be (Dodsworth and Laliberté, 2014). Furthermore, with the limited time of the "one-shot" class, metadata often does not get the time it deserves, but it must, at the very least, be highlighted. With the enormous amounts of digital spatial information available to students, it is critical to understand that "information has value." Therefore, it is imperative to state that metadata describes the resource (title, author,

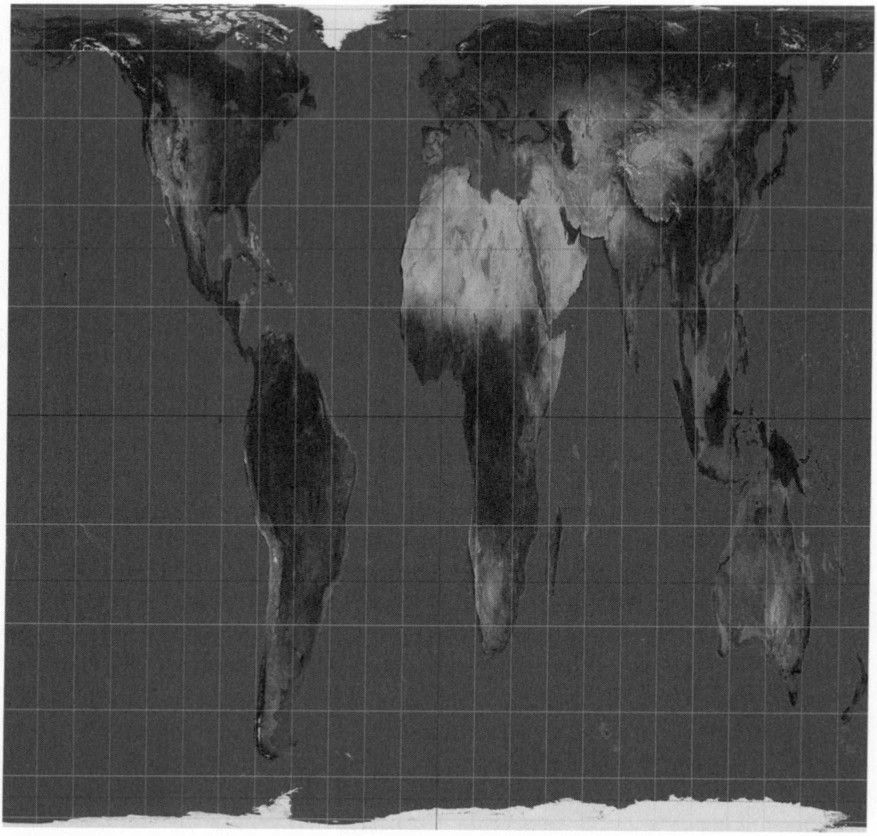

Figure 11.2. Peters projection. ***Source:*** **Wikipedia.** ***2015. "Gall-Peters projection." http://en.wikipedia.org/wiki/Gall-Peters_projection***

year, and keywords) and forms the foundation required to discover and identify material. Metadata also indicates how the materials are put together and linked, essentially the digital version of how pages are ordered to form chapters, and where footnotes and the bibliography reside in a book (Metadata Basics, 2007). Metadata provides information on how a resource was created, its associated file types, and other technical information, including rights management, which provides information on licensing and intellectual property rights (Metadata Basics, 2007).

Of the six frames, the one-shot session can highlight that "scholarship is a conversation" by showing that everyone has a voice, that everyone is embedded within space and as such, at any time, their voice can be added to the ongoing conversation related to this space. The one-shot can also highlight that not only are spatial literacy conversations happening in traditional media like journal articles and books but that these conversations related to visual literacy have been ongoing for hundreds of years in the form of printed maps. After all, mapmaking is about effective communication, and these conversations now continue online as data visualizations and as such run the gamut of literacy types including those grouped under media, digital, and cyber. From getting directions in your daily life to the thousands of spatial visualizations generated by governments, media organizations, academia, not-for-profits, and community groups, there is a spatial conversation unfolding at a rapid pace that requires an individual's active participation, and can be summed up by Bernard Nietschmann's statement, "Map or be mapped" (Stone, 1998).

TRAINING THROUGH A FULL-SEMESTER LECTURE COURSE

In the past there have been opportunities to be embedded as part of a course to add a geospatial component that is woven through the use of ArcGIS (a commercial desktop GIS program used by most academic institutions for map making and spatial analysis). Essentially, this entails providing graduate students an introduction to ArcGIS in the first week and then increasing the depth of coverage as it relates to the subject material. This involves growing the use of GIS as the course progresses and also provides more flexibility in integrating geospatial literacy throughout the course and allows for a more direct feedback loop from students in the class.

School of Library and Information Science

Geospatial information literacy courses are taught at a number of ALA-accredited library schools, with each course focusing on varying aspects of spatial literacy, including cartography, mapmaking, GIS data and software, and theoretical frameworks that link the topics to uses in libraries. The end goal of many of these courses is to sensitize librarians to mapping and spatial opportunities in their subject specialties and to provide the training required to enable librarians to embed geospatial literacy concepts and tools into classrooms, in reference and consultation services, and in digitization projects.

The ALA-accredited library and information science course highlighted in this chapter is taught as an eight-week online course at the University of Wisconsin, Madison, entitled "Introduction to GIS and GeoWeb Technologies." The course is an introduction to geospatial literacy, GIS technology, and GIS in libraries. Through hands-on exercises, lectures in prerecorded podcast format, and virtual discussions, students develop an understanding of spatial thinking and spatial mapping. Students also acquire skills in several online geoweb tools and applications as well as learn how to visualize data using the open source GIS software Quantum GIS.

Course Objectives

The chief aims and objectives of the course are to develop the spatial literacy skills required to answer map/GIS-related queries from faculty and students, especially when embedding spatial content into multidisciplinary course curricula. Knowledge of GIS data and applications will likewise benefit spatially related digitization projects and collection development and management responsibilities. Although this course and others similar to it have helped some students gain GIS librarian titles, this course is designed to focus on spatial information literacy rather than advanced GIS software training. That being said, when the course was first developed, many of the objectives closely paralleled the Core Competencies for GIS Librarianship, as outlined by the ALA Map and Geospatial Information Round Table (MAGIRT) Education Committee. The following is a list of competencies that students will have acquired after successfully completing the course.

Reference and Research Consultation

- Knowledge of basic cartographic concepts and techniques
- Awareness of different types of maps
- Knowledge of map and data resources and discovery tools
- Working knowledge of data organization and data manipulation
- Working knowledge of map-related project planning and implementation
- Knowledge of GIS tutorials and training courses specific to patron needs
- Working knowledge of a number of GIS-related software programs (Quantum GIS, Google Earth, ArcGIS Online, Google Fusion Tables)
- Knowledge of geocoding and georeferencing

Data Acquisition

- Knowledge of spatial data resources and data discovery tools
- Government resources, including local, state, national, and international
- Data repositories, including the web, academic/research community, and offline data resources
- Competence in data reformatting, manipulations (changing projections, converting file formats, editing shapefiles, etc.), naming conventions
- Knowledge of spatial metadata standards

- Knowledge of licensing matters
- Broad knowledge of data quality, data types, data storage requirements, and backups
- Knowledge of map scanning and digitization processes
- Knowledge of collection development principles

Teaching and Instruction
- Knowledge of subject-specific GIS-related resources
- Knowledge of crowdsourcing and web mapping
- Knowledge of GIS-related training resources
- Knowledge of best practices for GIS-related instruction and training

Every library and information science program has a set of program objectives that need to be met. The specific course objectives and assignments need to tie into the LIS Program Level Learning Objectives. Table 11.1 provides the program objectives met by this course.

Planning and Content of the Course

The course has evolved over the years since its first offering in 2011. With many new GIS-related technologies released every year, students are being exposed to a greater representation of different applications and digitization projects. Additionally, maps and data are easily available online now, providing students with much more variety and customizability of their projects in the course and also with work projects in the future. With this increase in data availability, the course has expanded to include collection development and curation, teaching students best practices in data management, especially when working with cloud services. Crowdsourced maps and cloud storage has increased significantly over the last few years, enabling students to not only be consumers of data, but rather, to focus on being creators, sharing the data and digital projects with others.

One last change to the course is the significant move from proprietary ArcGIS software to open source Quantum GIS, which occurred due to more and more students favoring the Mac over the Windows operating system. ArcGIS is Windows-based, whereas Quantum GIS supports both platforms.

Developing the eight-week course entails creating course content; lectures, demonstrations, and recordings of both; and assessment in the form of mapping assignments, completed tutorials, and discussions. Evaluation criteria are included as well. The lectures are created as PowerPoint slides and are recorded with voice narration. Many demonstrations are included to show students how to navigate around websites and how to use mapping

Table 11.1. Program Objectives Met by the Course "Introduction to GIS and GeoWeb Technologies"

LIS Program Level Learning Objective	*Course Objectives*	*Assignments That Provide Evidence*	*Criteria for Assessing Evidence in the Assignment*
1a. Students apply key concepts with respect to the relationship between power, knowledge, and information.	Students are able to systematically and critically analyze and evaluate information presented in a map format.	Discussion Post 1 Discussion Post 2	Discussion Post 1: To what degree does the post reflect findings that relate to crowdsourced community initiatives? What information is it sharing? Discussion Post 2: Post is assessed based on the detail provided in the description of the data discovered. Does it include qualitative factors like metadata, projection, and currency?
3a. Students organize and describe print and digital information resources.	Students are able to objectively critique and evaluate online digitized resources.	Discussion Post 2	Discussion Post 2: Post is assessed based on the detail provided in the description of the data discovered. Does it include qualitative factors like metadata, projection, and currency?
3b. Students search, select, and evaluate print and digital information resources.	Students are able to evaluate, select, and use digital resources across a variety of platforms.	Online Map Assignment and QGIS Assignment	Online Map Assignment: Do the maps include data resources that contribute to the purpose of the map story? Did the student create customized files (e.g., tables or images) to add to the overall user experience?
3d. Students understand and use appropriate information technologies.	Students are able to use a variety of online tools to manipulate and convert data files as well as use a variety of tools in GIS software.	QGIS Map	QGIS Map: Was the map created using advanced tools discussed in lecture, either within the program or online? Was effort put forward to create a map that includes several elements of the technologies discussed in the course?
4b. Students demonstrate good oral and written communication skills.	Students are able to describe their learning process and technical steps in mapmaking.	QGIS Map Report	QGIS Map Report: Does the report fully describe the user experience and step-by-step actions taken from data collection to final map touches?

applications. The course content is managed using Desire2Learn (D2L), which supports large file sharing, virtual forums, assignment uploads, and an assignment evaluation system. A teaching assistant (TA) is assigned to help instructors with technical issues.

There is a lot of administrative support available at Wisconsin. The associate director of the School of Library and Information Studies keeps in touch via e-mail and phone and assists with the development of the syllabus, especially with mapping learning outcomes to the program-level ones. She also connects the instructor with a library representative for library course reserve needs. There is also a clear handbook available that guides the instructor through the teaching policies, program goals, and teaching best practices.

The course itself consists of weekly prerecorded lectures that are approximately ninety minutes in length. Weekly readings are from the course textbook, written by the instructor, and roughly every second week has an assignment or discussion question assigned. The course is designed to introduce students to spatial literacy and GIS, showing them relevance through library examples. The weekly topics are as follows:

- Week One: Introduction to Spatial Literacy. This introductory lecture provides students with an overview of how maps and GIS are used daily. Students are introduced to basic geospatial literacy and are shown examples of how libraries are using mapping technologies in projects.
- Week Two: Introduction to Crowdsourcing. This lecture demonstrates to students how society plays a role in contributing information to consumers. They are shown several examples of volunteered geographic information (VGI) and are assigned the task of contributing information themselves using Google Map Maker. This lecture teaches the students to consider being not only consumers of data but creators as well.
- Week Three: Introduction to Cartography. This lecture teaches students how to read a map. It provides a detailed overview of the many different types of maps (exploration, township, cadastral, etc.) and the elements of a map. Projections, datum, and scale are introduced, as well as map design. Students learn about the essential components of a map and how to properly use them in order for the map to communicate effectively. Map digitization is discussed, including proper specifications for scanning, creating metadata, copyright, and citations. Online historical mapping projects are reviewed as well.
- Week Four: Introduction to GIS. The concept of GIS is discussed, including examples of real-world applications. Students learn how to frame GIS questions and learn more about projections, especially common ones used in GIS.

- Week Five: Geospatial Data. Students learn about databases, vector, and raster files. They are introduced to metadata and a wide variety of online data resources. They learn about numerical data and the importance of normalization. Map interpretation is discussed along with the importance of accuracy and reliability.
- Weeks Six and Seven: Introduction to Online Mapping and Quantum GIS. Students are exposed to online map applications that support GIS files. They are also introduced to the desktop GIS program Quantum GIS and are assigned exercises in geocoding and georeferencing.
- Week Eight: This wrap-up lecture brings all lectures together and discusses how the skills can be used in libraries. Library repositories for data and maps are shown, including digital map projects. Staff development and training are also discussed as students are encouraged to share their skills with others.

The assignments in the course provide a different element of learning as students develop hands-on experience with data creation, data acquisition, troubleshooting, and mapping. The students are required to become familiar with citizen mapping/crowdsourced projects, as well as identify properly created maps. Two major term projects include creating a map online in Google Earth using KML files and HTML code, and creating a map in Quantum GIS using GIS files obtained from a reliable source. For the latter, students are graded based on the complexity of the theme, appropriate use of GIS files, advanced uses of the program (clipping, joining tables, converting files, geocoding), appropriate cartographic elements, and originality. A report is submitted with this map detailing the steps taken to acquire the data and to create the map.

Upon completion of this course, students will have developed geographical and geospatial information literacy skills, including specific skills in the uses of online applications and Quantum GIS. Whether they will use their new skills in their workplace to promote their own subject-specific resources, or use GIS in their own professional research, their new knowledge set will hopefully ignite an interest to continue learning and sharing their knowledge with others.

Assessment

Teaching a course that focuses on technology is best suited in a classroom environment and ideally where a portion of the class can be spent in labs working on the tutorials and assignments. Students can have their questions answered easily and can replicate any problems they may be having with the software programs. In an online course, the instructor typically tries to troubleshoot problems by analyzing screenshots and steps and processes the students share via e-mails or in the online course forums. It can be difficult to understand what the student is trying to describe, especially when the instructor is not familiar with the student's technical ability. Sometimes the struggles are not with the applications taught in class, but with simple computer-related features, like unzipping files, downloading large files over the Internet, or forgetting passwords. It can be a challenge to teach online, especially when the online course is prerecorded and not live. Alternatively, some library and information science online courses are taught synchronously, where students meet for three hours once a week and listen and watch the instructor present live over the Internet. This provides the students and the instructor with different experiences, such as being able to ask questions or make clarifications, make comments in class, or offer a dedicated lecture for troubleshooting problems. These courses are better suited for technology-rich material; however, not all students or institutions can take advantage of this.

At the University of Wisconsin, Madison, academic administrators realize that asynchronous courses are not the easiest to teach, so they offer peer observations to assess the course and to provide suggestions to the instructor to improve the learning experiences of the students. The peer observer has access to all the course material by entering the D2L platform, and reviews some of the lectures, discussion forums, and assignments and provides feedback to the instructor when the visit is completed. The feedback received from the peer observer in the last course offering suggested correcting some of the audio in the recording as there were inconsistencies in the sounds. This will be corrected for the next offering. The observer was satisfied with all other elements of the course.

At the end of the course, students are encouraged to provide course evaluations. However, because it is an online course, the evaluation becomes optional and not compulsory as it often is in classroom settings. Very few students have provided feedback for the course, but those who did rated the course very positively and have stated that they have learned a lot.

CONCLUSION

Although not explicitly outlined in the ACRL *Framework for Information Literacy for Higher Education* (2015), spatial literacy is interwoven into all six frames, offering opportunities to gather and gain information through a spatial lens. Following the ACRL standards, spatial literacy skills can be gained in a number of ways, from reading papers, to watching online webcasts, to participating in online and/or in-class instruction. This chapter describes two contrasting approaches of teaching spatial literacy, from the "one-shot" where scholarship as a conversation underpins the more intimate setting of positioning students within the spatial landscape in order to understand how we are all innately spatial beings, to the other scale of a distributed and engaged online community. Both settings reinforce the two extents embraced by the core components of spatial literacy (scale, distance, as well as touching upon the six ACRL frames) and promote the development of a critical consciousness that fuels an understanding of the spatial information so that students can use it in an empowering and participatory manner (Mackey and Jacobson, 2011).

As the need for spatial literacy increases in recognition, more courses of these types will be offered to university students and library staff. Embedding GIS resources into course curricula is one of the best ways to ensure spatial literacy is not only being taught, but also practiced by students, scholars, and information professionals.

REFERENCES

ACRL (Association of College & Research Libraries). 2015. *Framework for Information Literacy for Higher Education*. American Library Association. Association of College & Research Libraries. http://acrl.ala.org/ilstandards/wp-content/uploads/2015/01/Framework-MW15-Board-Docs.pdf.

Dodsworth, Eva H., and L. W. Laliberté. 2014. *Discovering and Using Historical Resources on the Web: A Practical Guide for Librarians*. Lanham, MD: Rowman & Littlefield.

Kim, Minsung, and Robert Bednarz. 2013. "Effects of a GIS Course on Self-Assessment of Spatial Habits of Mind (SHOM)." *Journal of Geography* 112, no. 4: 165–77.

Mackey, Thomas P., and Trudi E. Jacobson. 2011. "Reframing Information Literacy as a Metaliteracy." *College & Research Libraries* 72, no. 1 (January): 62–78.

Metadata Basics. 2007. "3. Metadata Types and Functions." Accessed May 14. http://www.metadataetc.org/metadatabasics/types.htm.

Sinton, D. S. 2011. "Spatial Thinking." In *21st Century Geography: A Reference Handbook*, edited by J. Stoltman, 733–44. Thousand Oaks, CA: Sage.

Sriskandarajah, Dhananjayan. 2003. "Long Underwear on a Line? The Peters Projection and Thirty Years of Carto-controversy." *Geography* 88, no. 3: 236–44.

Stone, M. 1998. "Map or Be Mapped." *Whole Earth Quarterly* 94 (Winter): 54–55.

Tuan, Yi-Fu. 1977. *Space and Place: The Perspective of Experience*. Minneapolis: University of Minnesota Press.

12

Best Practices for Teaching with Primary Sources

Ellen D. Swain,
University of Illinois at Urbana-Champaign

Over the past fifteen years, the Student Life and Culture (SLC) Archives at the University of Illinois at Urbana-Champaign has worked closely with the university's Undergraduate Rhetoric Program to educate undergraduates about the value of primary sources and assist them in integrating these materials into their research. This chapter provides an analysis of this collaboration, specifically in light of recent SLC Archives assessment activities and a change in rhetoric program leadership and philosophy. As the SLC Archives transitions from providing large numbers of students with an introduction to the archives to giving more in-depth orientations to students in a smaller number of classes, its instruction programming has begun to more effectively implement best practices for teaching with primary sources that are grounded in the Association of College & Research Libraries' (ACRL) best practices standards (2012) and the *Framework for Information Literacy for Higher Education* (2015).

TEACHING WITH PRIMARY SOURCES: SOME CONTEXT

Information literacy librarians have led the way in creating literacy standards for instruction. The ACRL's "Information Literacy Competency Standards for Higher Education" (2000) are adapted and incorporated widely. The most recent ACRL *Framework for Information Literacy for Higher Education* (2015) is also an excellent resource for teaching and learning. However, library literature has not adequately addressed strategies for teaching with primary sources, and these ACRL documents do not address this type of learning in a meaningful way. Archivists have written a great deal about the instructional value of primary sources. New contributions, such as *Past or Portal? Enhancing Undergraduate Learning through Special Collections and Archives* (Mitchell, Seiden, and Taraba, 2012) and an upcoming Society of American Archivists (SAA) module book project on best practices (Chute, Morris, and Swain, 2016) are two examples of the momentum and growing interest in this area. For a full review of library and archives literature concerning primary source teaching, see Hensley, Murphy, and Swain (2014). But it is only this year that archivists are uniting with librarians to create guidelines for primary source instruction.

SAA's Reference Access and Outreach (RAO) Section has played a critical role in providing support, strategies, and direction for teaching with primary sources. In 2010, RAO established a working committee, which over the course of two years created a bibliography of works about teaching with primary sources and a report of findings and analysis from a survey of archivists regarding practices for such teaching. In 2013, this group became a standing committee of the RAO Section (http://www2.archivists.org/groups/reference-access-and-outreach-section/teaching-withabout-primary-sources-committee). Rooted in RAO's early efforts, the resolve to establish guidelines for teaching with primary sources is just in the beginning stages. The Society of American Archivists–Association of College & Research Libraries/Rare Book Manuscripts Section (SAA-ACRL/RBMS) Joint Task Force on Primary Sources, proposed by RAO leaders and others, was approved by the SAA Council in November 2014. Over a two-year period, September 2015 to August 2017, the group will develop guidelines and competency standards for primary source literacy. Guidelines will consider and address a student's ability to interpret and analyze primary sources and a student's understanding of and ability to apply effective research skills across multiple disciplines (SAA, 2014). The guidelines certainly will assist all who teach with primary sources in creating curricula and formulating learning objectives more effectively.

Archivists and librarians from across the country are using primary sources in innovative ways. The following is an account of an instruction program that is reinventing itself to meet the changing needs of program directors, instructors, and students by applying new guidelines and learning outcomes to instruction practices and drawing on the experiences and expertise of others in the archives and library fields for inspiration.

THE SLC ARCHIVES INSTRUCTION PROGRAM

A program of the University of Illinois (UI) Archives, the SLC Archives was founded in 1989 through the Foundation of Stewart Howe, class of

1928, an alumnus who established and operated a public relations firm for national fraternities and sororities from the 1930s through the 1970s. The SLC Archives includes Howe's world-renowned collection of fraternity and sorority records and publications as well as twenty national Greek-related organizational and personal collections. It also documents all aspects of student life and culture at the University of Illinois. Although most academic archives collect student-related materials to some extent, the SLC Archives is the only documentary program in the country dedicated to that purpose. A full-time SLC archivist, with the assistance of two graduate assistants and three undergraduate student workers, provides reference service; processes archival materials from national organizations and UI student offices, student groups, and alumni; develops and teaches archival instruction; and promotes the archives through events, workshops, and social media.

The collaboration between the SLC Archives and Undergraduate Rhetoric Program began in the early 2000s upon the arrival of the current archivist. Through word of mouth and networking efforts, the SLC Archives built a strong following among rhetoric instructors and directors as its holdings on student life appealed to their desire to move students from published sources to more personal primary materials about university and student experience. During this time, the Ethnography of the University Initiative (EUI), an interdisciplinary, multicampus endeavor in which classes from a wide array of disciplines use ethnographic methodology to explore and question issues relating to the local university, community, and environment (Swain, 2012), was established. Founded in 2002, EUI was a logical archives partner. Each semester, starting in 2003, six to ten classes explored the university in disciplines as diverse as anthropology, English, kinesiology, and urban planning. The rhetoric program was an early subscriber to EUI, and many of its instructors volunteered to take the EUI training and teach through the Initiative.

The Classes: Objectives and Planning

Rhetoric students use SLC archival materials (administrative files, student organization records, oral histories, personal papers, photographs, and ephemera) to investigate topics such as student protests in the 1970s, current dress trends, dining hall dynamics, and interracial and culture relations. Research assignments typically require students to analyze three or four primary sources with additional secondary sources on a topic related to the University of Illinois. The program coordinators for the rhetoric program have worked with the archivist "to heighten students' experience and knowledge of forming original research questions, using primary and secondary sources effectively and creating original content" (Hensley, Murphy, and Swain, 2014:

97). Assignments take the form of traditional papers, short essays that analyze two to three primary sources, or on-site exercises to evaluate an array of primary sources selected by the archivist for the class.

The archivist teaches instruction classes at the Archives Research Center or in the classroom. These sessions involve forty-five- to sixty-minute presentations that define primary sources, describe what the archives contains and how to find materials online, demonstrate search strategies, and explain logistics for using materials on-site. The class instruction session connects specific materials to student assignments (sent by the professor in advance) and includes time for questions and discussion of potential topics. Instruction objectives are threefold: students should know what an archives collects and does; how archival materials are arranged and can be found; and what to expect logistically when visiting the SLC Archives.

For fifteen years, the program has been quite successful, particularly in terms of introducing large numbers of undergraduate students to the SLC Archives in their first semesters in college and for generating excitement among instructors and students for primary research. From 2004 until 2012, class use and archival instruction sessions in the University Archives (including SLC Archives) rose by 94 percent. Students using the archives to complete a class paper during the same time period rose by 674 percent (Hensley, Murphy, and Swain, 2014). In 2009, the rhetoric program introduced an e-textbook that included a unit on primary sources. The director, who was also a director of the EUI program and through her work with SLC Archives a big supporter of primary source investigation, felt that the program "needed a book sculpted to its particular student body; one that assumed students had a high degree of formal knowledge about writing but little research or analytical skills" (Swain, 2012: 153). All newly hired teaching assistants were required to use it their first year; approximately 1,000 students used the book each fall.

Archives Resources

Working with such a large volume of students required major preparation, work, and planning. Because of the nature of rhetoric classes and the material each needed to cover in the semester, the archivist had little time to spend with the classes as a group. Instruction sessions could be characterized as "one and done." To help instructors and students prepare for this valuable meeting time, the SLC Archives staff created a number of online resources.

The Primary Source Tutorial

The Primary Source Tutorial offers instructors and students an introduction to primary source research focused specifically at the University of Illinois.

Three modules investigate different research components. Module One takes students through an in-depth discussion of the definition of primary and secondary sources using examples from the SLC Archives collections. Module Two introduces the students to the processes of finding primary sources at the University of Illinois and beyond. Finally, Module Three explains the step-by-step process of analyzing a primary source, again using SLC Archives materials as examples. The tutorial has been a great success in terms of instructors' use and appreciation. Those instructors who have devoted class time to taking the tutorial together prior to the archives visit have found it the most useful (see figures 12.1 and 12.2).

The Cold War Resource Guide

Archives staff noticed that rhetoric and EUI students gravitated to topics related to race, gender, and specifically student protests of the 1960s and 1970s. In 2005, in consultation with instructors, staff created Cold War Research Guides to help students find materials on these topics. Each subguide provides an overview of the topic, linked series or collections from the archives database, and a listing of related secondary sources (see figures 12.3 and 12.4).

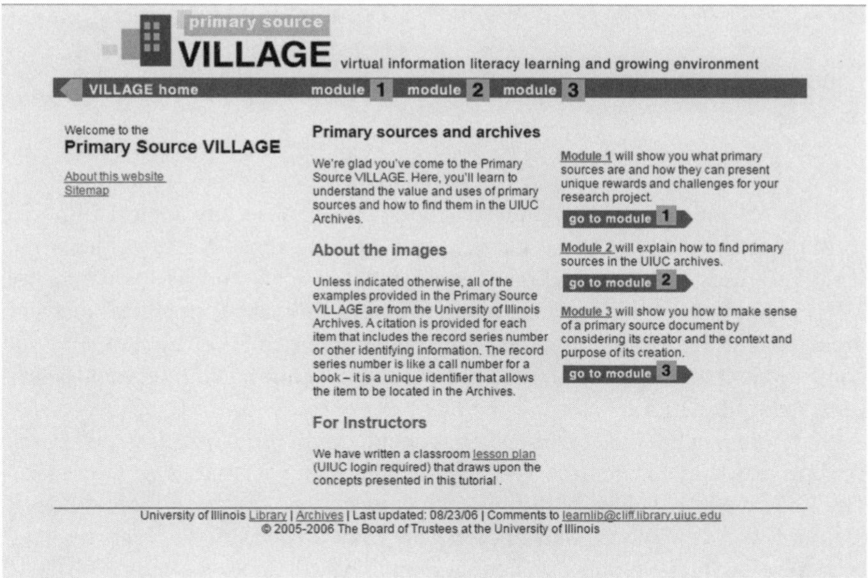

Figure 12.1. Primary Source Village. ***Source: http://www.library.illinois.edu/village/primarysource/***

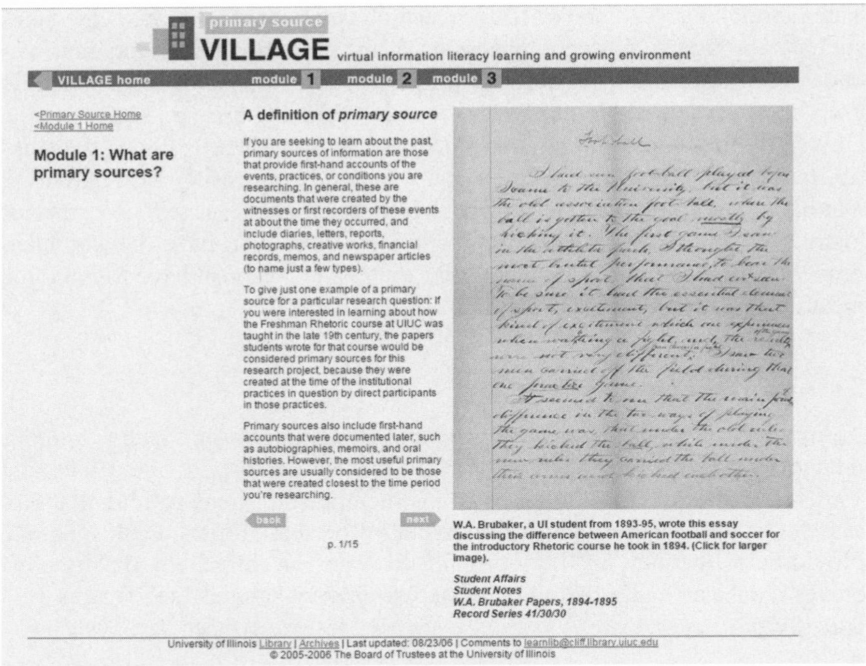

Figure 12.2. Primary Source Village: Module 1: What Are Primary Sources? ***Source: http://www.library.illinois.edu/village/primarysource/mod1/pg1.htm***

Topics in the Archives and the UI Student Timeline

Many of the instructors allowed students to choose any topic of interest throughout the history of the university (1867–present). Since students had little knowledge of the local past happenings, in 2007 archives staff created a "Topics in the Archives" list to help them think about potential research areas. Staff followed up with a UI Student Timeline in 2009, again to provide some context about UI's history and help students think about topic possibilities (see figure 12.5).

Staff also created LibGuides on general archival work and processes, finding statistics in the archives, and World War I resources at the university (http://archives.library.illinois.edu/slc/research-education/tools-guides/). Through word of mouth and one-on-one work with students, archives staff felt these sources greatly assisted students. However, it was not until 2012 that the archives undertook a formal assessment of its teaching effectiveness.

Cold War Research Guides
click below or on sidebar to access guides

Conflict over Academic Freedom and Free Speech at U of I

The Broyles' Bills
Clabaugh Act (1947)
The Leo Koch Case
The Fight for Freedom of Speech and Expression in the 1960s

Student Life during the Cold War Era

The GI Bill and the U of I
Sex, Censorship, and the College Scene
Conservatives on Campus
The Black Athlete at the U of I
Women's Athletics at the University of Illinois

Civil Rights on Campus

The Struggle for Integration in the 1940s and 50s
Affirmative Action at the University of Illinois
Project 500
Second Wave Feminism on Campus
Gay Rights on Campus
Latina/o Students at U of I

Vietnam War Protests

Students for a Democratic Society (SDS) at U of I
U of I students and the draft
1967 Protest-Sit-In against DOW Chemical
Publication of "Walrus"
October 15, 1969 Moratorium
March 1970 Rally Against GE
March Riots (1970)
May Student Strike (1970)

University Politics

The Rise and Fall of President George D. Stoddard
The U of I and the Defense Department
Surveillance, Discipline and the University of Illinois

Figure 12.3. Cold War Research Guides. ***Source: http://archives.library.illinois.edu/slcold/researchguides/coldwar/***

ASSESSMENT

In 2012–2013, the archivist collaborated with the university library's instruction librarian and a graduate student on a project to assess the effectiveness of the SLC instruction work with the rhetoric program. Through the years, the

Second Wave Feminism on Campus

Women's Student Union publication, 1977

Whereas the main thrust of first-wave feminism had centered on suffrage, the second-wave feminism emanating in the 1960s focused on a host of issues including economic parity, educational equity, and reproductive rights. At the University of Illinois, female students energized by the Civil Rights movement and the anti-war activities formed a host of women's groups on campus and pushed for gender equity. In 1972, Title IX (the Equal Opportunity in Education Act) prohibited gender discrimination in American educational institutions, opening up new opportunities in academics and athletics from college women.

University of Illinois Sources:

Women's Resources and Services Subject File, 1964-1991 (RS 41/3/10)

Women's Student Union Records, 1974-84 (RS 41/66/100)

Assistant Dean's Subject File, 1969-1972 (RS 41/3/12): Subject File of Mary Pollack includes information on sex education, the University Women's Caucus, and Women's Week.

Women's Resources and Services Reference File, 1959-88 (RS 41/3/9): Contains clippings, booklets, articles, and brochures concerning issues of topical interest to women in general and the women's movement.

Student Organizations Publications, 1871- (RS 41/6/840): Includes information from the Abortion Rights Coalition, National Organization of Women, and Women's Independent Student Association, among others.

Student and Faculty Org. Constitutions & Registration Cards, (RS 41/2/41): Includes many women's organizations.

Graduate Student Association Subject Files, 1967-71 (RS 41/62/15): Box 3 includes information on women's groups on campus.

Daily Illini, 1874- (Microform in Newspaper Library)

Illio

Bibliography:

Robert Bell and Kathleen Coughey, "Premarital Sexual Experience Among College Females, 1958, 1968, 1978," *Family Relations* 29 (1980), 353-357.

Figure 12.4. Cold War Research Guides: Second Wave of Feminism on Campus. ***Source: http://archives.library.illinois.edu/slcold/researchguides/coldwar/civilrights/secondwave.php***

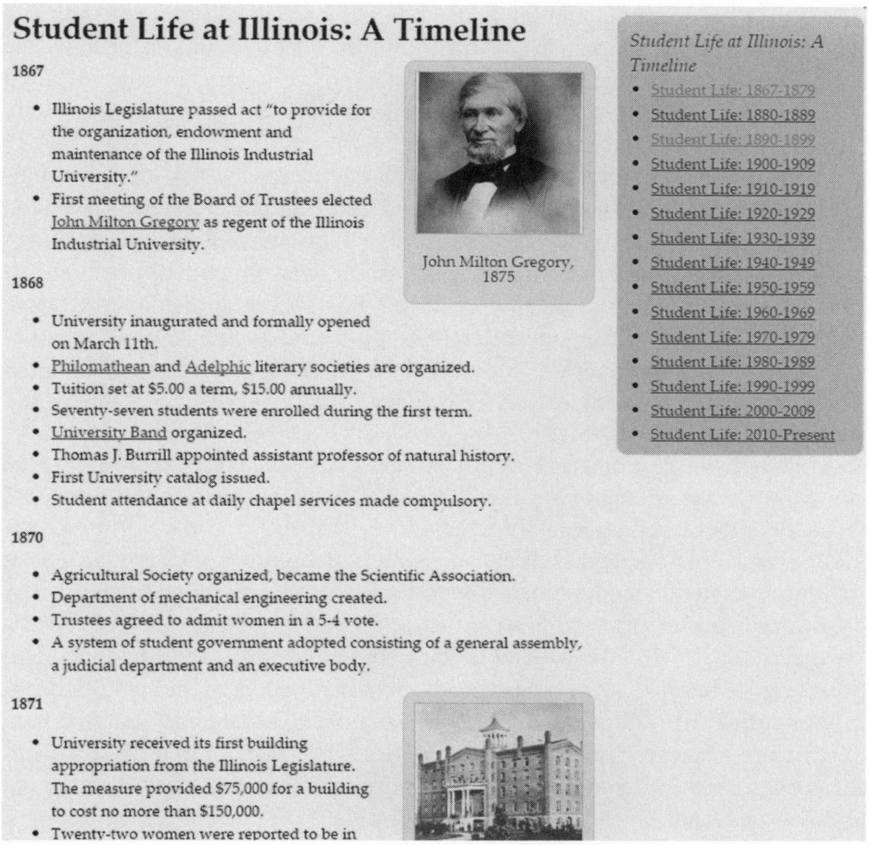
Student Life at Illinois: A Timeline
1867
Illinois Legislature passed act "to provide for the organization, endowment and maintenance of the Illinois Industrial University."
First meeting of the Board of Trustees elected John Milton Gregory as regent of the Illinois Industrial University.
John Milton Gregory, 1875
1868
University inaugurated and formally opened on March 11th.
Philomathean and Adelphic literary societies are organized.
Tuition set at $5.00 a term, $15.00 annually.
Seventy-seven students were enrolled during the first term.
University Band organized.
Thomas J. Burrill appointed assistant professor of natural history.
First University catalog issued.
Student attendance at daily chapel services made compulsory.
1870
Agricultural Society organized, became the Scientific Association.
Department of mechanical engineering created.
Trustees agreed to admit women in a 5-4 vote.
A system of student government adopted consisting of a general assembly, a judicial department and an executive body.
1871
University received its first building appropriation from the Illinois Legislature. The measure provided $75,000 for a building to cost no more than $150,000.
Twenty-two women were reported to be in
Student Life at Illinois: A Timeline
Student Life: 1867-1879
Student Life: 1880-1889
Student Life: 1890-1899
Student Life: 1900-1909
Student Life: 1910-1919
Student Life: 1920-1929
Student Life: 1930-1939
Student Life: 1940-1949
Student Life: 1950-1959
Student Life: 1960-1969
Student Life: 1970-1979
Student Life: 1980-1989
Student Life: 1990-1999
Student Life: 2000-2009
Student Life: 2010-Present

Figure 12.5. Student Life at Illinois: A Timeline. ***Source: http://archives.library.illinois.edu/slc/research-education/timeline/***

archivist worked closely with rhetoric directors and instructors whose classes visited the archives to gauge the usefulness of her archival instruction. However, this assessment study's objective focused on student perceptions of the instruction sessions' usefulness to determine what and how well they learned.

During fall semester 2012, the instruction librarian, archivist, and graduate student questioned all students who had attended the archivist's instruction sessions (approximately 220 students) via online survey, with a resulting participation rate of 11.4 percent. From that pool, those who had used the SLC Archives (as opposed to the University Archives, which is in a separate location) were identified and invited for postsurvey interviews to solicit student impressions of the impact of the archival instruction on their research.

The instruction librarian and graduate assistant interviewed four students; the archivist did not participate in the interviews in order to avoid influencing the results. Both the survey and the interviews were voluntary. A more detailed account of this assessment methodology and results was published previously (Hensley, Murphy, and Swain, 2014).

The assessment study focused on how well students learned archival intelligence (AI) skills. AI is a concept coined and outlined by Beth Yakel and D. A. Torres that describes the "researcher's knowledge of archival principles, practices and institutions, such as the reason underlying archival rules and procedures, the means for developing search strategies to explore research questions, and an understanding of the relationship between primary sources and their surrogates" (Yakel and Torres, 2003: 52). Specifically, the SLC Archives study centered on knowledge of archival theory, practice, and procedure.

Although the participation rate was small, student comments uncovered some important themes for improvement. Some students were confused about how the archives was arranged and described, even though the archivist covered this concept heavily in instruction sessions. Using an archives requires the understanding that materials are arranged by provenance (by creator, person, or organization), so materials on a specific subject such as "homecoming" will not be found together but across several separate collections (e.g., Alumni Association records, personal papers of students, Student Affairs office files). Student comments also indicated that understanding how to structure a research question was sometimes problematic. Third, some students expressed confusion about archival finding aids as surrogates for actual archival materials (also covered in the sessions). Finally, archival research requires mediation by the archivist. For students more familiar with library research processes, working with the archivist to find or access materials on-site (as opposed to checking out a book or accessing an online article through the catalog or Google) could be daunting.

A NEW DIRECTION BASED ON LESSONS LEARNED

Based on assessment results, the archivist, instruction librarian, and graduate student posited that four areas would be useful to consider for improving instruction: (1) borrow more aggressive pedagogical strategies from colleagues in library instruction and incorporate more active learning exercise into instruction; (2) partner closely with course instructors in developing and team teaching curriculum; (3) further develop online learning opportunities in order to better prepare students before they visit; and (4) consider alternatives for how instruction can more accurately model the archival research process for undergraduate students (Hensley, Murphy, and Swain, 2014).

In 2014, a new rhetoric director steered the program in a different direction. She discontinued the e-textbook, which all first-time instructors had been required to use, and that included the primary source unit. She wanted instructors to create their own lesson plans and teach what was comfortable to them. The new leadership required instructors to share their syllabi with them, but they were granted the freedom to teach with sources they chose. Part of the issue also involved the e-textbook's reliance on group project work. In this structure, the onus for creating the instructor's own syllabus and vision for the rhetoric class was on the instructor.

This change in rhetoric program curricula reduced both the demand for archives instruction sessions and student foot traffic greatly. However, it offered the SLC Archives some new opportunities to build on instruction components that have worked in the past and modify those that have fallen short. One of the biggest problems SLC staff has faced in the last years has been addressing the sheer volume of student use. Three hundred students through the doors in one semester has resulted in worn materials and extremely tired staff. Furthermore, using primary sources requires a different skill set than researching with library books and catalogs. Relying on instructors to teach primary source research and to some degree archival intelligence proved problematic. Based on assessment results, the archivist needs more in-depth time with students to make the interaction with primary sources more meaningful (Swain, 2012). Transitioning from high volume, scratch-the-surface instruction to more in-depth, targeted work is under way.

Establish Objectives and Goals for Instruction

The first steps in redefining the SLC Archives instruction program have been to establish objectives and goals for the instruction as per ACRL's guidelines and draft threshold concepts. In 1999, when the archivist first arrived at the SLC Archives, the position had been vacant for a few years, filled by an interim appointment and graduate assistants. The program did not have an active user base despite the rich and invaluable collections it held. The goal then was to explore potential user populations and promote the SLC Archives widely through networking and informational workshops concerning its general value for historical research. This macro approach resulted in a great interest in the SLC Archives that ultimately netted almost unsustainable use.

The SLC Archives program has stepped back to redefine its objectives in terms of developing a more in-depth involvement with classes and seeking opportunities to partner with faculty and instructors through embedded archival instruction. As part of this retooling, the archives is addressing the four areas uncovered by the assessment review by developing plans to carry out new directives and goals for each.

Partner with Course Instructors

The critical component to a successful instruction program is understanding the goals and objectives of the teaching faculty and instructors. Also crucial is identifying faculty or instructors who are truly interested in the archives and want to explore new teaching techniques and possibilities. The most successful collaborations are those in which the instructor has buy-in and will work with the students and the archivist to understand and use primary sources in creative ways. Certainly, the ACRL principles attest to the importance of collaboration and outreach.

Ohio State University history professor David Staley suggests that targeting faculty who receive good course evaluations and are popular with students is a great way to identify teaching partners. Faculty who like to teach and are good at it are more willing to try new things and teach creatively (Chute, Swain, and Morris, 2016). The SLC Archives plans to implement this approach in conjunction with mirroring the University of Illinois Library Rare Book and Manuscript Library's "coffee with the curator" program. Each month, a staff member is responsible for inviting a faculty member out for coffee to discuss possible teaching opportunities. This directed approach requires the curator/archivist to research faculty interests and course work offerings and to identify relevant archival holdings prior to the meeting. The SLC Archives will continue to highlight its instructional resources and offerings through its widely dispersed newsletter, but it will focus primarily on these more directed, targeted actions and will start on a small scale. Conducting assessment reviews as the program develops will be important for monitoring progress but also for modifying aspects of the program that are not working.

Borrow Pedagogical Strategies from Colleagues

In fall 2015, the SLC Archives, in collaboration with the rhetoric program, will be offering archival workshops to rhetoric instructors concerning different ways to integrate primary sources in their curriculum. Unlike past archives workshops, which were more general and informational in nature, these presentations will offer specific examples of archival exercises based on historical materials from the archives. For example, drawing from excellent presentations at the 2012 Midwest Archives Conference "Teaching with Primary Sources" symposium, staff are in the process of creating a history detective session on the topic of the university's 1897 freshman social affair expulsion case. Groups of students each will investigate different aspects of the story, in which students were expelled for rioting at a freshman event, through newspaper accounts, signed testimonials, photographs, and president's correspondence. Together, the class will piece together the entire story using primary source analysis.

This exercise is meant to provide hands-on exploration of source analysis as opposed to previous archives instruction sessions in which the archivist explained this kind of analysis through lecture examples. It also will be designed to instill in students the ideas outlined in ACRL threshold concepts: Authority Is Constructed and Contextual and Research as Inquiry (ACRL, 2015). These workshops will be voluntary, thus drawing instructors who are truly interested in this type of archival approach.

Develop Online Learning Opportunities

As mentioned earlier, understanding the teaching needs and objectives of faculty and instructors is critical to any partnership. The SLC Archives will conduct an online survey, in collaboration with the rhetoric program director and assistants, of instructors who have utilized or are interested in utilizing the archives. The survey, on the one hand, will seek to determine what archives sources instructors found most useful and how these sources were and could be best integrated into their teaching. It also will determine what types of materials or resources instructors would like to see digitized. Online sources such as the SLC Archives' Primary Source Tutorial, research guides, and the student timeline have been invaluable tools for helping instructors and students understand and access archives materials. The survey will help staff develop other online tools and set priorities for digitizing specific archival holdings.

Paramount to this work is the idea of "flipping the classroom," or providing materials for learning outside the classroom. One aspect of archival instruction that is critical but time consuming is the description and review of logistical information about using the archives. Archives staff are developing a YouTube video concerning archival use and rules that demonstrate these points in a fun or at least interesting way and that can be viewed outside the instruction session, freeing time to cover analysis and content issues during face-to-face archives instructional sessions.

Find Alternatives for How Instruction Can Model the Research Process

Students can be intimidated by archival research. The idea that they must work closely with archivists to access the materials, observe rules about handling and reproducing materials, and work with boxes of papers and photographs as opposed to books is intimidating. A big part of the archivist's job in introducing students to primary sources and historical research is to put them at ease about the process of using the materials. Archivist Jamie Nelson at DePaul University argues that teaching skills that are transferrable to any archives is invaluable. Instruction must model the research process. Nelson and her staff do not pull materials from boxes for show-and-tell during archives presentations. Students are treated as researchers. They are presented with a box of materials, use gloves to handle photos, and fill out user cards and research forms. In this way, they become comfortable with archives and understand the basic protocols for using any repository they may choose to visit (Chute, Swain, and Morris, 2016).

The SLC Archives will more fully integrate this philosophy into its instruction work. Even though the archivist has demonstrated the relationship between an online finding aid and the physical box it represented by showing both as part of the presentation, students who took the assessment survey expressed confusion. The solution to this problem may be to spend more dedicated time with the class. One new component to instruction sessions held at the SLC Archives is to take the class to the research room and into the vault. This mini field trip down the hall not only gives students a break but also helps reinforce the archival research procedure so students are comfortable coming back to do research. The vault tour is always impressive; it brings home the idea that archives deal with boxes of material that must be accessed with the archivist's assistance. It also reinforces the notion that since archives have a lot of material, advance searching in and familiarity with the SLC Archives' online search tools is critical to a successful research visit.

In the fall, the archivist will work with an instructor to hold a class period in the computer lab to help students formulate questions and conduct searches. This approach also will enable the archivist to spend more one-on-one time with students and help make future archives visits more meaningful and productive.

CONCLUSION

The integration of primary sources into course curricula is worthwhile and rewarding if archivist and instructor are truly committed to working together to achieve course goals and objectives. New guidelines for teaching with primary sources will be an invaluable resource for establishing and implementing goals and learning objectives. Key tenets in this process include the following:

- Target faculty or instructors whose work and interests connect strongly with materials in the archives. (Partner with course instructors)
- Communicate in person with faculty or instructors about learning outcomes for the assignment or project. Invite faculty and instructors to the archives to familiarize them with the space and ensure that they understand how to conduct primary source research. (Partner with course instructors; Establish objectives and goals)
- Use active learning techniques, in combination with lecture if applicable, to engage students with materials. Lecture alone is usually not an effective means of communication. Draw on colleagues' experience with pedagogical strategies. (Pedagogical strategies)
- Focus in depth on specific primary sources, chosen for the assignment or project, as opposed to "show-and-tell" approach with large variety of materials. (Pedagogical strategies)
- Convey basic archival intelligence information (concerning principles of arrangement and description, methods of searching, etc.) through active learning exercises. Challenge students to think about sources. (Establish objectives and goals)
- Convey critical differences between library and archives operations through hands-on approach. For example, taking a break from the class session to tour the area where archives boxes are stored illustrates the vastness of holdings and the necessity to use a finding aid to locate needed boxes. (Pedagogical strategies)
- Mirror the research process in class sessions. Provide materials in their boxes and walk through the registration process to emphasize typical archival research procedures. (Find alternatives for how instruction can model the research process)
- Emphasize to faculty and instructors that online resources (such as a primary source tutorial) are most useful when they examine the tool or resource with their students in a class session prior to the archives visit. (Develop online learning opportunities)

With thoughtful planning and communication with faculty or instructors, teaching with primary sources has the potential for students to gain a lifelong appreciation for historical materials and acquire analytical skills and a curiosity for historical inquiry.

REFERENCES

ACRL (Association of College & Research Libraries). 2000. "Information Literacy Competency Standards for Higher Education." American Library Association. Association of College & Research Libraries. http://www.ala.org/acrl/standards/informationliteracycompetency.

———. 2012. "Characteristics of Programs of Information Literacy That Illustrate Best Practices: A Guideline." American Library Association. Association of College & Research Libraries. http://www.ala.org/acrl/standards/characteristics.

———. 2015. *Framework for Information Literacy for Higher Education.* American Library Association. Association of College & Research Libraries. http://acrl.ala.org/ilstandards/wp-content/uploads/2015/01/Framework-MW15-Board-Docs.pdf.

Chute, Tamar, Ellen D. Swain, and Sammie Morris. 2016. "Helping Students Learn: Cases and Examples." In *Teaching with Primary Sources*, SAA Trends in Archives Practice Series. Chicago: Society of American Archivists, under contract.

Hensley, Merinda K., Ben Murphy, and Ellen D. Swain. 2014. "Analyzing Archival Intelligence: A Collaboration between Library Instruction and Archives." *Communications in Information Literacy* 8, no. 1: 96–114.

Mitchell, Eleanor, Peggy Seiden, and Suzy Taraba. 2012. *Past or Portal? Enhancing Undergraduate Learning through Special Collections and Archives.* Chicago: American Library Association: ACRL.

SAA (Society for American Archivists). 2014. "Call for Volunteers: SAA-ACRL/RBMS Joint TaskForce on Primary Source Literacy." http://www2.archivists.org/news/2015/call-for-volunteers-saa-acrlrbms-joint-task-force-on-primary-source-literacy.

Swain, Ellen D. 2012. "Making It Personal: Engaging Students with Their University." In *Past or Portal? Enhancing Undergraduate Learning through Special Collections and Archives*, edited by Eleanor Mitchell, Peggy Seiden, and Suzy Taraba, 151–55. Chicago: American Library Association: ACRL.

Yakel, Elizabeth, and D. A. Torres. 2003. "AI: Archival Intelligence and User Expertise." *American Archivist* 66, no. 1: 51–78.

13

Digitizing History

A New Course That Brings History to Wider Audiences

Patrick Ragains,
University of Nevada, Reno

This chapter describes the creation and delivery of Digitizing History (HIST 300A), a new undergraduate course at the University of Nevada, Reno (UNR), which is cotaught by history faculty, media production specialists, instructional designers, and librarians. In the course, students plan and create documentary websites incorporating text, images, audio, and video. The cohort of co-instructors designed the course, taught lessons in their individual areas of expertise, and collaborated with the lead instructor to grade the student websites and assess and revise the course. This effort exemplifies the information literacy best practices of collaboration, pedagogy, and assessment.

Documentary portals like American Memory have been available since the mid-1990s until the present, when there are really too many such sites to survey adequately. Also, there are notable examples of history faculty and their students creating well-focused documentary sites, such as Women and Social Movements in the United States, 1600–2000, begun by historian Kathryn Kish Sklar, which has expanded greatly as a licensed collection available from Alexander Street Press (http://womhist.alexanderstreet.com). Many college and university history programs have revised or added courses to give students experience creating documentary websites.

DESIGNING THE COURSE

Digitizing History was developed in the context of the University of Nevada, Reno's undergraduate history program, which promotes development of specific intellectual skills through reading, discussion, and writing. By majoring in history, students are expected to develop informed perspectives on the past via specific activities:

1. Critically analyzing and questioning primary sources
2. Critically analyzing and questioning secondary sources
3. Writing historical analyses
4. Analyzing cultural texts such as literature, film, art, etc.
5. Researching historical subject matter and learning to utilize a variety of bibliographic tools
6. Making effective oral presentations (Curcio and Hildreth, 2002: 2–3)

Writing historical analyses and making effective oral presentations are essential forms of discourse, although students also may create exhibits while enrolled in a public history course or an internship. Exhibits in museums and other settings translate historical analysis for nonscholarly audiences. Documentary websites serve a similar purpose, although prior to 2014, no course or internship at UNR provided students with the experience of creating an online "exhibit." The new course emerged from this background.

Nationwide, faculty in the humanities and social sciences are concerned about the relative decline of undergraduate majors in their fields (U.S. Department of Education, NCES, 2013), and are looking for ways to attract more students. UNR's history faculty articulated Digitizing History within the department's undergraduate major, knowing it would be quite different from any course they had previously taught, and largely experimental. The faculty decided to make the course an alternative to Historical Research and Writing (HIST 300) and designated it as HIST 300A. Although students could take this course instead of HIST 300, which exposed them to historical scholarship, a wide range of information sources, and required research and writing culminating in a prospectus, Digitizing History did not displace any topical upper-division courses. Also, the course would have no prerequisites.

Once the history faculty agreed to offer this new course, one faculty member worked with several librarians, media production professionals, and instructional designers to draft a syllabus. Everyone in this working group recognized the importance of a broad-based approach, but there were differences about what topics were essential. Some participants emphasized students' need for foundational knowledge about presenting historical scholarship and representing artifacts online, while others stressed the need for them to understand concepts related to describing artifacts or to learn technical and conceptual aspects of documentary videography (both video cameras and audio recorders were available for loan in the Knowledge Center at no charge). In preparing the syllabus for review and approval by the History Department, the College of Liberal Arts, and the University Courses and Curriculum Committee, the planning group agreed on a balanced coverage of topics and then sequenced these and related assignments, week by week. The sidebar reflects the topics and details of lessons as taught the course's first semester.

The amount of technical work to be required in the course drove another decision—the optimal maximum enrollment. Considering the digital media lab's capacity, the team of instructors decided to limit the course to seventeen students. This number seemed appropriate when estimating the amount of time that the media production specialists could devote to helping students individually and still meet their other work commitments. Seventeen students could work together in the lab during scheduled class meetings, each on a Mac Pro workstation. Eight students enrolled the first time the course was offered (seven completed), and six enrolled the second time. The co-instructors found these numbers manageable.

TEACHING

Below are descriptions of three instructional units or related lessons illustrating the scope of Digitizing History, followed by a summary of students' final presentations.

Foundations: Historical Research in the Online Era and Overview of Documentary Websites

Since HIST 300A was an optional substitute for another course, Historical Research and Writing, it was appropriate for the new course to expose students to a comparable range of concepts. The instructors sought to convey not only the range of documentary sources online, but an analytical perspective on online historical sources. Early activities in the course were designed to help students develop and demonstrate a foundational understanding of digital historical collections, including planning and building such collections and what digital collections can offer researchers, in contrast to collections in print or on microfilm. Students read David Thomas and Valerie Johnson's "New Universes or Black Holes? Does Digital Change Anything?" which identifies many challenges to today's historians, among them media formats that are unfixed, possibly unstable, or eventually rendered obsolete; funding of digitization projects; how selective presentation of sources influences meaning; and how online search capabilities influence both research behavior and discovery (Thomas and Johnson, 2012). Students also listened to or read a transcript of a radio interview with Arun Chaudhary, President Obama's

DIGITIZING HISTORY: SEQUENCE OF COURSE TOPICS

1. Course overview. Taught by the lead instructor.
2. Readings on historical research in the online era. Open access and government-produced documentary websites. Taught by the history liaison librarian. Case studies: National Archives (http://www.archives.gov); Afghanistan Digital Collections (http://afghandata.org/).
3. Commercially produced documentary databases. Taught by history liaison librarian. Case study: Digital National Security Archive (http://www.proquest.com/products-services/databases/dnsa.html).
4. Oral interviews. Taught by history faculty specialist in public history.
   a. Preparing to conduct a historical interview
   b. Technical matters
5. Legal aspects of reproducing documents. Taught by the history liaison librarian and photo archivist.
   a. Introduction to copyright
   b. Reproducing photographs and other materials housed in repositories
6. Researching new historical primary sources on the Internet. Taught by the history liaison librarian.
   a. President Obama's videographer (http://www.npr.org/blogs/itsallpolitics/2013/08/22/214207910/future-historians-good-luck-sifting-through-obama-video)
   b. CNN's Our Nixon
7. Web design: basic concepts and WordPress. Taught by an instructional designer.
8. Creating web-based documentary source collections. Taught by the head of Special Collections.
   a. Defining the scope of a documentary collection
   b. Identifying a theme and related sources
   c. Curating artifacts
   d. Selecting documents for a web exhibit
   e. Image formats
9. Presenting website designs in progress, consulting, and troubleshooting with instructors. All co-instructors present.
10. Videography. Taught by the director of digital media technology.
    a. Developing a script, planning the video
    b. Videography: technical matters
    c. Videography: editing and producing video
    d. Embedding video on website; in-class work
11. In-class work on projects and consultations with instructors. All co-instructors.
12. Out-of-class work on projects and consultations with instructors.
13. Final project presentations. All co-instructors.

videographer, in which Chaudhary discussed the challenges of using a vast, unsearchable video archive (Shapiro, 2013).

With this background, students participated in two online meetings, the first with Atifa Rawan, creator of the Afghanistan Digital Collections site (http://www.afghandata.org). Rawan described the loss of much of Afghanistan's cultural heritage over more than three decades of war and occupation, sources of the site's core documents, the setup and operation of digitization labs, and the project's goals and accomplishments. Students asked her questions about all aspects of the project. Rawan met with the class both times the course has been offered. In 2014, students had an online meeting with a scholar who created documentary projects for the National Security Archive, and in 2015, they met with an executive with Readex Inc., who discussed developing collections in the digital Archive of Americana, composed of books, magazines, pamphlets, newspapers, and government publications. Thus, students were exposed to perspectives of developers of two types of documentary websites, an open access digital library and commercial online collections.

Following the second online interview, students were assigned to write a three- to four-page essay, evaluating one of three sites, the Afghanistan Digital Collections, Readex's U.S. Congressional Serial Set, or a thematic collection in the Digital National Security Archive. For the site chosen, students were asked to focus on its theme, the time period covered, the documents presented, and to address the following points:

1. What is the purpose of the site?
2. Have the aims of the project been achieved?
3. How might this project improve our historical understanding? Are you aware of other print or online collections with a similar theme? Can you compare these other projects to the one you chose to write about?
4. How do Atifa Rawan's comments, those of the Readex and National Security Archive research staff, the radio segment on President Obama's videographer, and Thomas and Johnson's chapter inform your understanding of digitized historical resources?

The history liaison librarian graded these papers, consulting with the lead instructor about her general expectations for the essays and strategies for handling late assignments. While students' literal comments cannot be quoted here, a few examples can be summarized to illustrate both their perceptions and misperceptions. One student noted that a Digital National Security Archive collection about Central America and U.S. counternarcotics policy achieved its purpose of informing the public, but that other primary and secondary sources should be consulted in order to understand the sources in the collection. This indicated the student had developed a good understanding of the complexity of documentary research, and that no cache of sources contextualizes or interprets itself; interpretation is the job of the researcher and, ultimately, his or her readers. Another student wrote that documents in a National Security Archive collection might have been selected to promote a particular point of view. The librarian responded that, since the documents were obtained through Freedom of Information Act requests, there was little opportunity for government officials to have this sort of influence. In contrast, another student claimed that documentary projects can produce "truth." The librarian told the history professor, "I think he means that these projects can aid objectivity." The librarian also noticed that some students misunderstood search interfaces and overlooked hyperlinked subject headings and name authorities. Overall, students' varying levels of analysis indicated the assignment was worthwhile as a means of developing their understanding. Several of ACRL's information literacy frames apply to this unit, although, because the guest website developers explained how they planned and created their own projects, Information Creation as a Process is the most applicable (ACRL, 2015).

Legal Aspects of Reproducing Documents: Introduction to Copyright; Using Photographs and Other Materials Housed in Repositories

Since students would be gathering digital surrogates of photographs, cartoons, holographs, and other documents for their websites, it was essential for them to understand pertinent aspects of copyright and related rights regimes. The frame Information Has Value, relates directly to copyright and other forms of intellectual property (ACRL, 2015). This teaching unit differed somewhat over two semesters, although in each case it began with an introduction to copyright, taught by the history liaison librarian, followed by a more detailed discussion of reproducing documents in repositories, presented by the library's photo archivist. The librarian defined copyright under U.S. law, how it applies to fixed works, and its duration. The archivist placed copyright in the context of reproducing photographs and other works. She emphasized that, while an image may be owned by its creator, a repository, or other entity, and versions of an image and the provenance of each version can be compared, it is often impossible to speak of an original photographic image—with the exception of negatives. She related the case of a dispute that arose over the reproduction of a well-known photograph of wild horses, one print of which was donated to the UNR Special Collections by the photographer's surviving daughter, and another, which the photographer himself gave to a third party and was subsequently reproduced on a book jacket. Another case she described involved not photographs but archived case records from a state mental hospital, restricted by a privacy-related statute. The central point of the session was that researchers cannot presume they may freely reproduce, use, or disclose all sources, and that they must investigate and secure the rights to do so. Students read material from Richard Stim's book, *Getting Permission: How to License & Clear Copyrighted Materials, Online & Off* (Stim, 2010), and a more focused discussion on legal and ethical issues concerning the use of photographs (Vogt-O'Connor, 2006).

Students taking the course in 2015 completed a related assignment, which required each one to assess every image, video, or other object on their documentary website, with respect to its ownership and the student's right to use it. One goal of this assignment was to alert students to any potential rights infringements on their projects and give them time to seek permissions or remove items before the final due date. It was graded pass or fail, since part of the letter grade for the final website evaluation would reflect the status of digital objects. The co-instructors agreed that a standard of copyright compliance for noneducational purposes was appropriate for the projects, first, since the websites are freely accessible (not just to instructors and students in the course), but also because they wanted students to have the experience of selecting and using content in a setting where more permissive standards of fair use for educational purposes do not apply. Some students had reproduced images from books (e.g., a photograph of an automobile, taken from a book published by the museum that owns the vehicle) and microfilm editions of newspapers, for which the microfilm publisher holds copyright.

In-Class Work on Projects and Consultations with Instructors

Digitizing History includes class meetings in a computer lab and a computer/media lab, where students design their websites and produce audiovisual content. No single information literacy frame characterizes the work done in these sessions, although several of Christine Bruce's conceptions of information literacy are evident (information technology, sources, process, and knowledge construction) (Bruce, 1997). Some lab sessions are led by an instructional designer, media production specialist, or videographer, but most co-instructors attend at least one meeting to view students' work in progress and advise them as needed. These sessions are important opportunities for instructors to prompt students to reflect on all aspects of their work, from framing a historical topic and presenting it to various audiences who may have no prior awareness of it, to editing media and placing it on the site. The goal is for words and media on a student's website to present an original and coherent narrative on a compelling topic, supported by research in primary and secondary sources. Students must grapple with an array of conceptual and technical work that is relatively complex when compared to researching and writing a coherent textual narrative. During these working sessions, students are often absorbed in one aspect of their project, for instance, mulling over site navigability, or editing a video interview. This is not unexpected but poses challenges for instructors to encourage students, when necessary, to attend to other aspects of their project. Instructors should be aware of the cognitive challenges posed by creating a scholarly multimedia project (Yancey, 2004).

Final Student Presentations

Students presented their final websites in a forum attended by all co-instructors and invited guests. The instructors were able to view the projects starting a few weeks earlier via links posted on the course's Blackboard site, although most students continued working on their sites until the end of the semester. In their remarks, many students stressed the importance of their interview subjects over other aspects of their work, including photos and other documentary evidence on their site, the technical skills learned, design choices, or the broader significance of the events studied. The instructors had emphasized all of these elements throughout the course. While most presentations showed considerable progress in crafting a story of historical significance, at least one student stood out, as his site presented altered photos and cartoons used as propaganda in the early Soviet Union. His interview subject was a scholar whose discussion of propaganda was supportive of the topic but did not dominate it. Other projects have presented profiles of a key organizer of the 1960 Winter Olympics, Nevada's Air National Guard, the origins of baseball in Nevada, and a well-known scientist.

ASSESSMENT

At the end of the course's first semester (spring 2014), the co-instructors met to discuss and grade the websites. They considered the purpose, coherence, documentation, design, and technical aspects of each student project but did not use a formal rubric. The instructors successfully determined the grades, although the discussion resembled a jury deliberation, as individuals focused on different elements of the assignment. This was natural, since each instructor brought a unique background and skills to bear in the course. In the spring

2015 semester, the instructors developed a rubric, based in part on a scheme suggested by an English and digital humanities librarian at the University of Illinois at Urbana-Champaign (Green, 2014). The lead instructor weighted each element equally:

1. Concept, including power of theme and effectiveness as a community project
2. Design
   a. Innovative visual layout, color, etc.
   b. Images: variety juxtaposition, placement, relevance
   c. Text: appearance, readability, logical and balanced ordering of text blocks
3. Functionality: links, HTML coding, etc.
4. Structure and navigation: consistency, effectiveness, logical order of menus
5. Multimedia integration: proper display/play of all elements
6. Legal status of images (permission obtained; student's own; public domain)

Instructors used a second rubric to score the videos embedded in each site. That rubric is not reproduced here, but it isolated technical, conceptual, and creative aspects of the video segments and other required elements, such as audio quality, "B-roll" or supporting video, still photos, music, sound effects, narration, graphics, use of text, and credits.

In both semesters, co-instructors met after the students' final presentations to grade the websites. Using this rubric as a criterion-referenced framework (i.e., referring to performance standards rather than norms), many grades in 2015 were in the B range, with fewer receiving As, and one C. That same year, the instructors also reviewed the semester's assignments and drafted recommendations for a new history faculty member, who would lead the course the following year. They suggested requiring practice sessions for both the audio interviews and video component of the website project, where classmates would interview each other and shoot a practice video. These activities would require students to become more familiar with the equipment before meeting with their subjects to record media for their site. The instructors also agreed that a midsemester status check of students' progress should continue, but that this preliminary review should be graded, in order to encourage students to complete more work on their sites before running out of time at the end of the semester.

LESSONS LEARNED

Other chapters in this book have stressed the importance of librarians developing strong relations with faculty. These connections strengthened the environment for collaboration and enhanced student learning; further, they enabled the creation of this course. Following are general recommendations for creating a new course with disciplinary faculty and other professionals:

1. Start with a statement of the goals for the new course. What knowledge and skills should students develop? All faculty, librarians, and other stakeholders in the course should understand and accept these goals.
2. Understand how the new course fits into degree programs. Are there prerequisite courses or skills? Is it a required course or an elective?
3. Be prepared to brainstorm about possible lessons and assignments. Questions to consider as you develop these ideas are: What sort of work should students do in order to attain the desired knowledge and skills? What concepts must students understand in order to perform the work successfully (such as knowing about rights and permissions for using images and other documentary resources)? Should fundamental concepts be introduced via lectures, readings, and class discussions? Will students choose their own topics or will topics be assigned? If students choose their own topics, will they have opportunities to revise their plans? How can instructors check students' progress and provide feedback several times throughout the course? Should students critique their peers' work and, if so, how? Realize the purpose of brainstorming and its limitations: it is a means to identify possibilities, many of which will not be used. Ideas that are used will likely be changed substantially to fit the instructors' overall vision and goals for the course. Idea-generating sessions may be cut short in order to facilitate planning but can resume as needed. Co-instructors should feel free to make suggestions but rely on the lead course instructor to guide the process.
4. Sequence the lessons and assignments, keeping course goals and objectives in mind. Acknowledge time limitations, both in scheduled class sessions and in your expectations for students to read, write, and develop their projects outside of class.
5. Consider developing rubrics to use for all graded work.
6. Determine who will grade each assignment. A rubric can greatly aid collaborative grading, even if it is only a set of guidelines. Each instructor should explain his or her grading rationale while being respectful of others'.

7. After the course ends and grades have been assigned, hold a debriefing meeting for co-instructors to share their impressions and recommendations for revising the course.
8. Celebrate your success!

CONCLUSION

After teaching Digitizing History twice, it is clear that students are interested in the course and that the current group of co-instructors can partner successfully to plan and teach it. Still, a number of questions are evident. The low number of students in both semesters reflects that it is a new course. Many students—perhaps most—select major courses before their junior year and may not feel they have the flexibility to take another course, either for additional credit or as a substitute for another one already in their plan. The course is not based on a historical theme or period, which may cause students to overlook it. In the future, it is possible that a greater number of students will select HIST 300A as they create degree plans and select their major courses. Making Digitizing History more attractive and integral to the curriculum is one challenge the faculty face. As a substitute for HIST 300, Historical Research and Writing, faculty teaching this new course must determine an appropriate emphasis on technical and design skills that does not overshadow the recursive practice of framing questions, gathering sources, and analyzing them, a process that is central to historical scholarship.

Well-considered curriculum planning, skilled teaching, organizational skills, and some luck combine to create a fertile seedbed for Digitizing History. The course is still largely experimental, but this is appropriate in academe, since curricula continually evolve to address development in the disciplines and students' learning needs. The course is relevant to the needs of students entering graduate study or various jobs requiring research, clear writing, and presentation skills. Digital humanities projects, including documentary websites, are well-accepted platforms for presentation of research and public outreach, providing a justification for instilling these workforce-related competencies in a history curriculum.

REFERENCES

ACRL (Association of College & Research Libraries). 2015. *Framework for Information Literacy for Higher Education*. American Library Association. Association of College & Research Libraries. http://acrl.ala.org/ilstandards/wp-content/uploads/2015/01/Framework-MW15-Board-Docs.pdf.

Bruce, Christine S. 1997. *The Seven Faces of Information Literacy*. Adelaide: Auslib Press.

Curcio, Linda, and Martha Hildreth. 2002. "Undergraduate History Assessment Plan." Reno: University of Nevada, Department of History.

Green, Harriett E. 2014. "Faculty-Librarian Collaborations in New Media Ecosystems: Developing an Assessment Rubric for Digital Literacy in the Humanities." Paper presented at the Library Research Seminar VI, Urbana-Champaign, IL, October 9.

Shapiro, Ari. 2013. "Future Historians: Good Luck Sifting through Obama Video." National Public Radio. http://www.npr.org/blogs/itsallpolitics/2013/08/22/214207910/future-historians-good-luck-sifting-through-obama-video.

Stim, Richard. 2010. *Getting Permission: How to License & Clear Copyrighted Materials, Online & Off*. Berkeley, CA: Nolo.

Thomas, David, and Valerie Johnson. 2012. "New Universes or Black Holes? Does Digital Change Anything?" In *History in the Digital Age*, edited by Toni Weller, 173–93. Hoboken, NJ: Taylor and Francis.

U.S. Department of Education, NCES (National Center for Education Statistics). 2013. *Digest of Education Statistics*. Table 318.20. "Bachelor's, Master's, and Doctor's Degrees Conferred by Postsecondary Institutions, by Field of Study: Selected Years, 1970–71 through 2011–12." https://nces.ed.gov/programs/digest/d13/tables/dt13_318.20.asp.

Vogt-O'Connor, Diane. 2006. "Legal and Ethical Issues of Ownership, Access, and Usage." *In Photographs: Archival Care and Management*, by Mary Lynn Ritzenthaler, Diane Vogt-O'Connor, Helena Zinkharn, et al., 298–349. Chicago: Society of American Archivists.

Yancey, Kathleen Blake. 2004. "Looking for Sources of Coherence in a Fragmented World: Notes toward a New Assessment Design." *Computers and Composition* 21, no. 1: 89–102.

Index

Page references for figures are italicized

About the Editors and Contributors

Sara Arnold-Garza earned her master's degree in information studies from the University of Texas at Austin in 2011. She completed a two-year appointment as residency librarian for diversity and innovation at Towson University and now works there as a research and instruction librarian. Sara supports the university's political science department and provides research help to students and faculty across disciplines. Sara's work with the flipped classroom for library instruction earned her a 2014 Innovation in Teaching Award from her institution's Office of Academic Innovation.

Heidi Buchanan is a research and instruction librarian and professor at Hunter Library, Western Carolina University, where she also serves as information literacy instruction coordinator. Her MSLS is from the University of North Carolina, Chapel Hill. She is a graduate of the ACRL Information Literacy Immersion Program and a certified North Carolina Master Trainer. Together with Beth McDonough, she has written a book, *The One-Shot Library Instruction Survival Guide* (2014) and regularly coteaches an ALA Editions e-course, *Dynamic Library One-Shot Instruction*. The goal is to help librarians provide meaningful, relevant, and student-centered library instruction.

Eva Dodsworth is the geospatial data services librarian at the University of Waterloo Library where she specializes in teaching GIS and map-related content to the university community. Eva's interests include historical cartographic research and teaching geoweb applications and historical GIS. Eva is also a part-time online instructor for a number of library schools and continuing education organizations where she teaches the use of GIS (geographic information system) technology in libraries. Eva has also written *Getting*

Started with GIS: A LITA Guide, and has cowritten *Discovering and Using Historical Geographic Resources on the Web*, as well as *Using Google Earth in Libraries*.

Mary E. Edwards is the distance learning and liaison librarian at the University of Florida Health Science Center Library, where she has worked since 2004. Mary serves as liaison to a number of clinical and research departments in the Colleges of Medicine and Public Health and Health Professions and collaborates extensively with faculty from her departments on both instruction and research projects. She is currently teaching in the course "Interdisciplinary Family Health," which is the cornerstone of the academic health center's interprofessional education program. Mary holds an MA in library and information science from the University of South Florida and an EdD in educational technology from the University of Florida.

Laura Ferguson is assistant dean for faculty affairs, Texas A&M Health Science Center, College of Medicine, Round Rock Campus, and is a professor in the Texas A&M College of Medicine Department of Pediatrics. She received her MD from the University of Texas at Houston Medical School, completed a pediatric residency at the University of Texas Medical School at Houston Affiliated Hospitals, and is board certified by the American College of Pediatrics.

Sara Russell Gonzalez is the physical sciences, mathematics and visualization librarian at the Marston Science Library, University of Florida. She serves as the liaison to the Departments of Astronomy, Mathematics, Physics, and Statistics and coordinates the UF Libraries' 3-D services and the MADE@UF mobile application lab. She developed and teaches the UF Honors course "Discovering Research and Communicating Science" along with workshops on 3-D printing, modeling, data management, and visualization. Sara received her PhD in geophysics from the University of California, Santa Cruz, and an MLIS from Florida State University.

Cindy A. Gruwell is an associate professor and faculty librarian at St. Cloud State University in St. Cloud, Minnesota. In addition to reference and teaching responsibilities, she coordinates instruction and provides leadership for information literacy. Other responsibilities include staffing the reference desk, consultations, liaison to the Colleges of Science and Engineering and Health and Human Services, and participation on a wide array of library and university committees. Prior to her current position she was an associate librarian in the Bio-Medical Library at the University of Minnesota, Twin Cities. She received both her BA and MLS from the University of California, Los Angeles, and recently completed her MEd at Bemidji State University.

Benjamin R. Harris is an associate professor and head of instruction services at Trinity University in San Antonio, Texas. His research interests include the alignment of visual literacy and information literacy teaching and learning, the challenges of creating educational standards designed to facilitate assessment goals rather than learning, and critical pedagogy in library instruction.

Larry Laliberté has over ten years' experience working with GIS and spatial data. Currently he is the GIS librarian at the University of Alberta where much of his work revolves around analyzing and synthesizing spatial information at many scales, across many disciplines, in various formats. Over the last decade, he has developed and maintained an online collection of historical maps of Manitoba and in 2014 cowrote *Discovering and Using Historical Geographic Resources on the Web*. Recently he has taken a great interest in developing best practices for the long-term preservation of digital geospatial data.

Scott Martin earned an MSI from the School of Information at the University of Michigan in 2005. Since then, he's served as the biological sciences librarian at the University of Michigan Library. His duties include reference, instruction, and collection development in support of the biology departments in the College of Literature, Science, and the Arts; the Museums of Zoology, Paleontology, and Natural History; the Herbarium; and the University of Michigan Biological Station. He has coauthored articles in *Genome Research* and the *Journal of the Medical Library Association* and presented at the 2015 ACRL Conference and the 2014 CLI Conference. Scott also holds degrees in biology from Kalamazoo College and the University of Chicago.

Beth McDonough is a research and instruction librarian and associate professor at Hunter Library, Western Carolina University. Her MLS is from the University of North Carolina at Greensboro. Beth recently completed her EdD in leadership of curriculum and instruction at Western Carolina University. Her dissertation focused on critical information literacy. Together with Heidi Buchanan, she has written a book, *The One-Shot Library Instruction Survival Guide* (2014) and regularly coteaches an ALA Editions e-course, "Dynamic Library One-Shot Instruction." The goal is to help librarians provide meaningful, relevant, and student-centered library instruction.

Elizabeth McMunn-Tetangco is an instruction librarian at the University of California, Merced. She holds an MLIS from San Jose State University, an MAT from the University of San Francisco, and a BA in English from the University of California, Berkeley.

Susan Mikkelsen is an instruction and scholarly communications librarian at the University of California, Merced. She completed an MLIS at the University of North Carolina, Chapel Hill, a Multiple Subject Teaching Credential from the University of California, Riverside, and a BS in human development at the University of California, Davis.

Hannah F. Norton is a reference and liaison librarian at the University of Florida Health Science Center Library, where she has worked since 2010. Hannah serves as liaison to the College of Veterinary Medicine, the Department of Medicine, and the College of Medicine class of 2015, and has taught within various courses in the medical and veterinary curricula. She serves on the Curriculum Committee for each college as well as the Graduate Medical Education Committee. Hannah holds an MS in information studies from the University of Texas, Austin.

Jo Angela Oehrli is a former high school and middle school teacher who helps students find information on a wide range of topics as a learning librarian at the University of Michigan Libraries, Ann Arbor. In addition, she supports the students in the Women in Science and Engineering Residential Program and the students in the Michigan Research Community Residential Program as well as undergraduates across campus. She has published articles on library instruction, served as chair of the ALA LIRT (Library Instruction Round Table) Top Twenty Committee, and serves as an adjunct lecturer at UM's School of Information and also in the College of Literature, Science, and the Arts. She also supports the research and instructional needs for those throughout the university community who are studying children's literature at any level.

Michelle Rachal is the health sciences librarian at the University of Nevada, Reno. She holds a bachelor's degree in Spanish from the University of Nevada, Reno, and a master of library and information science from the University of Wisconsin, Milwaukee.

Patrick Ragains is business and government information librarian at the University of Nevada, Reno. He holds an MLS from the University of Arizona (1987) and an MA in history from Northern Arizona University (1984).

He has edited *Information Literacy Instruction That Works: A Guide to Teaching by Discipline and Student Population* (2013) and has published articles in *American Libraries*, *Communications in Information Literacy*, *Journal of Government Information*, *portal: Libraries & the Academy*, and *Research Strategies*. He is former chair of the ACRL Research Committee and is active in the ACRL Instruction Section.

Suzanne Shurtz is an associate professor, instructional services librarian at Texas A&M University's Medical Sciences Library and is a codirector of the Evidence-Based Medicine, Scholarship & Research curriculum at Texas A&M's College of Medicine. She is a senior member of the Academy of Health Information Professionals. Ms. Shurtz earned her master of library and information science degree from the University of South Carolina and a bachelor of science degree in elementary education from Brigham Young University. Previous to being a medical librarian, she taught four years in public schools, earned her English as a second language (ESL) teaching endorsement, and taught English overseas.

Heidi Slater is a reference and instruction librarian at the University of Nevada, Reno. She holds a BA in history from Yale University, an MEd with K–12 library certification from Portland State University, and has over twenty years of teaching experience. She recently coauthored a report with Ithaka S+R that examines how students engage in academic group work with their peers.

Ellen D. Swain serves as archivist for student life and culture at the University of Illinois at Urbana-Champaign where she administers the Student Life and Culture Archival Program, an archives dedicated to documenting student experience nationally and at the University of Illinois. Prior to this position, she was project archivist/assistant archivist (1996–1999) at the Evangelical Lutheran Church in America (ELCA) National Archives in Elk Grove Village, Illinois. She holds a BA from Earlham College, an MA in American history from Indiana University, and an MS in information science from Illinois. Ellen is a former president of the Midwest Archives Conference (MAC) (2011–2013) and is an SAA (Society of American Archivists) fellow (2013).

Michele R. Tennant is the associate director of the Health Science Center Library at the University of Florida. Since 1996, Michele has provided information literacy instruction in undergraduate genetics, using authentic experiences to engage students and reinforce learning. She provides instruction in the use of genetics and bioinformatics tools to graduate and professional students and faculty in the biomedical sciences, and provides students guidance on the role of librarians in information literacy by serving on graduate committees in UF's College of Education. Michele received her PhD in biology from Wayne State University, and her MLIS from the University of California, Los Angeles.

M. Sandra Wood, MLS, MBA, is librarian emerita, Penn State University Libraries, and a fellow of the Medical Library Association. Ms. Wood is founding and current editor of *Medical Reference Services Quarterly* (in its thirty-fourth volume). She was a librarian for over thirty-five years at the George T. Harrell Library, Milton S. Hershey Medical Center, Pennsylvania State University, specializing in reference, education, and database services. Ms. Wood has written or edited more than twelve books, the latest two entitled *Health Sciences Librarianship* and *Successful Library Fundraising: Best Practices* (both with Rowman & Littlefield Publishers, 2014).